ASSASSINATING THE PRIME MINISTER IN WHITEHALL

For
Donna, Lorne and Natalie

ASSASSINATING THE PRIME MINISTER IN WHITEHALL

THE VICTORIAN MURDER THAT SHAPED THE INSANITY DEFENCE

MARTYN FROST

PEN & SWORD
TRUE CRIME

First published in Great Britain in 2026 by
PEN AND SWORD TRUE CRIME
An imprint of
Pen & Sword Books Limited
Yorkshire – Philadelphia

Print ISBN 978 1 03612 952 1
ePUB ISBN 978 1 03612 953 8
ePDF ISBN 978 1 03612 955 2

A CIP catalogue record for this book is available from the British Library.

Typeset in Times New Roman 10.5/14 by SJmagic DESIGN SERVICES, India.
Printed and bound in the UK by CPI Group (UK) Ltd.

The Publisher's authorised representative in the EU for product safety is Authorised Rep Compliance Ltd., Ground Floor, 71 Lower Baggot Street, Dublin D02 P593, Ireland.
www.arccompliance.com

For a complete list of Pen & Sword titles please contact
PEN & SWORD BOOKS LIMITED
George House, Units 12 & 13, Beevor Street, Off Pontefract Road,
Barnsley, South Yorkshire, S71 1HN, England
E-mail: enquiries@pen-and-sword.co.uk
Website: www.pen-and-sword.co.uk

or

PEN AND SWORD BOOKS
1950 Lawrence Rd, Havertown, PA 19083, USA
E-mail: uspen-and-sword@casematepublishers.com
Website: www.penandswordbooks.com

MIX
Paper | Supporting responsible forestry
FSC® C013604

CONTENTS

FOREWORD

"M'Naghten Rules OK" was the favourite piece of graffiti for the law student in the 1970s. That itself was a testament to the astonishing longevity of M'Naghten's case in the annals of English law. The decision, formulating the M'Naghten Rules on insanity in criminal trials, had by the 1970s lasted for more than 125 years. Now the Rules are heading strongly for the 200-year barrier. Very few legal decisions from so long ago cast such a long shadow. It is striking that the case of M'Naghten, and the subsequent civil case of Banks v Goodfellow, some 27 years later in 1870, should have laid down the principles which guide the modern law of insanity in both criminal and civil fields. Yet modern psychiatry itself is unrecognisable from the so-called psychiatry of that era.

Even more extraordinary is that the course of English law on insanity should have turned, not on some wretched, tawdry murder in a dark Victorian backstreet, but on M'Naghten's mistaken assassination of the unfortunate Drummond in Whitehall; mistaken for the man whose secretary he was, the great British PM Sir Robert Peel. The story has the makings of a Hollywood blockbuster: threat to the prime minister, personal interest of the young queen of England, shooting of the PM's secretary in broad daylight in the centre of one of the greatest cities of the world, his apparent good chances of survival very possibly (as Martyn compellingly argues) ruined by the surgeons. Their medical skills were, if anything, even more backward than those of their colleagues, the psychiatrists. And then, the public baying for blood – for the execution of the murderer. Onto that stage, as M'Naghten's "brief", stepped one of the outstanding men, and certainly one of the most outstanding lawyers of the nineteenth (or any other) century: Alexander Cockburn. I leave it to you to cast the actor to play him.

How excellent it is then that Martyn Frost should have chosen to write this scintillating book. He is a historian whose life has been steeped in law. His first historical work was – like this – a book of huge erudition, yet an absolute page-turner, too: *A Victorian Tragedy*. It covers the seminal and also-still-authoritative case on insanity in wills: Banks v Goodfellow. That case was presided over by Chief Justice Cockburn, M'Naghten's barrister 27 years earlier. Martyn is a master of the subject. He has a depth of understanding only achievable through his researches into the Victorians' attempts to grapple with insanity from both a medical and legal viewpoint, and his mastery of all aspects of Drummond's murder and M'Naghten's trial. Complementing that, as gin to tonic, is his knowledge of Cockburn's life, career and personality. And his light, deft touch keeps the pages turning.

You, dear reader, would have to be criminally insane not to be fascinated by this book. But in the improbable event that you are not fascinated, you will at least have a perfect understanding of your criminal insanity, and the remarkable case which gave birth to the law's definition of it.

Tom Dumont KC
Radcliffe Chambers

AUTHOR'S PREFACE

The trial of Daniel M'Naghten for the shooting of Edward Drummond has long held a fascination for me. The drama of an assassination in the heart of political London was then followed by one of the most important, and sensational, criminal trials of the nineteenth century.[1] Both events created huge public interest in early 1843. The public's appetite for news of the killing, and then the trial, was almost insatiable and the press reporting was most extensive. For one of the barristers involved, he would obtain a verdict that would give a greater impetus to his already flourishing career. It would soon bring him the posts of solicitor general and then attorney general. He would later in his career be appointed Lord Chief Justice of England.

Many in this country had expressed simplistic views on M'Naghten's guilt – they only required a public hanging of the assassin, and the sooner the better. The widespread view was that the assassin's guilt was so obvious that a trial was almost superfluous. It would have been much better for those who cried out for a hanging, to have taken heed of a warning within the *Babylonian Talmud*[2] that directed: "A deaf-mute, an idiot and a minor are difficult to deal with, as he who injures them is liable [to pay], whereas, if they injure others they are exempt."

This was an approach to dealing with the insane criminal that was over a thousand years in advance of nineteenth-century Britain.

From the result of his trial came forth the so-called *M'Naghten Rules*, which gave a supposedly new approach to the law and insanity. This, however, was far from perfect, but no one seemed to mind the probability that M'Naghten would have been hanged if he was judged against these new rules – which would become named after M'Naghten. The new code was seen as a major step forward, although the exact terms of the Rules would later cause more difficulties, particularly in the twentieth century.

Initially the movement towards a recognition of the complexities of partial insanity was a huge step for the law and the people of this country – it was in fact a watershed in English criminal law. At the time of the trial, a large proportion of the British public, Parliament and even the monarch, were appalled at the court's verdict, and all expressed their views accordingly. But gradually, as the century progressed, the populace would start to appreciate that it was much more humane not to kill the mentally ill.

The reform of the law also caused a major change in the practice of medicine for those with mental illnesses. There was a long way for knowledge and medicine to advance in this area, but the M'Naghten verdict at least started an irreversible process – thereby helping to push forward the understanding of the legal relationship between crime, psychiatry and the treatment of the insane.

The outcome of the trial also started an important shift in the practice at the Bar. Trying to move away from the simple "tell right from wrong" test for insanity meant that the Bar had to begin to engage much more with the medical profession, now that medical diagnoses could well become a matter of life and death for the accused.

There is another important theme within this book and that is the actions of the surgeons who treated Drummond after he was shot. There were many conflicts and untruths in the evidence they gave in court, and in their public pronouncements on the health of the victim. It is perhaps unlikely, but certainly not impossible, that Drummond could have survived his wound if doctors had been included in the medical team, which was instead wholly composed of surgeons. Not surprisingly, this absence was later pounced upon by *The Lancet*.

I have tried throughout this book to use contemporary sources, particularly newspapers and periodicals. This is an attempt to reflect contemporary attitudes to the killing and the trial, in order to give more context to the then prevalent attitudes towards mental illness. Some of the contemporary attitudes have the capacity to shock even today. There is always a difficulty attached to using contemporary sources – they are often hurriedly published without sufficient verification. I have tried to correct the more obvious errors.

I must express my thanks to:

Colin Holburn, MB ChB FRCS(Ed) FRCEM for his advice on trauma injury

Professor Robin Jacoby for his ever-reliable help on issues of insanity

Tom Dumont KC for providing a foreword for this book and offering much sensible advice.

Without the generous help from all three this book would be much the poorer.

The Spelling of M'Naghten's name

Ever since M'Naghten's trial, there has been no agreement as to the correct spelling of his name. Being something of a traditionalist, I have used the spelling that has been used in the British, American and Commonwealth law reports – "M'Naghten."

CHRONOLOGY OF EVENTS

January 1843	On various dates in this month, M'Naghten was seen walking around Whitehall, while he was trying to identify Sir Robert Peel.
20 January (Friday)	Edward Drummond was shot once in the back by M'Naghten, following which M'Naghten was arrested. Surgeons gather at Drummond's house to assess his injury. An interview that evening took place between Inspector Tierney and M'Naghten.
21 January (Saturday)	Second interview between Tierney and M'Naghten. M'Naghten finds out that he did not shoot Sir Robert Peel. M'Naghten appears in Bow Street Magistrates' Court. Surgeons consider "Mr Drummond is doing very well".
22 January (Sunday)	M'Naghten's appearance at Bow Street Police Court. Queen Victoria records that Mr Guthrie, surgeon, "had but little hope from the 1st" for Drummond.
23 January (Monday)	Queen Victoria records Drummond as being worse. Doctors' note that bleeding Drummond has been "beneficial".
24 January (Tuesday)	Drummond's decline is now accepted to be terminal.
25 January (Wednesday)	Death of Drummond.
26 January (Thursday)	Coroner's inquest into Drummond's death; Coroner hears report on Drummond's post-mortem. Surgeons' evidence is that Drummond's wound was "inevitably fatal".
29 January (Sunday)	M'Naghten committed to Newgate, pending trial.

31 January (Tuesday)	Funeral of Drummond.
1 February (Wednesday)	M'Naghten committed for trial at the Old Bailey.
2 February (Thursday)	First appearance at the Old Bailey, trial put back to 3 March.
18 February (Wednesday)	M'Naghten examined by medical experts.
3 March (Friday)	Trial begins at the Old Bailey
4 March (Saturday)	Old Bailey trial stopped by judges and M'Naghten found not guilty on grounds of insanity.
10 March (Friday)	James Stevenson first appears in Lord Mayor's Court, charged with threatening to kill the Queen and Sir Robert Peel.
11 March (Saturday)	Guthrie lectures on bullet wounds at the Westminster Hospital.
14 March (Tuesday)	House of Lords debate on M'Naghten decision.
15 March (Wednesday)	M'Naghten removed from Newgate to Bethlem Hospital.
17 March (Friday)	James Stevenson again in Lord Mayor's court.
18 March (Saturday)	James Stevenson again in Lord Mayor's court. Found to be insane.
24 March (Friday)	M'Coleman appears in the Sheriff Clerks Court.
25 May (Friday)	M'Coleman arrested.
26 May (Friday)	House of Lords resolves to take the opinion of the judges on the implications of M'Naghten's acquittal.
19 June (Monday)	Judges attend House of Lords and five questions are put to them without argument regarding the law and partial insanity.
26 March 1864 (Saturday)	M'Naghten transferred to the newly built Broadmoor Asylum.
3 May 1865 (Wednesday)	Death of M'Naghten, aged 52.

PART I

Chapter 1

A DINNER AT WINDSOR CASTLE

In the early evening of Saturday, 20 January 1843, Queen Victoria and Albert, the Prince Consort, were at dinner at Windsor Castle. They had invited a few relatives and some members of their household to dine with them. Queen Victoria had ascended the throne in June 1837,[1] after the death of her uncle King William IV, only a month after she had turned 18. She had proposed to Albert of Saxe-Coburg and Gotha and they were married on 10 February 1840.

A Note is Received

During the dinner, shortly before 8 pm, Prince Albert was called away from the dining table and was handed a note from Sir Robert Peel, the prime minister.[2] The note was addressed to Prince Albert in order that he could read it first and decide when, and how, the queen should be informed of the note's contents. The note informed Prince Albert that Peel's private secretary, Edward Drummond, had been shot in the back that afternoon, at around 3.15 pm, while he had been walking along Whitehall. From the outset, there was some confusion about the time of this shooting, for example the *Morning Post* on the 21st reported it as having happened at 4.30 pm. The more likely time was 3.50pm – the time Drummond is known to have started to walk back to Whitehall after visiting his brother's bank.

Peel's note read:

> Sir, – I have the painful duty of acquainting your Royal Highness that Mr Drummond, my Private Secretary, was shot at this day about quarter past three o'clock, in the neighbourhood of Charing Cross.
>
> Two pistols were discharged, the first close to Mr Drummond's back, the second after the assassin had been seized by a policeman.

The ball entered in the back and has been extracted, after passing round the ribs.[3] I have just left Mr Drummond's house. No vital part appears to have been injured, and there is no unfavourable symptom whatever.

The assassin gives his name as MacNaghten, and appears to be a Glasgow man…….

We have not hitherto been able to discover that this man had any alleged grievance or complaint against the Treasury or any public office.

He has been loitering about the public offices for the last fortnight, and being questioned, I understand, some day since, by the Office Keeper of the Council office, said he was a policeman. This, of course, for the purpose of evading further enquiry.

The policeman who apprehended the man, says that he heard the man exclaim after firing the shots: "He or she (the policeman is uncertain which) shall not disturb my peace of mind anymore."

These are all the particulars I have heard or learned. I am afraid I have given them to your Royal Highness in a hurried manner. I have thought it better to convey this information to Her Majesty, through the kind intervention of your Royal Highness, than by a direct communication to the Queen.

I have the honour to be, Sir, with sincere respect, your Royal Highness's most faithful and humble Servant,

Robert Peel

Prince Albert decided, quite reasonably, that this unwelcome news must be brought to the queen's attention forthwith, and she was called from the dining table to join him. Both were shocked at the news that such a significant political figure had been shot in daylight, on a main thoroughfare, in the heart of London's government quarter. The shock for the queen was all the greater, as not only did she know Mr Drummond, but also because there had already been four unsuccessful attempts on her own life since she had ascended the throne.[4]

No matter how dreadful this news was, it was necessary for the royal couple to conceal their shock and outrage when they returned to the table. There was more discretion needed, as dining with them that evening was Drummond's younger brother, Colonel Berkeley Drummond, Groom in Waiting to the queen.[5] Colonel Drummond had only taken up this post the previous day. He remained oblivious to what had happened in Whitehall, until Prince Albert broke the news to him at the conclusion of the dinner, soon after 8 pm. Upon being told of the shooting, Colonel Drummond was greatly distressed, and he set off immediately for his brother's house, in Lower Grosvenor Street.[6]

The queen recorded the information she had been given about the shooting in her *Journal* later that evening:

> The bullet had passed through the ribs but had been extracted – no vital part had been touched & it was hoped he would do well. We were horrified & all the more so as his brother was sitting opposite to us. My good Albert was going to break the news to him, after dinner. When he had done so, he told me that poor Col. Drummond had been dreadfully overcome & was setting off at once for London, as he felt he could not rest easy here. We & everyone, were much distressed.[7]

By late that afternoon, the news of the shooting had spread rapidly around the West End and the government offices.[8]

Reaction to the News

The shooting of the prime minister's private secretary was an alarming event, particularly given that assassination of public figures was so rarely encountered in England. It was also alarming as being a potential threat to the stability of British politics, depending on who shot Drummond and who else might have been involved in a conspiracy. To most people, the shooting must have been seen as the action of a madman. It was an apparently motiveless attack on an affable private secretary who, all agreed, had no obvious enemies. Others might have been more disturbed, given the recent political and social unrest at that time in Britain (see Chapter 2).

Sir Robert Peel

On the afternoon of the shooting, Sir Robert Peel had been walking with his son Frederick in London. When they reached Cockspur Street, Peel was accosted by a stranger,[9] who asked Peel if he was aware that his private secretary had been shot in Whitehall that afternoon. Cockspur Street was at the south-west corner of Trafalgar Square, linking the Charing Cross with the eastern end of Pall Mall. Peel was therefore very close to the scene of the attack on his secretary, albeit a little after the event. Peel was not previously aware of this news and he made haste on to Lower Grosvenor Street to see how seriously injured Drummond was. Peel was reported as being very shocked by the news. According to *The Times*: [10]

> ...both Her Majesty and His Royal Highness Prince Albert manifested the most intense anxiety for the fate of the unfortunate sufferer. Early the following morning a messenger was despatched from the Castle to Grosvenor Street to ascertain the state of Mr Drummond; and a second messenger arrived at Windsor late the same afternoon, despatched by Sir Robert Peel to Her Majesty. Two communications also arrived at the Castle in the course of yesterday from the residence of Mr Drummond; and it is highly gratifying to state that the accounts transmitted to Her Majesty (who feels the most lively, yet painful, interest for the restoration of Mr Drummond) were of a very favourable and satisfactory nature.

Sir Robert Peel was in his second term as prime minister. He had previously, briefly, been prime minister for 120 days, ending at the start of April 1835. His second ministry lasted much longer – almost five years. In between Peel's two ministries, the Whig politician, Viscount Melbourne, was prime minister. Melbourne had been prime minister when Victoria ascended the throne. She had relied upon Melbourne to guide her through the intricacies of government, as she had received no training to ready her for the duties of a monarch. Victoria formed a close bond with Melbourne, which contrasted with her initial antipathy towards Peel. However, by the time of this shooting, Victoria had begun to recognise Peel's qualities. King Leopold I of Belgium[11] wrote to Victoria:[12]

> It was natural at first that you should not have liked to take him as your Premier; many circumstances united against him. But I must say for you and your family, as well as for England, it was a great blessing that so firm and honourable a man as Peel should have become the head of your Administration...
>
> I believe, besides, Sir Robert is sincerely and warmly attached to you, and as you say with great truth, quite above mere party feeling.

Peel's pragmatism and steadiness in his advice was properly recognised by both Leopold and Victoria. The queen was now becoming able to rely on his advice.

In the entries in Queen Victoria's *Journal* after the day of Drummond's shooting, the queen wrote that both she and Prince Albert were struck by how unwell Sir Robert Peel looked after the shooting. Many who met Sir Robert at this time were also concerned at his appearance and the obvious shock and strain that the killing of Drummond had placed on him. The shock of Drummond's death was magnified for Lady Peel, particularly with her strong belief that Sir Robert had quite probably been the assassin's real target.[13]

Colonel Drummond was back at Windsor the following day with the news that his brother was considered to be out of danger and that "his ultimate recovery might therefore be anticipated."[14]

The event of 20 January would, in due course, lead to a criminal trial at the Old Bailey that absorbed the public's interest and dominated the press. The outcome of the trial would change the criminal law of England for years to come.

Chapter 2

THE STATE OF BRITAIN IN 1843

Changes

Fundamental changes were taking place throughout Britain in the nineteenth century and they would affect the way of life for all classes of the population. Changes of such widespread nature and rapidity had not been seen in this country before. Their significance cannot be underestimated, as they impacted on all areas of British life. Not all changes were universally supported, but the extent of the changes generated their own momentum for further changes in the future.

Politics did not develop and change as fast as industry did, and this had led to an inevitable increase in political tensions. By 1843, the political atmosphere in Britain was tense. At the same time as Drummond's assassin went on trial, over fifty Chartists were on trial in Lancaster for incitement to riot and other offences connected with strikes and civil disorders in the North. But this discontent, which was across many classes of society, went back further than 1843, but the first half of the nineteenth century was a period of increasing political turmoil, working class unrest and a severe financial hangover from the wars against Napoleon.

The French Revolution and Politics

The economic difficulties in Britain, following the defeat of Napoleon in 1815, naturally had an impact on British politics. The discontent generated was increased by the political exhilaration that had been introduced earlier into Britain by the principles of the rights of man and the French Revolution's creed of *liberté, égalité, fraternité*.[1] Although Britain was later to be at war with the French, the original ideals of the French Revolution impressed many of those who sought greater social justice and political improvement in Britain. This impression was particularly strong on those intent on increasing the size of the (male) electorate. As Lord Cockburn,[2] the Scottish Whig judge and politician, put it:

> …everything was connected with the Revolution in France, which for twenty years, was, or was made, all in all, everything; not this thing or that thing, but literally everything was soaked in this one event.

In 1790, Edmund Burke[3] published his *Reflections on the Revolution in France.* He supported the status quo in British politics and opposed the principles of the French Revolution. His book was highly influential for those who were opposed to revolution within Britain. In the following year, the radical Thomas Paine[4] published his support for the French Revolution in *The Rights of Man.* Both books were widely read and discussed by those on all sides of the political debate. The growing awareness of the new political ideas not only inspired new aspirations, but, at the same time, pushed the ruling and professional classes towards repression of the new political demands. These issues would later help significantly with the rise of Chartism as a political reform movement.

The growing violence attached to the French Revolution, and the public executions by guillotine, disillusioned some who originally welcomed the new ideas and there would be others who turned away once there was war between Great Britain and France.

The rise in England of the Corresponding Societies also helped to politicise the previously less engaged levels of society and to fuel national debates on political reform. In 1817, the government's concern at the level of disaffection among the populace led to the suspension of *Habeas Corpus* in England (and in Ireland in 1822).

The Weather

Even the weather now seemed to be against British wellbeing. Bad harvests in 1809–1811 fuelled discontent, hunger and an increase in the number of those reliant on poor relief. Then came 1816, which became known as the "year without a summer". The prime cause of this disastrous year for European farming was that Northern Europe had to endure its coldest summer for centuries.

Much of this disaster was caused by the enormous and violent eruption of Mount Tambora.[5] This began on 5 April 1815, continued until the 10th, and its effects were devastating. The eruption is thought to have been the largest in human history. It was heard 1,200 miles away and volcanic ash, heavy volcanic rains and debris fell widely throughout the region. The eruption reduced the height of Tambora from 4,300m to 2,850m. The minimum estimate for casualties was 71,000.[6]

The effects of this volcanic explosion were made worse by the still lingering after-effects of the powerful eruption of Mount Mayon,[7] exactly one year earlier. These two eruptions, together, distributed vast amounts of volcanic dust high into the atmosphere. The upper atmosphere winds then spread the dust widely, thereby blocking much of the heat from the sun that would usually have reached the earth. The Central England Temperature showed 1816 to have been the eleventh coldest year since 1659, the third coldest summer, and the coldest ever July. Most of Northern Europe was badly affected by the cold, directly in health and hunger because of the widespread crop failures. Such a natural disaster naturally tended to hit the poor harder than the wealthy, who could purchase food at price levels that the poor could not.

Politics

In 1819, after the Peterloo Massacre in Manchester, the Conservative Government pushed through their *Six Acts* legislation. The repressive nature of this legislation inspired yet further resistance to the government. The Peterloo Massacre had horrified Britain, and this helped to generate further demonstrations for political reform. The demonstrators in Manchester in 1819 were approximately 60,000 strong. At that time there was little of what would now be called riot control. The mounted troops that were there could do little but charge to disperse the demonstrators. The lack of order among the troops, as well as too much alcohol, particularly within the Manchester and Salford Yeomanry, led to hundreds of demonstrators (men, women and children) being injured.[8]

Later, in 1830, the east and south of England were the setting for the Swing Riots. These were uprisings of agricultural workers, protesting about working conditions and the increasing use of agricultural machinery. Wider use of machinery had reduced the need for agricultural employment. Often there were warning letters, sent by workers to landowners and magistrates, demanding better treatment, and better wages, as well as the abandonment of the new machinery. Such letters were often signed "Captain Swing", hence the name given to the riots. The riots had some success, especially over the question of wages.

The political atmosphere at the time might not have been improved by the July Revolution of 1830 in France, which removed Charles X from the French throne and, at the same time, the Belgian revolution that separated Belgium from the Netherlands. Revolutions have always made neighbouring countries nervous.

Parliament Burned Down

On 16 October 1832, the Palace of Westminster was destroyed by fire. Lost in the conflagration were both Houses of Parliament. It is now accepted that the fire was started by the careless burning of old wooden tally sticks stored in the Palace of Westminster. The spectacle of Parliament ablaze attracted vast crowds and Parliament Square was filled with spectators, as was Westminster Bridge and the Embankment. Within the crowd were Prime Minister Lord Melbourne and most of his cabinet. Also present was Thomas Carlyle,[9] who later wrote about that night:

> The crowd was quiet, rather pleased than otherwise, whew'd and whistled when the breeze came as if to encourage it – "there's a flare up for the House o' Lords" – "A judgment for the Poor Law bill" – "There go their hacts" (acts). Such exclamations seemed to be the prevailing ones. A man sorry I did not anywhere see.

Others saw the crowds as being less anti-Parliament, but there still seems to have been a significant number rejoicing at the conflagration. The pride that Britain took in its Parliamentary system was dented by this conflagration.

Reform

As the nineteenth century progressed, three great questions came to dominate British politics:

> Greater political emancipation within Britain;
> Free trade (and the consequential repeal of the Corn Laws);
> Catholic Emancipation.

The first eventually gave rise to the Great Reform Act of 1832.[10] While this act was recognised as a major step in reforming the parliamentary franchise, like many reforms, it only paused the pressure for further reform for a little while. More demands would be formulated under the banner of Chartism. The main criticism of the 1832 Act was that it failed to extend voting rights beyond those with property ownership. The public's sense of betrayal by a Whig Government was soon after increased by the passage of the Poor Law Amendment Act 1834.[11] The harshness of this reform alienated the lower classes[12] and fed into the rise of Chartism.

The Great Reform Act also, for the first time, explicitly barred women from voting in elections. This was done by defining a voter as being a male person. This did not change matters, as far as women were concerned, as previously they had not been allowed to vote, but such an explicit legal ban caused more women to begin to question its unfairness. Although it would take a long time to bring about enfranchisement of women, the position after this act was one of increasing debate of women's rights.[13]

The roots of Chartism were originally in the industrial centres of the North and Midlands of England, but then they rapidly spread out from there to other centres of industry. It was the most significant movement for political reform in the first half of the nineteenth century. The Chartists sought:

1. Universal male suffrage at 21.
2. Secret ballots.
3. Abolition of property requirement for an MP.
4. Salaries for MPs.
5. Equalisation of constituency sizes.
6. Annual Parliamentary elections.

It would take a long time to achieve most of these aims (even in part) – the sixth was never realised. When the 1839 *People's Petition* in favour of the six demands in the 1838 *People's Charter* was presented to parliament, it was claimed to have 1.3 million signatures on it. Parliament refused to hear the petitioners and mutterings began in favour of a general strike.

A rising in Newport was followed by other attempts to pressure the government, in Bradford and Sheffield for example, but all were suppressed. However, through 1842 and 1843, strikes and protests continued. There was a General Strike called in 1842 which was connected to the Plug Plot Riots. The strike began in the Staffordshire coalfields and soon spread to the Stalybridge cotton mills. Yorkshire mills walked out and there were stoppages, of different strengths, throughout British coalfields. At its height, it was claimed that

500,000 strikers were involved (a figure that may have been fairly accurate). After riots in the Potteries, 116 strikers were sentenced to imprisonment and a few dozen were sentenced to transportation – some on perjured evidence.

The third major reform was that of emancipation of Roman Catholics. From the nadir of Catholic freedoms at the time of the Gordon Riots (1780), gradual steps were taken to increase the freedoms of Catholics in Britain. While this was gradual, the Roman Catholic Relief Act (1829) was a major step forward for Catholic rights. The passing of this act was bitterly contested and the change of the attitudes of the Duke of Wellington and Sir Robert Peel were pivotal. George IV, while being strongly anti-Catholic, was forced by cabinet pressure to give the Royal Assent to the Roman Catholic Relief Act.

Burgeoning Industry

The first half of the nineteenth century was a period of increasing progress in innovation in industry and transport in Britain. By the time Queen Victoria came to the throne in 1837, Britain already led the world in the development of the steam railway. This was not merely a revolution in steam transportation of passengers, as this was initially a minor event when compared to the impact on freight transportation, which had far wider effects on the British way of life.

The rapid increase in industrial development was the start of a new economy where industry would increasingly displace agriculture in financial importance. The early beginnings of this change might have been towards the end of the eighteenth century, but in the nineteenth century, with the pace of change quickening, there were ever greater effects on the national way of life.

The rapid growth of railways made newspapers easier and quicker to distribute, resulting in sales increasing by over 400 per cent from 1820 to 1850. This increase in sales was also facilitated by the reduction of the stamp tax on newspapers to one penny. A direct consequence of cheaper newspapers was that more people became more aware of political issues, as well as becoming better informed about Britain and its place in the world. New newspapers coming onto the market offered a wider spread of opinions on politics. At the same time, regional newspapers could provide local news more easily. The introduction in Britain of the uniform penny post, in January 1840, also helped to facilitate the spread of discussion and ideas.

The greater mobility offered by railways increased the movement of the population. Thomas Cook was the first to see the possibilities of train travel for leisure and he exploited the growing rail network for early excursions and tourism. This would continue to grow throughout the century.[14] The new accessibility of travel also enabled businessmen to travel more easily and develop new markets for products. Even new ways of trading such as mail order could be established.[15] The new railway lines helped to promote greater cohesion between different parts of the country. 1843 saw the opening of the Manchester and Leeds Railway, the Great Western Railway (between Bristol and London) and the London and Brighton and South Coast Railway. The new railways got the royal mark of approval when the queen travelled on the Great Western from Slough to Paddington.

A railway network required extensive civil engineering work in order to create it.[16] Therefore, the expansion of the network across the country required much hard physical labour, as initially the work was nearly all by pick and shovel. Hard working, hard drinking, and hard fighting gangs of "navvies"[17] provided the muscle. Some mechanisation was introduced in the 1840s with, for example, the development of the steam shovel. Opposition to railways being built (or despoiling the countryside, depending on one's point of view) often led to violent confrontations between landowners' men and the railways' navvies and surveyors. While these battles were being fought in the countryside, Parliamentary authorisation of new railway routes was fought in Parliamentary committee rooms by lucratively remunerated barristers. Generally speaking, the railways usually won these skirmishes.

A railway expansion on this scale meant the rapid development of heavy industry was necessary to create the new infrastructures. The quantities of iron and coal which were then required vastly changed the scale of iron ore extraction and coal mining to increase the production of metal. Not only was more iron and coal required, but industry also increasingly wanted better quality of both.

The capacity of the railways to transport much heavier goods than could be moved on roads (by horse) and on water (by canal) revolutionised the size and weight of freight that could then be moved by the new railways. The increasing speed of the newer steam engines enabled quicker delivery times for freight to be moved to customers in Britain and, significantly, to ports for export across the world. As Britain was the leader in railway design and engineering, engineers (and their construction companies) were in demand in Europe and throughout the Empire.

The ironworkers' increasing skills were also in demand for better iron, and later steel, products. Steam power was needed to drive the new screw propellers and replace older paddle wheels. This was to be revolutionary for both the Royal Navy and for the British merchant navy. Better quality steel transformed armaments for the Royal Navy and also began to change ship design – leading, as the century progressed, to the ability to replace wooden hulls with metal hulls[18] and to protect the ships further with armour plating.

The need for more raw materials, to make more engineered products, placed a strain on the ability of financial institutions to lend money to finance this progress. This was by no means a risk-free area for lending and there would be some notable insolvencies along the way. Nevertheless, the rewards could be substantial, and this provided impetus for the expansion of the British banking system at home and abroad. Not everyone profited from railway expansion, but the gathering pace of progress in science and new industries was too rapid to be slowed down, increasing particularly in the second half of the century. The woollen and cloth industries that had formed part of the first wave of industrial development also benefitted as the mills increased in size and production capacity, particularly to meet export markets. But amid all these changes, wages, safety and working conditions became an area of labour vs capitalism.

Assassins

With the political tensions in Britain there was an unwelcome trend for assassins to seek to influence politics through violence. At the start of the century, James Hadfield, an ex-Dragoon sergeant in the British Army, shot at King George III in London. Hadfield had received several severe sword wounds to his head in 1794, at the Battle of Tourcoing. At that time he was serving as part of the Duke of York's bodyguard in the Flanders campaign (1793–1795) against the French. The result of these wounds was that Hadfield became prone to violent outbursts – during one such episode he threatened to kill his own child because "God had ordered him to do so". After his return to England, Hadfield became involved in millennialism[19] and he believed that the second coming of Christ would be brought forward if he, Hadfield, became a martyr.

However, given his belief that his death must not be by his own hand, Hadfield planned to be killed by the British Government. On 15 May 1800, Hadfield fired a pistol at King George III, as the king entered the Royal Box at the Drury Lane Theatre. He had deliberately aimed to miss, hoping thereby to force his own execution by the government for attempting to kill the Sovereign. It was reported that his shot missed the king by 12 inches. He was charged with treason, but he was saved from execution by the brilliance of the barrister, Thomas Erskine, who defended Hadfield. Erskine's arguments were powerful and well-presented and led to the trial being stopped by the presiding judge, Lord Kenyon. Hadfield was acquitted by reason of insanity.[20] It was a startling conclusion that was far from universally approved.

Soon after Hadfield's trial, in 1802, the Despard Plot for the assassination of George III was foiled by the authorities. The plot took its name from Colonel Edward Marcus Despard, a former army officer and colonial official, who had been removed from his post for refusing to recognise any distinction between races.[21] He now sought the abolition of the monarchy and its replacement by a republic. The plot was known to the government for at least five months before the planned attack. The conspirators were seized one week before the attack on the cabinet was due. The conspirators were then tried and found guilty and the seven conspirators were executed. Political turbulence was very much in the air.

1812 saw the mysterious assassination of Emmanuel Henri Louis Alexandre de Launay, Comte d'Antraigues in Barnes. He was a colourful character, well known on the continent with many political contacts there, but he was perhaps too incautious in some political matters in Europe. The bloody murders, of the count and his wife by his valet, created a sensation. In the same year Spencer Perceval, then prime minister, was assassinated in the Lobby of the House of Commons. His assassin was convicted of murder, despite him being clearly insane.

In 1818, there was an attempt to assassinate Lord Palmerston,[22] who was then the secretary at war. On 1 April, Lieutenant Davies, an officer on half pay, shot at Palmerston, who had just reached the top of the stairs in the War Office. Davies shot as Palmerston turned towards his office, which meant that the pistol ball only grazed his back.[23] Davies was clearly mentally ill, and was soon found to be insane. He was confined in Bedlam for the rest of his life. Palmerston ensured that Davies was treated fairly by paying for Davies's defence in court.

A more ambitious attempt at assassination soon followed in 1820, with the Cato Street Conspiracy targeting the prime minister[24] and his entire cabinet.[25] This conspiracy was linked to the government restrictions on dissent and demonstrations in the previous years. The killings were prevented by the presence of an informer within the conspiracy. The informer was George Edwards, a police spy. The leader of the conspiracy was Arthur Thistlewood and Edwards became his second in command. During the arrest of the conspirators, a Bow Street Runner was killed by Thistlewood. Five of the conspirators were later hanged and, when dead, decapitated.[26] A further five conspirators were transported to Australia for life. In 1832, there was an "attempt" on the life of William IV by Dennis Collins, who threw two stones at the king.

Finances

In 1815, Britain had emerged victorious from the Napoleonic Wars, but had in fact been at war with France since they helped to create the first anti-Revolutionary France coalition in early 1793. Britain was then at war with France, and her allies, for virtually the whole time until 1815.

As well as financing the British Navy and Army, Britain became a paymaster for the anti-French forces' struggle in Europe. This major role reflected Britain's financial standing as the leading mercantile and banking country opposed to French hegemony. Britain at this time was also the possessor of an extensive non-European empire that would grow further as a result of the victory in the war against Napoleon. The Empire remained a major economic asset for Britain. The most important part of the Empire was what is now India, Pakistan, Afghanistan, Bangladesh, Burma and Ceylon. The conquest of these areas was still progressing in 1843.

The financial strain of the support for the anti-French alliances required both tax increases (including the imposition of an income tax[27] as a "temporary measure") and a major increase in the national debt. The temporary nature of income tax appeared to be confirmed by its abolition in 1802 by Prime Minister Henry Addington.[28] Addington was enabled to do this by the short period of peace provided by the Treaty of Amiens. The peace lasted scarcely more than a year.

Unfortunately, the breakdown of the Peace of Amiens meant that war was resumed with France in May 1803 and Addington, through financial necessity, had to reintroduce income tax in 1803.[29] It was later abolished in 1816. A measure of the public's view of income tax as being un-British can be gathered by the demand in 1816 that, not only must the government repeal the tax, but also that it should destroy all records of the tax assessments and payment. The government, to satisfy public opinion, duly destroyed the records in a public bonfire. However, this was not done without squirrelling away copies of the details of the assessments and payments in the Treasury records.

The demobilisation of soldiers and sailors, after peace in Europe was established in 1815, added to the rise in unemployment in Britain. At the same time, the economy was trying to recover from the war-time financial demands, which had resulted in the British national debt rising to £1bn by 1815. As with too many wars, the lack of employment for discharged soldiers and sailors helped to fuel further political unrest in Britain. Armed forces, of different times and different wars, have always seen the post-war lack of adequate employment as betrayal by the monarch/government of the day. The Luddite movement, opposed to the effects of growing mechanisation on employment, also rose and fell before 1820.

The growing financial needs of government had, by 1842, produced a substantial annual budget deficit. The prime minister at the time, Sir Robert Peel, an avowed opponent of income tax, had little choice but to reintroduce income tax in 1842.[30] To try to expand trade, at the same time as introducing income tax, Peel would eventually reduce a wide range of trade tariffs. He also attempted to repeal the Corn Laws, but this was lost against strong resistance from the Commons and many within his own party. Although Peel had previously been against this repeal, he now recognised the urgent need for repeal – even if his party did not.

Armed Forces

The role of the Royal Navy had been of huge importance in Britain's victory in the wars against the French and their allies. It was, at this time, the most powerful and well-trained navy in the world. It provided protection for Britain against invasion from the European continent and defence (and acquisition) of British colonies. The Navy also provided some security for the British merchant fleet thereby helping this fleet with some security of trade. At the same time, the Navy also enforced the blockade against continental trade. This trade blockade was a useful economic tool to use against Napoleon and his allies and it harmed continental economies, but it was also very unpopular at home.

The economic strains on the national economy from this long running war, followed by the difficulties of adapting British economic policy to peace time needs, helped to fuel discontent at home, particularly within the working classes. The level of unemployment served to suppress wage levels and aggravate unrest among the employed.

The lead taken by British politicians in the abolition of slavery and the slave trade led to the Royal Navy creating their West African Squadron which was highly effective in capturing slave ships and liberating slaves.[31]

The British Army that performed so well under Wellington in Spain and France was disbanded with alacrity, so much so that when the Waterloo

Campaign in 1815 required British troops, many of the experienced soldiers had already been discharged from the army. This reduced the number of British soldiers that were available for this campaign, while increasing the number of unemployed ex-soldiers who were looking for jobs in England.

Turmoil

It was against all the above background of demands for change and social unrest that the assassination of Edmund Drummond took place. The changes to the structures of society, and the pressures for more changes and more civil rights, all made the ruling and middle classes uneasy. The killing of the prime minister's private secretary was therefore, to these classes, yet another frightening event. Only thirty years before, Spencer Perceval,[32] the then Tory prime minister, had been assassinated by a pistol fired in the lobby of the House of Commons. That event in itself shocked the country, but while the reaction of the upper classes was one of horror, the working classes were jubilant. Perceval was, to the working man, an obstacle to all political reform and his administration had brought on the poor nothing but hardship after hardship. The London crowd quite literally danced outside Parliament in celebration of Perceval's death, while at the same time trying to reach the assassin, John Bellingham, to shake his hand and free him from his arrest. The mob forced a number of the mounted Life Guards to retreat from the scene. Bellingham was later taken by coach to Newgate Prison under an escort of Dragoons. While Bellingham was in jail awaiting trial, the risk of an attempt to free him was considered so likely that the 1st Regiment of Horse was deployed on the Surrey side of Blackfriars Bridge and 250 men of the 1st Regiment of Foot stationed in the Brunswick Street riding school – such was the feeling against the execution by the working classes.

By 1843, there was further political ferment, as a major attempt to repeal the Corn Laws was being proposed. These laws had protected the British farmers from grain prices being depressed by the importation of cheaper grain from abroad. If free trade in grain was allowed there would be much advantage, for example in cheaper bread, for the poorer classes. However, for the British farmers more competition from cheaper grain imports would force down their profits. Although Sir Robert Peel, as prime minister, would eventually split the Conservative Party and force through the repeal of the Corn Laws, until 1843 he had voted consistently against repeal. However, Peel was nothing if not a realist and, despite his previous support for the protectionist duties, he had come to recognise the much greater potential for Britain in the wholesale abolition of duties. The consequential rapid increase in trade proved him to have been correct. His original support for high tariffs had originally made Peel something of a hate figure for the reformers and their supporters. The *Weekly Chronicle* commented that:

> Anti-Corn law meetings in town and country multiply at such a rate that it is impossible for a weekly newspaper to chronicle even their names.[33]

On 17 February 1843, the leading Radical MP Richard Cobden, during a debate in the Commons, caused uproar on the Tory benches when he claimed that Peel was:

> ...individually responsible for the present condition of the country....I tell him that the whole responsibility of the lamentable and dangerous state of the country rests with him.

This apparently personal attack on Peel caused the Tory MPs to turn on Cobden. Cobden attempted to explain that he was referring to official responsibility resting with Peel, and that he did not mean personal responsibility. This sort of half-apology infuriated the Tory members still more. That this heated exchange occurred very soon after the assassination of Peel's private secretary probably accounted for some of this display of bad temper, on both sides of the House. When the Corn Laws were repealed in 1846, Peel's Conservative party was split and Peel resigned from office. In his valedictory speech, Peel acknowledged that it was Cobden, more than any other individual, who should take the credit for the repeal of the Corn Laws.

At the same time as the Anti-Corn Law campaign, the Chartist movement was also increasing the pressure on the government for more radical political reform. 1842 had seen the submission of the second Chartist petition to Parliament. There was an economic depression in the country that produced significant hardship for the working class and a rise in industrial unrest. All these events made for Peel's administration becoming ever more unpopular. But, from the point of view of the gentry and mercantile class, Peel was a man who could protect them.

It is worth noting that the *Morning Herald* carried an article just before the trial of M'Naghten. It began by observing that:

> The statement made at Bow-street on Saturday as to the intention of the murderer M'Naughten in shooting at the lamented Mr Drummond has produced a profound and most painful sensation throughout the metropolis and increased the general anxiety to know the actual state of the prisoner's mind. But whether he committed this atrocious crime when sane or insane, its perpetration will surely give some check to the dangerous agitation and seditious and treasonable style of public oratory so much in fashion now-a-days? Be the man a lunatic or a rational being, when his thoughts turned on public affairs, the act by which he deprived the public service of an excellent officer, the Prime Minister of an able and confidential helper, and his relatives and friends of a gentle and valued kinsman and acquaintance, was originally provoked by the violence of liberal politics.[34]

The final sentence is undoubtedly incorrect, as there is little evidence that the Act was inspired by violent rhetoric on the part of liberal politicians. It does however indicate a tendency in the politics of the day towards greater aggression in personal attacks. As such, it served to poison the English political atmosphere still further.

Chapter 3

THE VICTIM

Edward Drummond was an experienced civil servant with impeccable political and society connections. He was also a great-grandson of William Drummond, 4th Viscount Strathallan, a Scottish hero and Jacobite, who was killed by an English sword-thrust at Culloden in 1746. His life and death were remembered in Robert Burns's *Strathallan's Lament*.

William Drummond had a brother, Andrew Drummond, a goldsmith, who had left Scotland for London. Andrew founded Drummond's Bank in 1717 at Charing Cross.[1] The bank was a success – it still exists, but it was acquired by the Royal Bank of Scotland in 1924.

Edward, born 30 March 1792, was the son of Charles Drummond and Frances Drummond. Charles had been one of the original partners when the banking partnership was created and, for a time, he was manager of Drummond's Bank. There were nine children of his marriage, although only five survived childhood. One son, Edward, never married, nor did his sister, Charlotte Matilda. She lived with Edward at his leased house at 19 Lower Grosvenor Street and ran his household for him. This street was, at that time, considered to be a respectable area of central London.

Edward had matriculated on 23 October 1810 at Christ Church, Oxford, aged 18. During his brief time at Oxford, Drummond was reported as having been notable for the quality of his manners, conversation, discretion and his thoroughly good nature. He was therefore popular with his fellow students. However, the following year he left Oxford, returned to London, and joined the civil service, as a clerk of the Treasury. It is not known why he left college without taking a degree, but quite possibly it was due to a lack of funds and the necessity of earning his own living. The banking wealth appears to have been very much in the hands of those Drummonds who managed the bank.

Edward and Politics

When Edward moved to London, he began to move in fashionable and political circles.[2] He did well at the Treasury and, by the time of his death, he had risen to be the chief clerk in the Treasury – a position of no little importance within the Civil Service. Through his talents and ability, he attracted the attention of the Earl of Ripon,[3] the then Chancellor of the Exchequer, and in 1823 he was appointed to be Ripon's personal secretary. That he held this position at the age of 31 was a testimony to his capabilities.

Drummond would later be the personal secretary to three prime ministers,[4] and in 1843 he was the personal secretary to a fourth prime minister, Sir Robert Peel.[5] All of these prime ministers were Tories. The Duke of Wellington was said to have praised Drummond publicly when he declared that he had "unbounded confidence in [Drummond's] integrity" and he had, on another occasion, publicly expressed his great satisfaction that Mr Drummond had done him the honour of becoming his private secretary – high praise indeed from one who was known for his exacting standards.[6]

The Role of a Personal Secretary

For almost twenty years Drummond discharged the role of personal secretary to these politicians – duties which *The Times* described as:

> …only inferior to those of a Cabinet Minister, because they are less conspicuous…. As there is no connexion so close as that which binds the English statesman to his secretary – a connexion unknown and unappreciated in foreign courts – so perhaps, there is no grief so profound as that which an English statesman feels for the loss of him in whose person the qualities of friend and partisan have been harmoniously blended – who has been the associate of his public counsels, the confidant of his public cares, and the cheerful companion of his private life.

A former prime minister, Lord Melbourne, a Whig politician, held no partisan views against Drummond and said of him that he was "a very quiet, gentlemanly and agreeable man".[7] The *Morning Post*[8] described Drummond as "…no man could have been more generally deservedly popular than Mr Drummond." Thomas Raikes thought Drummond to be a "mild, inoffensive character" who could have had no private enemy.[9] There was no cross-party animus towards Drummond, as he was respected across the political spectrum.

After Drummond's death *The Spectator*[10] wrote:

> To the Minister, whose confidential helper he was, in the closet-labours which are the statesman's great toil, the loss, for the time at least, can hardly be overrated. It is losing another brain – another map of ideas, amplifying and often more perfectly expressing what forms but a section of the Minister's range of thought, necessary for perpetual reference to make clear the whole chart. The private secretary – the other self that stays at home to keep work going while the statesman is abroad – must be the greatest privation that a Minister personally can sustain; and Mr. DRUMMOND had been that other self to some of our most famous rulers.

Lord Ashley wrote to Sir Robert Peel:

> He was to you so true a friend and so valuable an assistant that I may venture to regard him as among those whom you most loved and honoured. God knows the loss is not yours only; everyone who enjoyed the acquaintance of the poor dear fellow must feel that society can ill afford the privation of so simple-hearted and so English a gentleman.[11]

Drummond's popularity was not confined to politicians. Peel, in a letter to Queen Victoria regarding Drummond's death, wrote of how much the killing had affected his wife, Lady Julia Peel. Not only was Lady Peel aghast at Drummond's assassination, but she was further distressed by suspecting that her husband was the real target of the assassin. Both Peel and his wife were due to stay at Windsor Castle very soon after the shooting, but this visit was cancelled as Julia Peel was left in a state of nervous collapse after the news of the shooting. It took some months before she was fully restored to health.[12]

Press Reaction

Because of Drummond's importance in British political life, his assassination instantly caused public horror. The arrest and trial of the killer gave rise to, for the time, very significant press attention throughout the country. The *Morning Post* leader described Drummond's popularity among his peers the day after the shooting. The paper spoke of his bonhomie, kindness, manners and courtesy. He was described in the press as being of "full habit of flesh" (portly).[13]

In his role as private secretary to the prime minister, Drummond travelled with Peel often and had occasion to meet Queen Victoria and the prince consort. The queen also held Drummond in high regard and she recorded in her *Journal*:

> …he had been a perfect gentlemen & that he could see anyone for Sir Robert. He had the most perfect temper, which nothing could ruffle. He had the rare advantage of never betraying anything, yet at the same time, mixing a great deal in society & talking upon all subjects. He remarked that he must have been an extraordinary man, else he would not have been chosen as Private Sec^y by 5 Prime Ministers.[14]

The *Illustrated London News* in an editorial comment on the death of Drummond considered that:

> A fearful impression is beginning to prevail that the stain of assassination is fixing its indelible blackness upon the land …….we have had now, within a short period of time, five black attempts at broad-day assassinations – all of the most revolting and motiveless description – all most base, foul and unnatural – and three of these have been directed against the person of a beloved and virtuous Queen.[15]

While there was much public anger towards M'Naghten, the same issue of the *Illustrated London News* displayed a more rational approach towards the forthcoming trial:

> We are content that the wretched man should abide the ordeal of his country's laws and, mercy forfend, that we should demand vengeance instead of justice when he is tried! If he really is mad – if reason is shut out of his brain – if his heart is blind – his mind sadly and hopelessly incoherent, irresponsible and void of thought – his soul darkened and prostrate under an almighty affliction – it is not for man to dole forth retribution unto such as him.

William Henry Stevenson, who replaced Drummond as Peel's private secretary, gave evidence at trial. He confirmed that Drummond had apartments allocated to him at 10 Downing Street, while Peel frequently worked from his home. Both, therefore, walked often between the two houses.

Charlotte Drummond

Given her lack of personal wealth, Charlotte Drummond was faced with immediate financial difficulties after her brother's death and needed to surrender the lease on their Grosvenor Street property quickly, despite having no other property to go to. Sir Robert Peel wrote to the queen asking for assistance for Charlotte. Queen Victoria quickly agreed to assist and noted in her *Journal*:

> Wrote to Sir Robert Peel, in answer to a letter I received from him, late last night, in which he expressed a hope, I might be able to give poor Miss Drummond an apartment at Hampton Court, which I said I would be happy to do.[16]

There were a number of grace and favour apartments at Hampton Court, which could be allocated to deserving individuals at the queen's discretion. Peel's letter of 25 January referred to Miss Drummond as living with her brother and being dependent upon him. He added that "it would be a very great comfort to a lady of most unexceptionable conduct and most deeply attached to her brother."[17]

Sir Robert Peel also assisted the Drummond family by arranging for Drummond's nephew to be appointed to a vacant clerk's position at the Treasury.

Chapter 4

THE SHOOTING

On 20 January, Edward Drummond had been attending to his official duties as private secretary to Peel at the Privy Council offices during the late morning. He left Downing Street at about 3.30 pm to call on his brother, Charles Drummond, at Drummond's Bank. He walked along Whitehall to the bank in Charing Cross. Peel later wrote in a letter that he believed that he must have walked within 3 yards of M'Naghten half an hour before the shooting, but M'Naghten either did not see him or, more likely, could not recognise him.[1] Presumably this would have been either when he left his house or when Peel left the Privy Council office.

Whitehall and Charing Cross were both, at that time, busy parts of London – these streets were described as "densely thronged" with pedestrians on that day. The difference then, when compared to today, was the number, and diversity, of small shops, workshops and offices, particularly in the northern sections of Whitehall and Charing Cross. Drummond's walk to his family's bank was therefore along crowded pavements.

Outside the Treasury, Drummond met the Earl of Haddington, then the First Lord of the Admiralty, and Haddington accompanied Drummond on his walk up Whitehall. The two parted company outside the Admiralty Building, and Drummond continued alone towards his brother's bank, which was near to the statue of Charles I at the Charing Cross.[2] Any conversation Drummond had with Haddington was unlikely to have been scintillating, as Haddington was reckoned by his contemporaries to be a most dull man indeed.[3]

The assassin had followed Drummond during his walk to the bank. While Drummond was inside the bank, M'Naghten waited in a doorway about two doors away from the bank. At around 3.40 pm[4] Drummond, having completed his business with his brother, left the bank and reversed his earlier walk to go down Whitehall, towards Downing Street. Very soon, at a point near the Salopian coffee house, M'Naghten approached Drummond from behind, then shot him in the left side of his back with a pistol. M'Naghten was so close to his quarry that when he fired, the powder-flash from his pistol caused Drummond's coat to start to smoulder.

Police Constable James Silver

Fortuitously, Police Constable James Silver of A Division[5] was on the other side of Whitehall, almost opposite the scene of the shooting. On hearing the shot, Silver immediately ran across the road to tackle M'Naghten. This was not without risk, as the roadway was very busy with horse-drawn traffic in both directions. As Silver reached Drummond, M'Naghten put the pistol that he had just fired into his jacket and was drawing a second pistol which he then pointed at Drummond. As the powder-smoke from the first shot cleared, Silver tackled M'Naghten and, during their struggle, the second pistol was fired but the pistol ball did not hit anyone.[6] Silver succeeded in holding down M'Naghten on the pavement. He then handcuffed him, with the assistance of a bystander.[7] Although they were not required to give evidence at trial, this second shot was also observed, according to the *Morning Post*,[8] by two witnesses. One was a shopman in the employ of Mr Mitchell the stationer at No 39 Charing Cross and the second was a clerk employed by Mr Groves the fishmonger at No 33.[9]

The Bystanders

Two bystanders later gave evidence in court about the shooting. Robert Hodge, a carpenter, saw M'Naghten's first shot hit Drummond, but then as Hodge approached M'Naghten, he stared back intently at Hodge. Fearing he would be the assassin's next target, Hodge fled into the road, ran into a horse-drawn omnibus, and fell over in the street.[10] A second bystander, Benjamin Weston, a porter at the nearby Ship Tavern, was outside the Salopian coffee house when he heard the first shot. He saw Drummond stagger, clutching at his left side. He also saw the gunman draw out his second pistol and start to aim it, moments before Silver grappled with him. Weston ran to the aid of the policeman and helped him to subdue the gunman.[11] The gunman was then handcuffed by Silver.

Where Exactly Did the Shooting Take Place?

There was, not unexpectedly, some divergence as to where the shooting took place in the different eye-witness accounts, and the contemporary reporting.

In 1843, the northern end of what is today called Whitehall was then known as Charing Cross, taking its name from the Charing Cross[12] originally erected there (Charing Cross is now the southern part of Trafalgar Square at the junction with Whitehall). In 1843 Whitehall ended and Charing Cross began approximately at Whitehall Place, opposite the Old Admiralty building, and ended at the Charing Cross.

Mr Drummond had walked north along the western pavement of Whitehall to Drummond's Bank (49 Charing Cross) and he then returned southwards on the same pavement until he was shot. The evidence of Benjamin Weston, who helped to capture the gunman, was that the shooting took place between the Salopian coffee house and the Ship Hotel. These two premises were numbers 41 and 45 Charing Cross respectively. These numbers place them among the buildings on the west side of the road which ran north from the Old Admiralty Building to Drummond's Bank. Weston worked for John Hill, the tenant of Nos 41 and 45, so it is most unlikely that he would have not been able to identify the place correctly.

The Times' *Correspondence*

In March 1891, *The Times* published an article about Sir Robert Peel and, embarrassingly, it incorrectly referred to Edward Drummond as having been shot in the lobby of the House of Commons. The author of the article had clearly confused Drummond with Prime Minister Spencer Perceval who was assassinated in the House of Commons lobby in 1812. This glaring error prompted further correspondence – and no doubt some harsh words from the paper's editor.

An eyewitness to the event, who was not called to give evidence at the trial, wrote to *The Times* on 2 April 1891 about the shooting, merely identifying himself as "P.H.A.". He had been travelling on a horse-drawn omnibus from Peckham which had made a routine stop "near the corner of the Admiralty". He said that the conductor jumped off the omnibus and followed the rapidly forming crowd to Drummond's Bank. The conductor quickly returned to his passengers with the news that the victim was "a cousin to Drummond, the banker, and secretary to Sir Robert Peel, from whom he had only just parted".

This account had some support from another letter to *The Times* on 28 March 1891 from "F.G.A.M.". He was not an eyewitness but he clearly recollected being told at the time that the shooting took place "near the lamp post at the north east corner of the Admiralty". He also believed that Drummond clung to the lamppost outside of the Admiralty after he was hit by the first pistol ball. While this is, of itself, worth little as evidence, it does match with other, more contemporary accounts, apart from hanging on to the lamppost (although this could be quite probable).

This 1891 correspondence also brought forth a letter from George Frederick Parratt. He had been a clerk working under Drummond in 1843. He claimed that Drummond had been shot on the pavement opposite the entrance to the Treasury. This claim is wholly inconsistent with all other witness accounts and Parratt's letter does not claim that he actually saw the shooting. This version of events must be discounted as it is so much at odds with the eyewitnesses' evidence. However, Parratt was correct in saying that earlier Drummond had crossed Whitehall to Whitehall Gardens to see Peel in the morning and this information appeared in a number of other accounts.

Other contemporary newspapers' reports described the shooting as taking place in the gap between the Horse Guards and the Admiralty, but this seems too far south to be correct. Another newspaper report[13] linked the shooting to a gunsmiths and a stationers in Charing Cross. The 1843 Post Office London Directory shows that No 39 Charing Cross was the premises of William Mitchell & Son, booksellers and stationers, and No 37 was the premises of Henry Tatham, gun, pistol and rifle maker. No 39 adjoined the Salopian to the south. *The Spectator*[14] also claimed that the shooting was near the Salopian. A second account in the *Morning Post* of 21 January 1843 located the shooting outside Mitchell's the stationers. PC James Silver's evidence at the coroner's inquest[15] was reported to have been that after the first shot, when he crossed the road, Drummond was at the door of the stationers and the gunman was by the door of the gunsmiths. Silver estimated that the two were about 4 yards apart.

There is little difference in the mention of the corner of the Admiralty and the Salopian coffee shop[16] as those locations were very close to each other. It seems that this is probably as accurate as the location can be identified. That the assassination took place fairly close to Drummond's Bank is given some support by the multiple reports that Drummond was able to walk, with some difficulty, to the bank after the shooting.

The Duke of Wellington

The disturbance in Whitehall, with shots fired and a policeman tackling the gunman, caused no little alarm among the pedestrians in Whitehall. One who was not perturbed, and was well acquainted with weapons being discharged, was the Duke of Wellington. At the time of Drummond's shooting, the Duke had just left his office in Horse Guards[17] and was walking towards St James's Park, across Horse Guards Parade, when a "stout youth about 16 or 17 years of age" ran into the duke, almost knocking him over. A policeman immediately came to the duke's assistance and seized the lad, who tried to apologise to the duke, but he would accept no apology and walked off towards the park and his residence, Apsley House, at Hyde Park Corner. The police held the youth in their cells for three hours to make sure that the duke did not want him charged (and probably to make absolutely certain that the boy had nothing to do with the shooting).[18]

Reaction

Despite being the victim of M'Naghten's attack, there was no possibility that there was anything personal in the attack. M'Naghten and Drummond moved in entirely different spheres of society and would never have met, nor would they have had social or business dealings, before this attack.

The *Morning Post* leader commented on 21 January:

> It is hoped and believed that the wounds inflicted on Mr Drummond are not likely to prove fatal, but this cannot lesson the disgust and horror we feel at the attempt to commit so atrociously un-English a crime. Both in private and in public life no man could have been more generally and deservedly popular than Mr E Drummond. His frankness and bonhomie had so thoroughly endeared him to his friends, and his kindness and courtesy gained him the respect of all who were brought into communication with him in his official capacity, that all suspicion of the assassin having been actuated by private vengeance is at once removed. The strong probability, therefore, is that he was instigated by political motives to the commission of this foul crime and that he mistook Mr Drummond for Sir Robert Peel, or some other member of the Government.

On the same day *The Times* expressed similar views on the shooting:

> But we cannot abstain from expressing our horror, not only at the present atrocious attempt, whoever may have been its designed

> victim, but at the dreadful imputation which this and similar attempts have fixed upon the national character. Formerly it was our boast that the weapon of the assassin – exercised for ready gain in all Europe besides – was unknown save by ignominious report in England: formerly Englishmen would have thought it a foul scorn that men in public station should be marked out for murder in the public streets.
>
> But events that have occurred within the present century may have disabused us of this cherished and exalted faith. The belief in the honour and manly courage of Englishmen is become one of those ancient superstitions, the memory of which provokes a painful comparison between the past and present times.

Both of these reports read very oddly today, with their references to the supposed virtues of the English national character and English scorn for the ways of foreign countries.

On 21 January, Peel sent a note to the queen about his meeting that morning with Home Secretary Sir James Graham. He told Graham that a Police Inspector Tierney had gone into M'Naghten's cell early that morning and had asked M'Naghten if he was aware of who he had shot. Tierney said that M'Naghten replied "Yes, Sir Robert Peel". Graham and Peel were quick to conclude from this that Peel had to be the original target; a conclusion that horrified the queen.[19] Two plain clothes policemen were provided straightaway after the shooting to act as bodyguards for Peel. There was further concern that drunks in the street were heard uttering threats against the queen and Sir Robert and "infirm brains began to work in that direction."[20]

It would be some time after the shooting before Peel was considered safe from any further attack.

Chapter 5

DRUMMOND'S FUNERAL

Edward Drummond died from the pistol ball wound in his back on 25 January 1843. Although initially the surgeons treating him were optimistic for his chances, Drummond steadily declined. There was little controversy over his treatment while he was alive, but now, looking more closely at his treatment, the surgeons' press releases and their other later statements, there are some serious issues that can be identified in his treatment. These issues are set more fully in Chapter 9.

Given the optimistic nature of so many of the surgeons' bulletins about Drummond's prospects, his death, when it came, was a blow to his friends and colleagues. Sir Robert Peel and Lady Peel were much distressed by his death. In a note to the queen on the day of the death, Peel wrote:

> This sad event has had such an effect on Lady Peel, and all the circumstances attending it are so distressing to Sir Robert Peel, that relying upon your Majesty's great kindness, he ventures to express a hope that your Majesty will have the goodness to permit Sir Robert and Lady Peel to remain for the present in London, or should your Majesty desire to see Sir Robert Peel before Wednesday next, to allow him to wait upon your Majesty in the morning of any day which your Majesty may be pleased to name.... He need scarcely assure your Majesty that nothing but such a sad event as that which has occurred would induce him to prefer this request to your Majesty.[1]

Funeral and Burial

Drummond's funeral took place on 31 January 1843. The service was held at Charlton-near-Woolwich, in Kent. The Reverend Arthur Drummond was the incumbent of this parish. It was the Drummond family's wish that only immediate members of the family would follow the coffin from Lower Grosvenor Street to the church.

The cortège left Drummond's home in Lower Grosvenor Street at 8 am. At the head of the cortège were funeral mutes,[2] and they were followed by a page bearing a plume of black feathers. Then came the hearse, drawn by four black horses, with eight hearse pages as bearers. There was then a mourning coach containing Colonel Berkeley Drummond, the Reverend Arthur Drummond and Mr Charles Drummond Jnr. At the rear was the private carriage of Edward Drummond.

The route taken by the cortège was via Vauxhall Bridge, through Camberwell and New Cross to Deptford. The cortège then passed over Blackheath to Charlton and arrived at the church at 11.10 am. Charlton-near-Woolwich church was, and still is, a building of no particular architectural importance or beauty.[3] At the churchyard, the coffin was met by the Honourable and Reverend Mr Boscawen,[4] vicar of Wooton, near Dorking, who then proceeded to start the reading of the service for the dead. The coffin was taken into the church and placed in the centre aisle. The church then filled with "the most respectable inhabitants of the neighbourhood – all of whom appeared much affected" for the service.[5]

At the end of the church service, the mourners moved towards a vault at the eastern edge of the churchyard for the interment. It was reported that the three Drummond brothers were very affected by the interment and that Colonel Drummond "was completely overcome". The coffin bore the simple inscription "Edward Drummond Esq died 25th January 1843 aetatis sum 50". The vault that was used was reported to be over 200 years old and it had fallen into considerable decay. As no one claimed ownership of the vault, the Drummond family arranged for it to be refurbished and they appropriated it for use by the Drummond family.

Many of the great and good wished to attend the funeral, but they complied with the family's wishes that the service be private. This was almost certainly why Sir Robert Peel, other distinguished friends and political grandees were absent from the service. The esteem in which Drummond was held can be gathered from *The Times* of 23 January 1843. In amongst the lengthy reports of the assassination was a list of those who either called at Drummond's house or sent their representatives to enquire after Drummond's health. The list contained a royal prince, two royal dukes, the dukes of Wellington, Buckingham and Dorset, the duchesses of Somerset and Norfolk, other members of the nobility, and most of the foreign ambassadors in London.[6] The stream of enquiries as to Drummond's health at his house continued until his death.

Connections

Inside the church, near where Drummond's coffin was placed during the service, there is a plaque and a bust of the only assassinated British prime minister, Spencer Perceval, who had been buried at this church in the Egmont family vault in 1812. The plaque reads:

> Near this place are the mortal remains of the Right Hon. Spencer Perceval, First Lord of the Treasury[7] and Chancellor of the Exchequer, who died on the 11th day of May, 1812, in the Commons House of Parliament, in the 50th year of his age. His noblest epitaph is the regret of his Sovereign and his country – his most splendid monument the glory of England – by his councils maintained, exalted, amplified; but the hand of the assassin not only broke asunder the brilliant chains of duty which bind the statesman to his native land, and made a void in the high and eloquent councils of the nation; it severed ties more tender and delicate – those of conjugal and parental affection, and turned a home of peace and love into a house of mourning and desolation.

Spencer Perceval KC is, to date, the only British solicitor general or attorney general to have later become prime minister.

There are curious connections between these two assassinated political figures.

- Spencer Perceval had eloped with, and married, Jane Wilson, a sister of Thomas Wilson of Cheshire.
- Edward Drummond's brother, the Reverend Arthur Drummond, had also married a sister of Thomas Wilson of Cheshire.
- Edward Drummond's uncle, Andrew Berkeley Drummond, was married to his cousin, Lady Mary Perceval. She was the daughter of the 2nd Earl of Egmont, John Perceval, and also a sister to Spencer Perceval.

At his death, Spencer Perceval left thirteen children, and one of his sons, John Thomas Perceval, later became a campaigner for reform of the lunacy laws, after spending three years in various asylums as a patient. He was a patient at Brislington House in Bristol and Ticehurst House in Sussex. He later wrote unflatteringly about both places.

Chapter 6

THE CULPABILITY OF THE POLICE AND CIVIL SERVICE

Commissioner Mayne

News of the shooting at Charing Cross had been relayed quickly to Sir Robert Peel's office and then to Mr Mayne,[1] one of the two commissioners of the Metropolitan Police. Mayne at once set off for Gardener's Lane Police Station where M'Naghten was being held and, from what he gathered from the police officers there, he began to believe that the intention to kill had been planned, in the prisoner's mind, against Sir Robert Peel, or another member of the government, and not against Edward Drummond.

Mayne's next step was to order enquiries to be made among officials at the Treasury and Home, Foreign and Colonial offices. His aim was to gather any information to support the early reports that M'Naghten had been reconnoitring Whitehall before the shooting. These particular offices of the government were all close to the scene of the shooting – as were Peel's official residence, 10 Downing Street, and his private residence, 4 Whitehall Gardens.

As a result of these enquiries, several members of Whitehall staff came to Gardener's Lane for the purpose of giving information to help to identify the assassin. A messenger from the Home Office at once identified M'Naghten as the man who he had seen for the last fortnight walking continually, during office hours, along Whitehall, between Lady Dover's residence, adjoining the Home Office, and the corner of Downing Street.

Those Who Saw M'Naghten Loitering in Whitehall

There was no apparent purpose involved in M'Naghten continually walking around Whitehall, but this had not been seen as providing cause for any concern at the time. The Home Office messenger, who had spoken to M'Naghten, said that at all times M'Naghten seemed to be rational, and yet all he would say was that he wanted to know, by sight, the various members of the government as they passed through Whitehall. That he offered no reason for wanting to gather this information caused the messenger no apparent concern. The lack of curiosity as to why M'Naghten wanted to identify government ministers, when he had no apparent business with them, seems to have been typical of police and civil servants.

Alarmingly, the information about M'Naghten lurking in Whitehall was fully corroborated by several porters and messengers from other government offices, who all identified the prisoner as being frequently seen in the neighbourhood of the Home Office.[2] No one from these offices, who saw M'Naghten or spoke to him, appeared to think that M'Naghten's conduct was evidence of any sinister purpose. Admittedly political assassination in London was not really a feature of British political life, but street robberies, with or without violence, were far from unknown. It is therefore rather odd that government employees should not have been alerted by this suspicious activity. It belies the commonly held notion that those in the capital were sharper, or more worldly wise, than others.

M'Naghten was certainly not dressed as one who ever associated with politicians, nor did he speak in a way that suggested this. There is no evidence of the police or the civil servants informing their superiors about M'Naghten's behaviour. There is no evidence that anyone sought advice from their superiors either. However, given M'Naghten's later shooting, it is unlikely that any superior would later admit to receiving such information and not acting on it.

There is a clue to the reaction of the civil servants to M'Naghten's behaviour. PC Drake's evidence, later in this chapter, deals with this issue. The *Morning Post* reported:

> It is said that M'Naghten had, for three weeks previous to the assassination, been seen as many as twenty or thirty times a day walking in front of the public offices, but he never made any inquiry. On Saturday week he was observed in Downing-street, at the time the Cabinet Ministers were assembling to hold a Council; on that occasion several other persons were standing near him, but with whom he did not appear to have any acquaintance or conversation.[3]

If the *Morning Post* was correct with their figures, then there should have been real concern at M'Naghten's constant wandering outside government buildings, apparently looking for someone who he would not identify when questioned.

Nor would M'Naghten disclose what his purpose was in walking every day over the same pavements.

Police and Civil Service Conduct

Police Constable 136 of A Division, James Partridge, later gave evidence against M'Naghten. This was reported as:[4]

> For some time past I have been doing duty in the neighbourhood of Whitehall, and during the last 17 or 18 days I have frequently seen the prisoner walking up and down near the [Privy] Council-office and the Treasury, and generally observed that he looked earnestly towards the residence of the Duke of Buccleuch.[5]
>
> I have several times seen him standing on the steps leading to the Council-office. I particularly recollect seeing him there on the morning of the 13th inst. I asked him whether he was waiting for any person, and I believe his reply was that he was waiting to see a gentleman, but he spoke in a hurried manner, and instantly walked away. On Friday morning last, about half-past 10 o'clock, I again saw him walking to and fro in front of the Council-office, and after watching him a few minutes I went up to him and asked him whether he had yet seen the gentleman he wanted, to which he hastily replied, "No" and walked hurriedly away. I saw nothing more of him for about half an hour, when I next saw him standing near the entrance to Lady Dover's residence;[6] he was eating a piece of bread. I then left the neighbourhood for an hour or two, and on my return, I saw the prisoner near the Treasury and between that time and half-past 3 o'clock I saw him several times in the neighbourhood.[7]

Partridge's evidence, while appearing to be admirably detailed, revealed that:

- an unknown person had continually loitered outside government offices for more than two weeks;
- this person did not reveal any real reason as to why he was there;
- no one challenged him to provide a proper, and credible, explanation for his conduct;
- no one even tried to discover his identity;
- no one asked for his name or address.

And yet none of this apparently gave rise to any suspicion on the part of the policemen on the beat during January. There was no admission by any senior police officers that the loiterer's conduct was brought to the attention of any of the supervisory officers.

Further police evidence came from PC John Drake. He first noticed M'Naghten on the 3rd or 4th of January, loitering in the same area as the other witnesses had mentioned. On the 18th, after complaints from staff in the Privy Council offices, Drake spoke to M'Naghten:

> "Some of the gentlemen inside have been speaking to me about your standing on the steps; they don't appear to like your standing here".
>
> M'Naghten said, "Tell them it is a notion I have taken".
>
> I said, "If you are waiting for any one you had better wait on the pavement, as they don't appear to like your standing on these steps unless they know your business".
>
> M'Naghten said, "You can tell them their property is quite safe".[8]

The underlined passage in Drake's evidence that there was some concern about M'Naghten's loitering in Whitehall strikes rather an odd note. There is no evidence that any of the "gentlemen" in the Privy Council offices could be bothered to follow up on any concerns and deal with the issue properly.

This rather truculent exchange on M'Naghten's part did not seem to have caused any suspicions in Drake's mind. Also, apparently, the idea of telling M'Naghten to stay away from the area unless he gave an adequate explanation for loitering so often outside government premises did not occur to Drake either. Later the same day, M'Naghten approached Drake again and asked if he would join him for a drink. M'Naghten repeated his invitation the following day. On both occasions Drake refused. Surprisingly M'Naghten was yet again not told to move away and there was no attempt to remove him from the area.

The police failings were noticed very quickly by the press. *The Morning Post*[9] correctly commented:

> We concur in thinking that police officers should receive instructions to be a little more on the alert with respect to persons whom they may perceive, for days and weeks at a time, skulking

> in the vicinity of particular neighbourhoods, without having any good reason to assign for their conduct. In the present case we have a man loitering about unwatched – almost unquestioned – when a little judicious reflection would suggest the improbability of his so demeaning himself unless for some sinister purpose. We are not of those who would encourage the stupid and discreditable prejudices that are so prevalent in some quarters against the efficacy and character of the Metropolitan Police Force, but we may not omit to remark that…… there are far too many cases of officers going too far, or not far enough. Here is a point of duty that requires intelligent supervision, and care should be taken that every officer, individually, has correct and specific notions of the nature and extent of his powers.

London's Metropolitan Police force had been in existence since 1829.[10] The Home Secretary responsible for the creation of this new force was Sir Robert Peel.[11] The creation of this new police force had faced opposition from those who saw the police as a threat to civil liberties (and those who saw it as a threat to their long-standing profitable criminal activities). Others opposed it because a standing police force was thought by many to be distinctly un-British. The *Morning Post*'s moderation in its criticism perhaps reflected its unwillingness to be seen as attacking the police too strongly, when the force was still trying to grasp the full breadth of what would be expected from them.

The Recruiting Sergeants

As more information was sought after the shooting, it soon came to light that M'Naghten had been seen by others when he reconnoitred the Whitehall area. He had been accosted, on separate occasions, by two cavalry sergeants, Richard Jones, of the 10th Hussars, and William Beale, of the 2nd Dragoon Guards,[12] who were both recruiting for their regiments.

Sergeant Jones had seen M'Naghten walking around Whitehall and Downing Street and concluded that he was a suspicious character. This accurate conclusion on Jones's part showed more concern for safety than any of the policemen who policed the area. Jones had approached M'Naghten and asked him if he would "serve the queen and enlist". This offer was refused and M'Naghten said he was waiting to meet a gentleman. Jones saw him again the following day and again he pressed him to enlist. He told M'Naghten that if he changed his mind, he could receive a bounty on enlisting and that the sergeant would buy him a drink.

Although he did not change his mind about enlisting, M'Naghten agreed to have a drink with Jones at Carpenter's Wine Vaults in King Street, near Downing Street. Jones asked him questions about why he was always in Whitehall, but M'Naghten simply repeated his original answer that he was waiting for a gentleman. He would not give Jones his name nor his business. Jones left Carpenter's now even more convinced that M'Naghten was up to no good. Jones next approached a police officer from A Division[13] and told him of his suspicions, suggesting that the police ought to keep an eye on M'Naghten. The police officer brushed off Jones's warning, telling him that it was none of the police's business and he would have nothing to do with it. Sergeant Jones had no civil or martial authority to arrest or detain a civilian.

To put it mildly, this was a very unusual view of the duties of the Metropolitan Police force. This exchange occurred only two days before the assassination of Drummond.[14] Queen Victoria later noted, with approval, the evidence that Sergeant Jones gave in court:

> There was nothing much more that had been found out about McNaughten [sic] excepting of the Xth,[15] which showed great negligence by the Police. This Serg^{t} had disliked the look of the man, & on pretence of asking him to enlist had entered into conversation with him, afterwards telling the Police that he did not like the look of the man, & advised their keeping a watch over him.[16]

This was not the sort of criticism of the new police force that its commanding officers would have wanted from their Sovereign – and no doubt the criticism, and a demand for remedial action, would have filtered down to individual members of A Division rather quickly.

Another Police Error

Unfortunately for the police, there had been an earlier attempt on the queen's life when they had failed to meet the standards expected of the new force. This had occurred on 29 May 1842, as the queen and Prince Albert were returning to Buckingham Palace via Constitution Hill. A young man, John Francis, stepped towards the royal carriage, but his pistol would not fire, and Francis was chased when he ran off and escaped his pursuers. The following day, the queen agreed to travel on exactly the same route in a deliberate attempt to lure the gunman into repeating his attack. This time the royal carriage was better guarded and driven at a faster pace. Francis did return to try again, but this time his shot missed. Francis was arrested, charged, convicted and, in June, was sentenced to death – to be hanged, drawn and quartered. This sentence was commuted on 3 July to one of transportation for life, with hard labour. [17]

While Francis had waited to take his first shot at the queen, he was spotted by Constable Trounce, who was on duty in plain clothes. Trounce was suspicious about Francis's agitated state and Trounce decided to watch him carefully. Francis, seeing he was being watched, tried to hide behind a tree – and occasionally peered furtively to see if Trounce was watching him. Trounce continued watching but took no action. As far as Trounce knew, Francis was not a wanted man – he was, but no one had told Trounce. Trounce had been given a description of Francis, but he had not been told why it was needed. Trounce was newly transferred to A Division, but had not been given any instruction of what his new duties were to be.

As the royal carriage approached Buckingham Palace at speed for the second time, Trounce did not seize Francis, but instead, he came to attention and saluted the royal carriage. Francis then fired and, momentarily, Trounce froze, but he quickly redeemed himself by chasing and arresting Francis.

Shortly afterwards a new police detective department was created as an experiment. There was much more for the Metropolitan Police to learn about royal protection.

Mr Howe

In the Bow Street Magistrates' Court, other evidence was given that M'Naghten had been seen loitering around Downing Street for over a fortnight. Mr Edward Howe, an office-keeper at the Board of Trade in Whitehall, had seen him daily on and around the steps of the Privy Council offices. This was an astonishing admission and shows how little awareness there was of the need for security of important government figures and their offices.

On the morning of the assassination, Howe said to M'Naghten that he presumed him to be a policeman in plain clothes and Howe received the reply, "Yes, I am". On hearing this, Howe replied that M'Naghten was "alright" – presumably accepting his explanation as satisfactory. Howe did not realise that his own question had been framed in such a way that it gave M'Naghten an obvious answer to it. Howe accepted the reply and apparently did not realise how naïve his conduct was. As for the police force, the civil servants also seemed unaware of any possible threat from the suspicious activity of one who constantly lurked around the government offices.

There was convincing evidence that the police and the civil service staff failed to think about what was happening before their eyes. Further, they did not really know what their duty was in the circumstances, even though there was an earlier warning, from 1812, with the assassination of the then prime minister, Spencer Perceval.[18]

It is very difficult to absolve the police of blame, when the conduct of Sergeant Jones clearly showed that he recognised the risk from M'Naghten's unusual conduct in Whitehall. Jones viewed it as being of sufficient concern to tell a policeman on duty in Whitehall of what he had seen and heard of M'Naghten's conduct. Jones had no legal powers to hold and arrest a civilian, but the police could arrest and interrogate. The policeman not only did nothing, but thought that the suspicious character was nothing at all to do with him. A clear chance to stop the assassination was missed. A similar view must prevail of the civil servants' conduct, particularly the ineptness of Edward Howe.

Chapter 7

THE ASSASSIN

The initial lack of information about M'Naghten did not prevent early press speculation about the man and his state of mind. *The Times*[1] produced a lengthy opinion piece which made clear the fears and opinions arising from the attack. It included:

> In the present state of the case, however, it would be out of our province to allege or to hint anything with regard to the prisoner's sanity or purpose. His criminality will be well examined, and his defence well weighed in a court of justice. But we cannot abstain from expressing our horror, not only at the present atrocious attempt, whoever may have been its designed victim, but at the dreadful imputation which this and similar attempts have fixed upon the national character. Formerly it was our boast that the weapon of the assassin – exercised for ready gain in all Europe besides – was unknown save by ignominious report in England: formerly Englishmen would have thought it a foul scorn that men in public station should be marked out for murder in the public streets.[2]
>
> But events that have occurred within the present century may have disabused us of this cherished and exalted faith. The belief in the honour and manly courage of Englishmen is become one of those ancient superstitions, the memory of which provokes a painful comparison between the past and present times. Twice has the life of the SOVEREIGN been attempted – once (and it may turn out twice) that of the First Minister of the Crown. In the former cases party feeling was never alleged or supposed to have instigated the assailants. We hope that the present attack may be proved to be independent of such a cause. But whether this be so or not, we know full well that

> there is not one class or party throughout England – be its object ever so wild, its conduct and language ever so violent – that it would not strongly denounce such a base and wicked attempt to further any political scheme – none but what would reject and disclaim all connexion with the wretched assassin in language of unequivocal indignation.
>
> But the subject still retains much to grieve the thoughtful and well-disposed. Can it be that we are approaching that fearful period in a nation's history when men become indifferent to right and wrong – when patience, charity and patriotism give way to pride, revenge, and selfish malice – when all thought and care for the honour of their country are merged in a rabid appetite for an evil notoriety, or a morbid craving after desperate vengeance? God forbid! We had rather see an England reft [sic] of all her glory, greatness, and possessions, than tarnished with the crimes of ancient Venice, or dishonoured by the wickedness of modern France.

This presentation of the English character and its values was akin to what would later come to be called Jingoism.[3] But there is little doubt that this view of the national character, and its comparison with that of the French, (with which Britain had finished a long and expensive war less than thirty years before) would have reflected the views of many in England at that time.

We now know that Daniel M'Naghten was, certainly by the time of the shooting, a very troubled soul. However, for the government, the press, and the public, the two more immediate questions were:

1. Who was the assassin?
2. What was his motive for killing the prime minister's secretary?

Both the Scottish and English press rapidly turned their attention to ferreting out all they could about him.

The Arrest

After he was overpowered and arrested in Whitehall, M'Naghten was taken in handcuffs by PC Silver to Gardener's Lane Police Station.[4] On the way there, M'Naghten was heard by Silver to say either "he" or "she" "should not break my peace of mind any longer". PC Silver could not make out which M'Naghten had said. Silver searched M'Naghten when they arrived at the police station and then M'Naghten was then charged with:

> …attempting to assassinate, by shooting at him with two loaded pistols, near Charing-cross, Mr. Edward Drummond, the Private Secretary to Sir Robert Peel.

He did not make any reply to the charge, nor would he give the police any information about himself. *The Spectator*[5] estimated M'Naghten's age between 30 and 40 years old (he was in fact 30). *The Times*' report differed, in that it reported[6] that the assassin had given his name as being Daniel M'Naghten, but that he would not give up any further information.

PC Silver and Police Sergeant Shaw, who was also from A Division, left M'Naghten in custody at Gardener's Lane Police Station and set off to No 7 Poplar Row, New Kent Road, where M'Naghten had been lodging in London. Although the press reports said that M'Naghten did not give any information at this police station, he must have given the address of his lodgings to the police for them to have been able to perform a search. On searching his room, Silver found two further pistol percussion caps and Sergeant Shaw found a powder flask, a gun case and five pistol balls. They returned to Gardener's Lane Police Station with this evidence. These items were kept alongside the two pistols that had been seized from M'Naghten when he was arrested.[7]

M'Naghten's Lodgings

M'Naghten had lodged at 7 Poplar Row for possibly sixteen weeks prior to the shooting. He had also lodged there on earlier visits to London. His weekly rent for his single room was 2/6d, which he always paid regularly. Mrs Dutton, the landlady, thought that M'Naghten had travelled to London looking for work, as he had yet no apparent employment, but he was out every day. Her view was reinforced by the very shabby clothes he was wearing when he arrived there. His wardrobe was miserable. He had one shirt, although he did buy a second after a fortnight. The shirts could then be washed alternately. He possessed two pairs of socks and a flannel waistcoat. His trousers were patched and darned, but other holes and tears were left undarned. His boots were falling apart, and he had to borrow an old pair to wear from a shoemaker while the shoemaker repaired them.

The Observer[8] printed further information about 7 Poplar Row and the arrangements with Mrs Dutton. It was apparently three years since M'Naghten had first lodged at this house and, on later visits to London, he would always use the same room when he lodged there. The room was not the best available in the house, but M'Naghten seemed to prefer it, probably because it was not close to other lodgers' rooms.

Mrs Dutton thought that M'Naghten was "of a quiet turn of mind". He seldom rose before late morning, but he then left the house immediately and did not return until ten at night. She also said of him that he was never seen to be anything but sober:

> I always thought he was rather reserved in his manner, he was a man that avoided conversation with people. He never appeared to wish to join in conversation; I never saw any companion of his during the whole time he was with me; I never saw him with a creature – not one.

Mrs Dutton was also asked if M'Naghten would look a person in the eye or avoid eye contact. Her reply was:

> Rather down, he answered shortly and quickly, as though he wished to get rid of a question. As far as I could judge I should say his habits were very penurious; he had only a change of linen, a change of flannel, and a change of socks in the house. I had no conception of his having anything like 700l. by him.

He left after about three months, telling Mrs Dutton that he was going to France. He was away for several months before he returned. It was later established that he made at least one, if not two, trips to France. But M'Naghten's demons drove him back to London each time. He then took the room again for a further three weeks before going, he said, to Scotland. At the start of October 1842 he returned to lodge again in the same room.

Mrs Dutton told an *Observer* reporter that M'Naghten's "gloomy temperament" was, after this return, more marked than previously, but despite this, he always remained civil towards her and her other lodgers. She also commented that he always appeared to have something on his mind and generally would not seek conversation with other lodgers. However, he mentioned to her when he returned in 1842 that he had recently been in Scotland. This was during the time that Queen Victoria had visited Scotland for the first time. M'Naghten told her he had seen the queen while he was in Scotland. It is not clear if there was any particular motive for his trip to Scotland.

Queen Victoria's Visit to Scotland

Queen Victoria's *Journal* provides different information for the day of the shooting, after her meeting with Sir Robert Peel:

> "I think I know, or can guess how it occurred" [said Peel]. The day of the attempt, he had walked with his 2 sons to the Treasury – & then left alone by a private passage into the Park, to go to $\mathrm{L^y}$ Chantrey's,[9] telling $\mathrm{M^r}$ Drummond he would be absent about an hour. Very soon after this $\mathrm{M^r}$ Drummond had left the Treasury with $\mathrm{L^d}$ Haddington, who happened to be about the same height as Sir Robert's son, poor $\mathrm{M^r}$ Drummond being something of the same height & size as Sir Robert Peel. $\mathrm{M^c}$Naughten mistook them. . .
>
> Sir Robert said that so many abominable, threatening anonymous letters have been written to poor $\mathrm{L^y}$ Peel, which is too wicked, & which have made her quite ill. These anonymous letters are such a horrid, base cowardly practice. Sir Robert said that he had felt so glad when we were safe out of Scotland again, for that he thought I had never been more exposed, than on that particular last day, when I was so nervous in going through Stirling & Linlithgow.[10]

The queen's views on Stirling and Linlithgow were indeed unfavourable after her first visit to Scotland in September 1842. Her *Journal* recorded:[11]

- [Stirling] *...where the crowd was quite fearful & the streets so narrow that it was quite alarming...order was not very well kept...I was quite overcome and most nervous...*
- [Linlithgow] *...the crowd was again dreadful & the people drunk & disorderly which made me quite nervous...*

These comments should be read in the light of Victoria being a 23-year-old who had already been a target for three assassination attempts – one assassin having made two attempts.

The *Spectator*[12] also reported that during this visit to Scotland, Sir Robert Peel invariably rode in one of the royal carriages, and Drummond travelled in Sir Robert Peel's own carriage. This article raised the possibility that, while Drummond was in Scotland, he could have been pointed out to M'Naghten as being Sir Robert. If this was true, the assassin's confidence could have been complete when he later saw Drummond leave the house of Sir Robert Peel in Whitehall Gardens. However, this is unlikely as, if it was correct, there would have been no necessity for M'Naghten to have loitered around Whitehall to try and identify Peel in January.

While in Scotland, M'Naghten lodged with Mrs Jane Patterson, who had previously provided lodgings for him when he was working in Scotland. Unfortunately for M'Naghten, she discovered his two recently purchased pistols. Not unreasonably, she was alarmed and challenged him as to why he had them. All he could manage was a rather limp reply that he planned to shoot some birds. Mrs Patterson was well-aware of his fondness for feeding birds, so she was most unlikely to have believed him. Within a few days he left her house, taking only few of his possessions with him and leaving most of his possessions behind. During this time in Scotland, M'Naghten had renewed acquaintance with some of his former friends. They later told the press that M'Naghten's eccentricities appeared to have become more marked during this time that he had been in Glasgow.

Police Interviews

M'Naghten was first questioned by Police Inspector Hughes at Gardener's Lane Police Station. He refused to give the inspector his name or any other personal information. From his accent, the police thought, correctly, that M'Naghten was Scottish, as did the press, who assumed from his accent that he was either "a Scotchman, or a native of the north of Ireland, who had been living in Glasgow."[13] He was described by the reporters who saw him at the police station to be:

> …a broad-faced man, with lightish hair, and bore the appearance of a gentleman's valet, or something of the kind. He was attired in a black coat, plaid waistcoat, and drab[14] trowsers [sic]. There was nothing whatever to indicate insanity in the prisoner's appearance, nor did he appear at all unnerved at the position in which he stood. He was at once placed in the cell, and information

> of the occurrence forwarded to Sir Robert Peel, and Mr. Mayne, one of the commissioners of the Metropolitan police.[15]

It seems clear from this that the police had allowed some reporters to have access to the police station to see the assassin, even if they did not allow the press to ask him any questions.

M'Naghten's demeanour while at Gardener's Lane Police Station was calm and collected. A reporter for *The Times* noted that M'Naghten did not appear to show any evidence of insanity. It is interesting that both the reporters for *The Times* and the *Spectator* commented on this. A lack of overt signs of insanity was a fairly meaningless concept in assessing insanity, but it did at least reflect public attitudes of that time generally towards lunacy – it was widely believed that lunatics should be raving or visibly behaving wildly. His calmness contrasted with the agitated figure described before the assassination. This might well be accounted for by his belief, at this stage, that he had shot Sir Robert Peel and therefore achieved his object.

The Times reported[16] that the assassin gave his name as Daniel M'Naghten, but with no other information at this time, the police could not form a view about his motive for wanting to assassinate Drummond, nor as to any possible co-conspirators and accomplices. The absence of any further information did not prevent *The Times* from advising its readers:

> ...that his purpose was carried out with the most cold-blooded determination, though, fortunately, no fatal results are expected to accrue from the wound which he succeeded in inflicting on his intended victim.[17]

Confirmation of M'Naghten's Error?

On 21 January, Queen Victoria recorded in her *Journal* that Sir Robert Peel had advised her, by letter, that Inspector Tierney had spoken to M'Naghten in his cell at Gardener's Lane Police Station. As previously mentioned, Tierney had asked M'Naghten if he was aware who he had shot and he said that M'Naghten replied, "Yes, Sir Robert Peel". This was the first time that the suspicion that Peel was the real target had been apparently confirmed. M'Naghten, during his trial, did not confirm this. Indeed, other statements made by M'Naghten, when interviewed by the doctors, did not corroborate Tierney's version.

The problem with Tierney's approach to interrogating M'Naghten in the way he did was that the conversation took place without any other persons being present. This was highly irregular and, in the absence of other witnesses being present, rendered the information obtained by Tierney useless for the purposes of any prosecution. That someone as senior as Inspector Tierney should make such a basic mistake is baffling.

M'Naghten's Money

In addition to the two pistols which were fired at Drummond, PC Silver found that M'Naghten had in his possession:

- two £5 Bank of England notes, four sovereigns, four half-crowns, one shilling, one four-penny piece, and a copper penny (total £14-11s-5d) and
- a receipt for £750 from the Glasgow and Shipping Bank [*sic*] in the name of "Daniel M'Naghten".

This was a surprisingly large amount of money for a woodturner to have saved. However, it was not outside the realms of possibility for a hard-working single-minded man, who had abstemious habits and no dependants, to have accumulated. The *Morning Post* referred to this money without any undue surprise. "He had when taken into custody, a sufficient sum of money to indicate that distress had not driven him to his desperate act."[18] Indeed, none of the press accounts expressed any surprise at the amount of money that he had in his possession.

The *Glasgow Chronicle*[19] clearly stated, from their own investigations, that M'Naghten "for years previously was in a state of mental aberration". The same article claimed:

> However much parties differ as to his sentiments in other matters, all are agreed in this – that he was from his youth upwards an exceedingly provident, careful and saving man – not a whisky drinker – not a jovial companion – not an attender of public entertainments.... The fact is he never spent money on any luxury at any time when he could avoid it...

This view of the *Glasgow Chronicle* was very firm and clear on M'Naghten and his money, and as a Glasgow paper, they were in a better position than the London press to write so firmly.

It was by no means outside the realms of possibility that, given the poverty of his life with his mother, he may have determined at an early age to save as much as he could and avoid the near destitution of his early childhood. The industriousness of his father's woodturning business almost certainly served to teach him the value of money. Similarly, politicians did not seem to have expressed any shock at the amount of his savings, nor assumed that it must have been financed by someone else. (There is more on M'Naghten's wealth at the end of Chapter 8.) The same *Glasgow Chronicle* article also made the observation that M'Naghten was "more than fastidious as to the getting in of his accounts at all times" no matter how many times it was necessary to remind the customer. This habit was not that of a spendthrift.

The Search for More Information

Inspector Hughes had tried to question M'Naghten further, but he resolutely refused to answer the inspector's questions. Mr Mayne, one of the two commissioners of Metropolitan Police, also went to the police station to check on what had occurred and review what the next steps should be. He, too, doubted that Drummond had been the intended target, already suspecting instead that Peel had been the real target. The police at the station told Mayne that they suspected M'Naghten had intended to kill the prime minister, or some other members of the government. There was not yet any confirmation of this, but it was certainly a reasonable assumption at this stage.

There then followed an attempt to establish if any of staff at the Treasury, Home, Foreign or Colonial offices had any knowledge of who the assassin might be and what his real intentions were. The initial result was that:

> ...several attended at the station-house for the purpose of speaking, if possible, to the identity of the assassin. A messenger at the Home Office at once identified him as a man whom he had seen for the last fortnight walking, without any apparent object, continually during office hours, between Lady Dover's residence, adjoining the Home Office, and the corner of Downing-street. The messenger states that at all times the prisoner seemed to be collected, and was supposed to be a person desirous of knowing by sight the various Members of the Government. This statement was subsequently fully borne out by several porters and messengers of the other Government offices who also identified the prisoner as being frequently seen in the neighbourhood of the Home Office.[20]

The main government departments checked their files to see if there had been any correspondence to or from M'Naghten, particularly concerning complaints against Drummond personally, or against government departments, in case he had ever sought a position in these offices, or if he had any grudges or grievances against. This search drew a blank.

By this time, others who had been in Whitehall at the time of the shooting had come forward, claiming to have seen the assassin follow Drummond from outside the Privy Council offices to Drummond's Bank. Some also claimed to have seen him waiting in a doorway near the bank while Drummond was in there. The news of him following and waiting for the victim pointed to a deliberate assassination attempt, rather than a spur of the moment action.

M'Naghten's receipt from the Glasgow bank confirmed the statement made with respect to his name, but M'Naghten still gave no information about his motives for the shooting. Research over the next few days would uncover no evidence that M'Naghten:

- had been in any contact with Mr Drummond – either by letter, or by meeting;
- had any connections with any civil servants in London;
- had referred any complaint to the government;
- was a disappointed applicant for any office position in Whitehall.

His demeanour throughout this time remained calm – unusually so for one who had just shot a senior government official. He displayed no overt signs of insanity, nor any particular interest in the investigation into the shooting. His calmness gave him an air of detachment from all that was happening around him which, for a man who was now in peril of his life, and was in police custody charged with murder, was rather unusual. The press did not seem to think that this detachment might be a symptom of mental illness.

Evidence of M'Naghten's Mistake

When exactly M'Naghten became aware of the true identity of his victim is not wholly clear from the press reports. The exchange with Police Inspector Tierney in the second meeting between the two would certainly have established that he had not shot Sir Robert Peel as he had thought. In a note to Queen Victoria on 21 January, Peel informed her that:

> Sir R. Peel begs leave to mention to Y^{r} Majesty a fact, which has not hitherto transpired, & which he was not aware of until he had an interview this morning, with Sir James Graham.[21] On the Inspector Tierney going into MacNaughten's cell this morning, he said to him I suppose you are aware who is the person you have shot? MacNaughten answered "Yes, Sir Robert Peel"… it would appear that Mr Drummond had been mistaken for Sir Robert Peel. The magistrate thought it better not to have this evidence at present placed on record.

The queen noted in her diary:[22] "This horrified us still more, as if Sir Robert had even only been wounded, what a terrible thing it would have been! I wrote to him, in both our names, to this effect."

Now that M'Naghten knew that he had shot the wrong man, he showed no alarm or contrition. It would be most unusual for an assassin to be so detached and this should have raised some question or concerns amongst those watching him.

The reason for M'Naghten's mistake probably starts with the point that, unlike their counterparts today, the politicians of the early Victorian age were not easily recognisable by the man in the street. In 1842 there were no photographs in the newspapers or periodicals. There were sketches drawn by some newspaper artists, but these were only recognisable as true likenesses when the subject has posed for a sketch.[23] Often there would be no accurate drawings of criminals until they were in court and they could be observed at more leisure by a press artist.

Peel and Drummond certainly did not look alike, although they were of a similar age and height, but Drummond would, on occasion, travel in Peel's carriage – sometimes alone and sometimes with Peel. This carriage clearly bore Peel's coat of arms on the doors and anyone seeing it could assume, fairly reasonably, that it was Peel who was travelling in it – but which person was in the coach on this occasion? Peel lived in his London residence in Whitehall Gardens, across Whitehall from 10 Downing Street. But Drummond lived, on occasion, in parts of 10 Downing Street where he had rooms for his own use. M'Naghten had seen Drummond on previous days walking between the two properties and could have assumed that he must be the prime minister. To be sure of this, M'Naghten once asked a policeman if the man he pointed out was Peel. The policeman, thinking he was actually pointing at Peel, who was, at the time, walking next to Drummond, confirmed that he was.

Queen Victoria's *Journals* provide different information for the day of the shooting, after her meeting with Sir Robert Peel:

As mentioned on p.47, The *Spectator*[24] had reported that when the queen visited Scotland, Sir Robert Peel rode in one of the royal carriages, and Drummond travelled in Sir Robert Peel's own carriage. This article raised the possibility that Mr Drummond was actually pointed out to M'Naghten as being Sir Robert during the trip to Scotland. The *Morning Post*[25] carried a report that M'Naghten had told Mrs Dutton, his landlady in London, that he had been in Scotland during the queen's visit to Scotland in 1842. If this was true, the assassin's confidence in having identified his target would have been complete when he saw Mr Drummond leave the house of Sir Robert Peel in Whitehall Gardens. However, the assumption that M'Naghten had already had Drummond pointed out to him in Scotland would then raise the awkward question – if he had already been identified to M'Naghten, why would he need to increase the risk to himself by asking people in Whitehall to point out Peel? The answer to this would probably be that M'Naghten had seen a figure in a carriage passing by in Scotland but could not see him clearly enough to be able to recognise him a year later.

There was an unsubstantiated report in *The Times*[26] that Drummond had received threatening letters which had later been mislaid:

> On Friday morning Mr Drummond stated to a friend that he had seen a man lurking about the Treasury, as he thought, somewhat suspiciously, and coupling this fact with threatening letters he had previously received, he remarked he did not like the appearance of the man. His friend replied carelessly, that he did not conceive the matter worth thinking about, and it was supposed it was subsequently dismissed from Mr Drummond's mind.

While it is quite conceivable that Drummond could have seen M'Naghten outside the Treasury, M'Naghten would not have been the one to send any threatening letters, as he was not concerned about Drummond. As there was no evidence produced by "the friend" at any of the hearings into the assassination – nor was the friend identified in the press – this report ought to be ignored.

M'Naghten's Early Life

Daniel M'Naghten was born in 1813 in Glasgow. He was the illegitimate son of a woodturner[27] of the same name. Daniel was brought up by his mother,

Ada, an unmarried dressmaker, until her death in 1821. Thereafter, Daniel went to live with his father's family. No more appears to be known of his mother.

A Mr Spalding, who had previously lived and worked in Glasgow in Stockwell Street, came forward shortly after M'Naghten's arrest. Spalding was a carpenter, now living in London, but he had lived for a number of years as a near neighbour of M'Naghten senior in Glasgow. When M'Naghten junior was a young boy, he would call at Spalding's workshop each day. Spalding said that M'Naghten was a mild and unassuming child, who was popular with the customers at his shop.

M'Naghten was soon apprenticed in his father's profession, and he proved to be very good learner. He became both a good woodturner and a valuable employee for his father. It is only supposition, but as his father's illegitimate son, M'Naghten may not have been welcomed into his father's household and business by any half-siblings, or by his father's wife. During M'Naghten's trial, his barrister, Alexander Cockburn QC, referred to Daniel's illegitimacy saying that he was:

> ...a natural son, and probably did not meet with that full measure of kindness which is usually shown to legitimate offspring.[28] Whatever might have been the predetermining cause, he appears from the commencement to have been a man of gloomy, reserved and unsocial habits.

For reasons unknown, instead of earning a partnership in his father's business when he came of age, he remained a journeyman in his father's workshop. It is possible that his father was pressured by his wife and children not to be generous to him. It could also be possible that his father could already detect early signs of mental illness in his son. Whatever the reason, he was disappointed with his father's decision and soon decided to move on. He left his father's house when he was 18 and began to prepare himself for the life of an actor.

Acting Career

M'Naghten used his savings from working for his father to support himself as he began to study plays, particularly those of Shakespeare. Later, a friend of his wrote of this time that M'Naghten was often to be seen in his lodgings studying plays.

M'Naghten began his stage career in 1832, when he was aged 19. Appearing as "Mr. Knight", he gave several readings and recitations. This first attempt was not a success, but he persevered and made progress, although he was always unlikely to make much of a career on the stage. He soon joined a travelling group of actors who worked the west coast of Scotland. The troupe was not particularly successful and M'Naghten left to tour on his own. This was never going to be a profitable proposition for him, although he did scrape by. After three years of acting, he returned to woodturning in Glasgow.[29] He kept a souvenir of this career – a pair of red leather sandals, such as were worn then by actors. He later abandoned this souvenir when he last left Mrs Pattison's Glasgow lodging house in 1842.

Business on His Own Account

With the end of his career on the stage, M'Naghten returned to woodturning and set up his own business nearby to his father's workshop in Turner's Close. From the outset his new venture was a success. Having already proved himself as a skilful woodturner when working for his father, he now applied himself diligently for his own profit. The difference in his approach to this work was now marked in that he would work harder and for longer hours. At the same time he lived frugally, even sleeping and eating, for a time, in his workshop.

Still estranged from his father, M'Naghten was increasingly becoming a man of very odd behaviour. He would spend his days at work and he claimed that he could do as much work in a day as two or even three other men could do, so hard did he apply himself. No one appears to have disagreed with this claim. He did not rest much away from his work and what little he did, he spent studying. The *Glasgow Chronicle*[30] claimed that M'Naghten would spend up to sixteen hours a day in working and reading. The same article claimed that he was a radical in politics and "inclined to infidelity in religion." That is to say he would attend churches of any Christian denomination, just to hear the sermons. Sermons clearly interested him much more that the denomination of the church.

Once when M'Naghten rented a room in Glasgow, he shared the room with William Gilchrist, in order to save money by splitting the cost of the room between them. Later, Gilchrist gave evidence at M'Naghten's trial that M'Naghten was prone to pacing naked up and down the room, all the while muttering incoherently. Later, at other lodgings in 1837, his behaviour had become so odd that his landlord gave him immediate notice to leave, so fearful was he of M'Naghten's state of mind. After leaving those lodgings, he returned to living in his workshop and worked and studied even harder than before.

Despite the success of his own business, M'Naghten remained a loner who formed few, if any, real friendships. He continued to work hard, and successfully, at his trade. In such leisure as he had, he would study what were described by others as "difficult and abstruse matters". He read widely across many subjects, and it is likely that there was no real consistency across his range of reading. It was not centred on one area of literature.

M'Naghten was known to take pleasure in watching the local birds, feeding them crumbs and discouraging others from robbing their nests. He was also said to feel a greater affinity for children than adults. It was well known that he took much delight in watching children at play, but there were no claims of impropriety in this pleasure. It probably merely revealed that this was something that had been absent from much of his own childhood. There was probably only meagre playtime when he was still with his impoverished mother and when at his father's house, he would soon be apprenticed to his father's trade.

Information from the young man who later took over M'Naghten's workshop was also reported in the press:

> [M'Naghten] was much devoted to bathing in the river [Clyde]……so much so that he is known to have bathed every morning for years, even during the coldest days of winter.... He was extremely acute and had a retentive memory not only in matters pecuniary, connected with his business, but also on the subjects of which he read.
>
> The same young man says he (M'Naghten) was more than usually fastidious as to the getting in of his accounts at all times, sending him fifty times for one account until it was obtained. Latterly, he (M'Naghten) assigned, as a reason for this anxiety, his belief some persons were disposed to do him an injury.
>
> When last in Glasgow he (M'Naghten) stated to the acquaintance formerly alluded to, that when previously in London, he had made many applications for situations of different descriptions. In particular, he had attended clearly to the advertisements of situations in the London papers, but found, after he called to offer himself as a candidate for any place, however humble, that hundreds of persons had applied before him."[31]

As M'Naghten was not the earliest of risers when he was lodging at Mrs Dutton's house, it is not surprising that many had got there before him for any vacancies. By now, M'Naghten's mental state was showing clear signs of the illness that would blight the rest of life. Something that would not have been helped by the apparently hopeless search for work in London.

M'Naghten's Politics

> M'Naghten mentioned to him, when last in Glasgow, that he had been infrequently in the House of Commons; and he not only saw and heard the leading members, but made very shrewd remarks on their several oratorical displays. He said that Sir R. Peel was a more polished orator than either Daniel O'Connell or Lord John Russell, although Dan was the ablest declaimer.[32]

The above passage on Parliament would appear to confirm that M'Naghten had visited the Commons and that he had seen and heard Sir Robert Peel in the Chamber. If this is true, and M'Naghten was not simply repeating what he had heard or seen in a newspaper report, why did he shoot the wrong man? After all, the press had made a point of reporting M'Naghten's "very acute, retentive memory".

> …a question suggested itself to his friend – could M'Naughten have mistaken Mr Drummond, secretary to Sir R Peel, for Mr Drummond Chairman of the Board of Excise? It may or may not be possible. Those who knew him in Glasgow, however, seem quite satisfied from their knowledge of his memory that he never could have mistaken Mr Drummond for the Premier.

The *Glasgow Courier* issue cited above also reported that a contemporary of M'Naghten had described him as a keen politician, a violent radical, who was extremely anxious to enter into controversy with all and sundry. The same article, however, went on to express some doubt on this point:

> Now this statement is altogether opposed to the experiences of any of his friends and acquaintances. So far from this, he is spoken of as a man who anxiously avoided controversy and even conversation with anyone. The extent of his violent Radicalism

> and hatred of Conservatism only amounted to his voting for Liberals at the Glasgow elections when his vote was called for and expressing his dislike to Toryism and the income tax (no very violent indication, we should think, either of furious Radicalism or insanity).

It is more than a little difficult to make out M'Naghten's true opinions. However, the remarks of those who knew him do give the impression of M'Naghten espousing particular subjects, depending on the views of the company he was in. He was all in for Chartists when in their company, apparently, but rarely, if ever, does he seem to have said anything on that subject when away from their company. He listened to debates in Parliament on a visit to London and formed opinions on the leading speakers, even rating Peel as the most polished speaker in the Commons. M'Naghten was keen to learn and enrolled in adult learning classes, but he did not continue with this after only a fairly short time. The only constant seems to be his growing belief in his persecution by the Glasgow Tories.

M'Naghten's Mental State

M'Naghten's belief that persons were persecuting him had started to grow when he was still in his woodturner business. He started to complain of pains, particularly in his head. He would spend long periods holding his head in his hands, speaking, largely to himself, of the tortures in his head and mind. Sometimes he would spring to life and run from his workshop to throw himself in the Clyde to try to relieve his mental torment. In describing this mental suffering to the jury at his trial, his counsel, Alexander Cockburn, did not claim that M'Naghten's odd behaviour was proof of insanity, but he did claim that it showed the unusual torment that he was in. He further suggested that it was a precursor to the disease that eventually led him to Whitehall with two pistols in his pockets.

It was reported that M'Naghten had asked the Glasgow police for protection against his Tory persecutors, who, he claimed, intended his death. The *Glasgow Chronicle*[33] also claimed to have seen a letter to M'Naghten written by Mr A. Johnston, a local MP, which expressed the view that M'Naghten was "not of sane mind." It was also claimed that, about two years before Drummond's murder, M'Naghten had told his landlady in Glasgow, Mrs Pattison, that there were devils in human form intent on killing him. Because of his fears, he approached various people in Glasgow for assistance, including his father, the Glasgow sheriff, the procurator fiscal,[34] the police commissioner, and M'Naghten's member of Parliament, but none of them would help him. Some of those who had been approached by M'Naghten advised his father to have M'Naghten confined in an asylum, but he declined, hoping his son would "grow out of it". It is noteworthy that those who M'Naghten approached in Glasgow were of the opinion that he was insane. This was of course only the opinion of men who had conversed with M'Naghten, but were by no means qualified to pass judgment on psychiatric illness. However, this is not sufficient for their views to be wholly dismissed. They were professional men used to dealing with a range of people who sought advice and heard complaints. The unanimity of their views that M'Naghten was insane must carry some weight, particularly as they were willing to give evidence in court as to how they viewed the accused.

M'Naghten also confided in his father in the summer of 1842 that he intended to call on Sir James Campbell, the lord provost[35] of Glasgow and this he did. Sir James's recollection was that M'Naghten did call that summer, and he received him in the hall of his residence in Bath Street. Sir James described M'Naghten as a jolly looking man who spoke very coolly. (No one else appears to have thought that M'Naghten was jolly looking.) Despite this, Sir James clearly thought that his visitor was "labouring under hallucination of mind."

> [M'Naghten] told the Provost, with great earnestness, that he had been incessantly watched and dogged by certain parties, who had an ill-will for him. He said they had forced him from his home by their spiteful machinations, and the very night before they had obliged him to fly to the fields in the suburbs for refuge. Sir James Campbell asked the name of the complainer… and afterwards reasoned with him as to the folly of his notions. Sir James likewise inquired, pretty broadly, whether he had ever been treated, as if it had been suspected there was anything wrong with his intellects, and being replied to in the negative, seriously advised him to consult his relations or some medical man as to the state of his health. At this visit he talked neither of religion nor politics; but just shook his head, and said that "he could not get rid of them at all".
>
> The father of the assassin says that he could not do with his son at all in his place of business, for although he was well behaved, so far as sobriety and industry were concerned, he was frequently reading books, and keeping others off their work. He is described

> as being most anxious to make money, and frequently wrought night and day for that purpose. He was a violent Radical, and spoke furiously against the Conservatives of this city (Glasgow}, frequently declaring that they and Mr. Lamond, their agent, were constantly against him.[36]

There was a letter from Mr Johnston, MP, to M'Naghten,[37] in reply to M'Naghten's letter of 3 May:

> I received your letter of the 3d May. I am very sorry I can do nothing for you. I am afraid you are labouring under a delusion of mind, and that there is no reason for you entertaining such fears.

M'Naghten brushed this aside, saying that he had tried his best to do, without any success. In this endeavour he was thwarted by "a parcel of devils" who persecuted and tormented him. To this he added that if the devils did not stop tormenting him, he would "blow their brains out".

Two years before the events in Whitehall, M'Naghten gave up his business,[38] despite the good profits he had been making. He did so because of his paranoia, and the continuing belief that he was being persecuted. A modern view of his mental state, and his difficulty in relating to others, would be that he was showing signs of a schizoid personality. This illness is today seen as a common precursor of schizophrenia.[39] The persecutors were initially perceived by him as being Catholic priests in Glasgow, aided by the inevitable Jesuits. However, this belief developed further (for reasons that are now not wholly clear) into persecution by the Conservative party in Glasgow. The Conservatives were, he believed, watching him, following him, mocking him, threatening him, libelling him and poisoning his food. He was convinced that they would injure or kill him if they caught him.

M'Naghten believed his persecutors followed him into Scotland when he went there during the queen's visit in 1842. Also during 1842, M'Naghten met with William Gilchrist, a Glasgow printer, who he had known since 1834. They had lodged together in the Gorbals for a time. Gilchrist gave evidence about their last meeting in July 1842:

> ...when we walked together for a short distance, I thought he was altered, both in manner and appearance, for when I looked at him he always dropped down his head and looked at the ground. His

> conversation was not so connected as formerly. I have known the prisoner burst out into immoderate fits of laughter without any cause whatsoever; at other times he would moan. I never knew him attend any political meetings or express any extravagant political opinions.

Gilchrist added in cross examination that the ejaculations and laughter that he mentioned "might have been caused by the recollection of something he had previously heard and I was not aware of."

Later, M'Naghten also believed that his persecutors followed him to London. He had tried to escape them by going to the continent – twice – but each time they followed him there as well. He returned to England and when he went to Liverpool, they followed – indeed, he found that he could not escape them anywhere. It appears to have been at this point that he decided on killing possibly the chief Tory, Sir Robert Peel. This, he believed, would be the only way to stop his torment and rid himself of his persecutors.

It may, or may not, be relevant to observe that there is no evidence whatsoever that M'Naghten had shown that he had any romantic interests.

M'Naughten Buys Two Pistols

Police enquiries soon after the shooting of Mr Drummond revealed that M'Naghten had recently acquired two pistols from a Mr Martin, gunsmith of High Street in Paisley. M'Naghten called at his shop, sometime during July 1842, seeking a matching pair of pistols. Mr Martin produced various pistols for M'Naghten's inspection, but none of them were a matched pair. One pistol caught M'Naghten's eye and he pressed Martin for another pistol that would match it. Martin had no matching pistol and instead urged him to take a different pistol that was only a half-inch shorter in the barrel. M'Naghten's reaction was that "he would look daft-like to have pistols that were not matched."[40] This seems to have been an odd flash of vanity on M'Naghten's part.

Mr Martin could not produce a matching pistol, but he offered to obtain one from his son, who was in the same line of business in Argyll Street, Glasgow. Two days later it transpired that Martin junior did not have a matching pistol, and M'Naghten finally agreed to take the unmatched pistols from Martin.[41] At the same time he bought a copper powder flask, a key for the pistol barrels and had some pistol balls cast to fit the pistols. The total cost was 17 shillings. Both pistols were quite new and were marked on the side with the name of the maker, "Martin, Paisley". One of the barrels was 6 inches long and the other barrel was an inch shorter. The pistols were described in the coroner's court as being of "elegant workmanship".

Later, Martin recalled that that during the transaction, M'Naghten's "demeanour throughout was composed and sensible". Curiously, Mr Martin could not tell from M'Naghten's visits that he was a Glasgow man. Martin also recalled that M'Naghten had mentioned that he would be leaving the country in about three weeks.

Mrs Pattison, M'Naghten's landlady while he stayed in Glasgow, was irate when she found out that he had brought pistols into her house. He tried to mollify her by saying they had only been bought for shooting birds. This was most unlikely, as shooting birds would have been against M'Naghten's character and he was known for urging others not to rob nests or shoot birds. There is also the point that, if shooting birds was his intention, two short-barrelled pistols were most unsuitable firearms for that purpose.

M'Naghten and Politics

A significant issue in assessing M'Naghten's conduct is the extent to which he was involved in Glasgow politics before his move to London. The 1830s and early 1840s were turbulent times in Glasgow and indeed in most industrial centres in England. The growth of the Chartist movement, and particularly its call for political reform, was much discussed by members of all classes. The extent to which M'Naghten was involved in Chartism is very much an open question. There is no doubt that he knew Chartist activists (indeed one, Abram Duncan, worked for him for a time) and it would be unusual if M'Naghten was not in general favour of Chartism's aims. However, this could apply to very many of the working class of Glasgow. After all, at the time of the shooting, Glasgow (and other manufacturing centres) were in a recession, which by definition gives rise to increased unemployment, shorter working hours and downward pressure on wages. Recessions always brought hardship.

The important question, however, is the extent to which M'Naghten might have been active in any workers' resistance, or even armed resistance – there is no evidence that he was. Despite the government's use of informants within the Chartism structure, no information linking Chartism to the assassin or the assassination was found (or was voluntarily admitted or disclosed by Chartist sympathisers). It is also pertinent that even if M'Naghten was fully involved in Chartism at some time, it is inconceivable that a person in M'Naghten's fragile mental state would be relied upon to handle an assassination. That he came near to assassinating Sir Robert Peel was more due to the ineptness of the police, not the support of Chartists assisting M'Naghten.

Clothes and Pistols

There are, however, two troubling aspects when trying to understand M'Naghten's actions before the shooting.

When M'Naghten appeared before the magistrates in London after the shooting of Drummond, he was described as being reasonably dressed. This was a correct observation of his dress when he appeared in court. However, it is at odds with other descriptions of him before the shooting. His landlady, Mrs Dutton, described him as being seen wearing shabby and much patched clothes. She said that when he first arrived at her house, he only had with him "a change of linen, a change of flannel and a change of socks in the house." The smarter clothes that he wore when he was walking around Whitehall might well be accounted for by M'Naghten having had the foresight to realise that he would not stand out in Whitehall if he kept more appropriate clothing for his reconnaissance. If this was so, and it seems a logical point, it is now not known where these clothes were stored, and where he could change into them each day.

If this was indeed what he did, then the address of that property would have been important information for the police, in case the address was occupied by another, or others, who might have aided M'Naghten while he was in London. It is possible to develop various theories around how M'Naghten might have concealed his respectable clothes and who might have assisted him to do so.

Clearly, various different scenarios can be built around changing/concealing his better clothes:

- M'Naghten had accomplices that were political enemies of the government e.g. Chartists, and they hid the clothes for him.
- M'Naghten had rented a second room elsewhere in London which he used during the day when he was away from Mrs Dutton's house, as he might need to hide from his "persecutors".
- There were no accomplices and M'Naghten merely rented premises to hide his better clothes – and anything else that he would not want to keep at Mrs Dutton's house, such as his pistols.
- M'Naghten's paranoia drove him to keep moving his clothes frequently to new hiding places.

All or any could be possible, but the events are now too far away, in time, to be proved or disproved.

Once M'Naghten had acquired his two pistols, the same question arises as to where these were kept. It is most unlikely that these were kept regularly at Mrs Dutton's boarding house. She described his lodgings as a single room (she called it a "back attic") that was away from other lodgers. She added "there was no sitting room, only one bedroom". She also said of his room, "he kept his things in three table draws, but no drawer that locked – his room was never locked." It seems quite safe to deduce that his pistols were never kept at his lodgings (particularly after his landlady in Glasgow had found the pistols in his room when he last stayed there).

Mrs Dutton later told reporters that Drummond had no boxes or other property of his own in his room during his last stay. If M'Naghten did not have any boxes containing the apparel that he wore on the day of the shooting, where was it acquired and where was it kept safe? This point was not apparently considered by the prosecution.

M'Naghten Appears in Court, Saturday, 21 January 1843

Once it was known that M'Naghten would appear in court at Bow Street, there was a considerable crowd waiting in the street for the court doors to be opened at 10 am. M'Naghten was brought to the court from the police station, where he had been held until he was required in court. He was accompanied on the journey to court by two police inspectors from A Division.

Mr Hall, who was the magistrate listed to hear the case, arrived at 10.30 am and the charge as entered in the charge sheet was:

> Daniel M'Naughten, aged 27, of No 7 Poplar-row, Newington, by trade a turner; from 90 Clyde-street, Anderston, Glasgow, about three months ago; charged with discharging two loaded pistols at Mr Edward Drummond, at Charing-cross and wounding him. Found upon his person: two 5l. Bank of England notes, a receipt on the Glasgow and Ship Bank for 750l. to the credit of Daniel M'Naughten, four sovereigns, 11s. 4d. in silver, 1d. in copper, a key, a knife, 10 percussion caps and a brace of pistols.

The press reported M'Naghten as young, of about 5 feet, 7 or 8 inches tall, and having "the appearance of a mechanic",[42] whatever that meant. He appeared to be of rather slight build, of fair complexion with light hair and whiskers. His face was described as having "long features." He was respectably dressed in a black coat, black cloth waistcoat, drab trousers with black boots and a black beaver hat. Reporters thought that his countenance betokened nothing ferocious or determined – implying that they did not perceive any visible signs of lunacy or anger.

Evidence of the events in Whitehall was given in court by PC James Silver; Robert Hodge, the carpenter who witnessed the shooting; Benjamin Weston, a porter at the Ship Tavern; PC James Partridge and Mr Harvey Drummond, a partner in Drummond's Bank. Also called was Mr Bransby Cooper, surgeon, who gave evidence as to the wound inflicted on Drummond.

M'Naghten declined to examine any of the witnesses as they gave their evidence, but as he was being taken back to his cell, he asked if he could return to the court to make a statement. He then read out this statement:

> I wish to say that it is the Tories of my native city who have driven me to this act. They follow me and persecute me wherever I go; and they have, by their treatment of me, already ruined my health and disordered my mind. I can't sleep at night and have no rest night or day. They have followed me to France, to different parts of England and to other places – in short wherever I go. The system they have pursued towards me was such that I could go on no longer. I believe I have been driven into a consumption by them. I believe I shall never be the same individual again that I was before. I used to have good health and strength. They have accused me of crimes of which I was never guilty. They have done everything in their power to harass and to persecute me; and, in fact, to murder me. That is all I have to say at present, and it can all be supported by evidence.

On the magistrate asking if he had anything more to say. M'Naghten added:

> Only that they have completely disordered my mind. I am quite a different man from what I used to be, before they commenced their persecutions.

The statement was taken down and M'Naghten signed it.

Tothill Fields Prison

After being remanded in custody, the gaoler at Bow Street Magistrates' Court, Tyrell, moved to take M'Naghten from the court, but as he did so, M'Naghten pointed to the small cell attached to the court. He asked Mr Hall, "Shall I be kept in that place for a whole fortnight? Because if I be, I'll not live." Mr Hall assured him that he would not be confined in that cell but instead would be taken to a prison "where you will be taken proper care of".

M'Naghten was held temporarily in the court cell where he had a substantial meal of beef, potatoes and bread. Afterwards he was allowed to wait in the jailer's room for the usual prison van to take him to Tothill Fields Prison. While waiting for this van, M'Naghten joined in the conversation with Tyrrell, and other court staff. He was attentive to the conversation which passed between other persons present at the gaol, and he frequently laughed at any jocular comment which happened to be made. His demeanour throughout the whole day was precisely the same, and he displayed no apparent anger towards the court or his jailer. *The Times* reporter observed that:

> … there was nothing in his appearance or behaviour, with the exception of the statement he made before the magistrate, from which it could be inferred that he was labouring under insanity.[43]

This observation would not be regarded as significant today.

After 5 pm M'Naghten asked if he might have his tea. He was provided with a pint of coffee, a penny loaf and some butter, all of which he happily consumed.

At Tothill Fields Prison

M'Naghten was collected from the court around 6 pm by the prison van and duly delivered to Tothill Fields Prison. A prison was first built on this site in Westminster in 1618. In 1834 the old prison was demolished and a new prison, with the same name, was built on ground below Victoria Street and close to Vauxhall Bridge Road.[44] The plan of the new prison followed the "panoptican" design, created by Jeremy Bentham, with the warders in the centre of the site and able to see all round the site. It had an initial capacity of 900 prisoners.

M'Naghten was received by the governor, Lieutenant Tracey. It had already been decided by the governor that M'Naghten would be placed in a particular cell. This was a cell that had previously housed several well-known criminals. Most notorious of all was Francois Benjamin Courvoisier, a Swiss valet. He had been executed in July 1840 outside Newgate prison. His hanging was watched by an estimated crowd of 40,000 people.[45] Courvoisier, when he came to England, had held various domestic positions with the aristocracy. By April 1840, he was valet to Lord William Russell at 14 Norfolk Street,[46] Park Lane. Lord William was the third son of the Marquess of Tavistock, his nephew was Francis, 7th Duke of Bedford, and another nephew was Lord John Russell,[47] then Secretary of State for the Colonies. That the victim was an aristocrat, mixed in with the very gory manner of his murder,[48] ensured that press reporting would hold the public fascinated by the investigation, arrest, trial and then execution. It was probably only overtaken for public interest by the Rugeley Poisoner's trial in 1856.[49]

The same cell had also recently been used to accommodate John William Bean, who tried to assassinate Queen Victoria in 1842. Publicising that M'Naghten was to be placed in such a notorious cell would have helped to create an impression of guilt by association in the minds of newspaper readers (and potential jurors).

M'Naghten declined an evening meal and, being tired, he asked to be left in his cell to go to sleep. He went to sleep almost immediately. During the night, as was then normal in the case of a notorious prisoner awaiting trial, a lit lantern was left in his cell and a turnkey was stationed outside the cell to watch him (without being seen). This was not only to foil any attempted escape, but also to prevent any attempted suicide.

On Sunday, 22 January, M'Naghten attended divine service in the prison. M'Naghten said to the warders that he was of no particular religious persuasion, but he would go anywhere to hear a good sermon. After the service, according to the prison staff, he was returned to his cell where he ate a dinner, with gusto, from a nearby public house. Afterwards he was visited by Mr Lavies, surgeon to the prison. From this meeting, Lavies apparently concluded that M'Naghten was not a lunatic and that he was fit to stand trial. The chairman of the visiting magistrates for the prison accompanied Lavies during this meeting and he was of the same opinion. It is fair comment to ask what a surgeon and a magistrate knew of mental illness. But *The Times*[50] did not think so:

> It seems very improbable from the taciturn and reserved demeanour of the prisoner, that he will say anything upon the subject ... it is understood that since his confinement in Tothill-

> fields, he has not shown the slightest disposition to make any communication beyond the very extraordinary and confused statement he made [in the magistrates court]……
>
> It appears to be the general opinion of many persons who were present during the examination of the prisoner, and who are competent to form an opinion upon such subjects, that in making the statement he did, it was his wish to lead the public to infer that he was labouring under insanity, although his previous conduct and behaviour, coupled by his general appearance, entirely negative such a supposition.

Quite who the other people present were is unclear. Unfortunately the press did not understand their limitations when it came to understanding insanity. At the time this article was published it was fairly clear that no one who had spoken to M'Naghten, so far, had any knowledge of mental illness; nor did Queen Victoria, when she noted in her *Journal*[51]

> …a letter relative to him, from a person in Glasgow, trying to show that he was odd in the head, & by that means, mad, – but this he is *not*. I wrote to Sir Robert Peel that no one's life would be safe, if people were continually being let off on the plea of insanity, & that I am anxiously hoping this will not be the case in this instance.

This comment was quite probably driven by her own justifiable fear of assassination. However, common sense ought to have restrained the queen from her comment that M'Naghten was not mad. There was a further entry in the queen's *Journal*[52]

> The wretch, Mac Naugthen, Sir Robert said, showed the greatest intelligence & was evidently not the least mad. That he owned at least £1,000, & that he was evidently a man of literary acquirements, which extracts from Voltaire &c, found in his lodging go to prove. Mr Allison, the author, & Sheriff for the County of Glasgow (really it must be sheer folly & madness) has, without being in the least acquainted with the wretch, collected all the evidence he can, in order to prove Mac Naughten's insanity, & sent it officially to the Secy of State. This, Sir Robert Peel says, is highly embarrassing to the Govt. How anyone can do such a thing, is quite inconceivable!

The above comments are a very sad reflection on both the queen and the prime minister. It is unfortunate that neither the queen nor the prime minister stopped to consider how little either knew of insanity. Neither appeared to understand basic principles of English law when it came to the application of the death penalty, but probably many, after reading the newspapers probably agreed with them.

Mr Spalding Calls

Mr Spalding, a carpenter, called at the prison.[53] He had known M'Naghten in Glasgow and he wanted to speak to the prison governor but, in Lieutenant Tracey's absence, he saw the deputy governor. From the information already published in the press, Spalding had recognised M'Naghten as someone he knew.

Spalding had previously lived and worked in Glasgow in Stockwell Street. When M'Naghten was a boy, Spalding said that he would call at Spalding's shop daily. From his time in Glasgow, Spalding also remembered M'Naghten senior well, and that his business was one that had prospered significantly. Spalding was also aware of M'Naghten senior taking young M'Naghten into his business and teaching him the skills of woodturning. On completing his apprenticeship, M'Naghten still worked for his father as a journeyman, according to Spalding. However this runs counter to information from others that M'Naghten senior would not take M'Naghten into partnership. This caused M'Naghten to leave both his father's house and his father's business and set up as a woodturner on his own account – near his father's workshop.

M'Naghten had learned his trade well and he now worked hard in his new premises. He quickly established a reputation for excellent workmanship and delivering his work on time. He also made it clear to customers that his bills were to be paid on time and defaulters would receive as many visits as it would take until they had cleared all amounts owing.

Spalding also claimed, correctly, that M'Naghten had saved a significant amount of money from his labours, both during his apprenticeship and later in business on his own.[54] This answered those who were incredulous as to the level of M'Naghten's savings from sheer hard work.

Spalding described M'Naghten during this time as being teetotal and one who would not waste time, or money, at inns or coffee houses. Nor did he think that M'Naghten had showed any interest in political meetings, but on Sundays he went to a Presbyterian church, usually attending two services.

The Times, when reporting Spalding's views, considered that it was very improbable, from the general taciturn and reserved demeanour of M'Naghten, that he would say anything concerning his attack on Drummond – at least not before the trial. Since his confinement in Tothill Fields Prison, M'Naghten did not show the slightest inclination to make any statement, beyond his statement where he revealed his persecution by the Tories. It was known that the Metropolitan Police had sent at least one police sergeant to Glasgow to gather what background information was known about M'Naghten that could explain the assassination attempt.[55]

Chapter 8

THE TRIAL

M'Naghten's trial opened on Friday, 3 March 1843 at the Central Criminal Court – The Old Bailey. Presiding was Tindal,[1] the Chief Justice of the Court of Common Pleas, assisted by Coleridge[2] and Williams,[3] both Justices of the Court of Queen's Bench. The public interest in this trial was by now immense, and this was driven not only by the assassination itself, but also by the extensive newspaper coverage, which had started immediately after the shooting of Edward Drummond.

Court Attendance

Well before the court doors were opened, the streets outside the Old Bailey were thronged with excited would-be spectators. The court doors were ordered to be kept shut until 9 am. The throng outside the court was claimed to be like nothing ever witnessed before by the court officials or the press reporters. The *Illustrated London News* thought that the press of people, and the crowding in the court, exceeded even that seen for the recent trials of Francois Courvoisier and Daniel Good.[4] The press reporters had difficulty in obtaining entry. Even members of the aristocracy, who had obtained passes for admission, had trouble making their way, through the crowd, into the court.

Albert, the prince consort, was reported by the *Canterbury Journal,* 4 March 1843, as being in court for most of the first day of the trial and that he appeared to take much interest in the proceedings. However, there is a problem with this report, as there is no corroboration of this in the entries in Queen Victoria's *Journal*. Instead, her *Journal* records that Albert was out shooting in the morning of the 3rd and that, in the afternoon, both Victoria and Albert went out for a drive in the "cold and snowy countryside".[5] Her entry for the following day makes no reference to the second day of the trial but confirms that Albert was at Windsor that afternoon.

There is an illustration in the *Illustrated London News* of the interior of the Old Bailey Court for M'Naghten's trial. The artist who drew this sketch placed, in the centre of the Bench, a man without a judge's wig. This man appears to be wearing a chain of office, which rules out Prince Albert, but makes it more likely that it is the Lord Mayor of the City of London, who was reported as being present in court. In two recent books on Drummond's assassination, this particular print was used as an illustration and dated 11 February 1843. This is a patently incorrect date, as the trial at the Old Bailey was held on 3 and 4 March. There is no date attached to the illustration on the original publication of the sketch in the *Illustrated London News.*

The Times, almost with disappointment, noticed that there were fewer ladies present than would usually have attended such an important trial. This point underlines how often sensational trials would attract society women as spectators. However, there were notables present in abundance: the Belgian, US and Saxony Ministers (ambassadors), members of the peerage and Parliament were present. The body of the court was full of young barristers, "the majority of whom we never before observed in court". The same paper added a footnote to its report of the first day, thanking the Lord Mayor and sheriffs for making sure the press were accommodated, but:

> ...we cannot help protesting at the extreme rudeness, in some degree approaching ruffianism, displayed by the underlings at the gates and inner doors.

The Preliminaries

Very soon after 9 am, the court was already uncomfortably crammed, with no further room for spectators. As was usual for a notorious trial, a great number of barristers crowded into court, although many claimed to have been inconvenienced by being required to stand. When Sir William Follett, the solicitor general, who was to lead the prosecution on behalf of the Crown, arrived just before 10 am, he had great difficulty getting through the throng to reach his seat at the counsels' table. Matters commenced with the arrival, at 10 am, of the three judges, accompanied by the lord mayor of London, the London sheriffs and some of the London aldermen. M'Naghten was then escorted into court and placed at the bar.[6] He was calm and dressed in dark, well-worn clothes – resembling "a decent mechanic" as the *Kentish Times* rather snobbishly put it.[7] He appeared to be in good health, with a slightly florid complexion. He entered:

> …with a firm step, although it was evident he was much excited; he was dressed apparently in the same clothes as when under examination at Bow-street and appeared to have altered very little, if any, in his general appearance.[8]

The indictment was read out, that M'Naghten did:

> feloniously assault Edward Drummond with a certain loaded pistol, which he then and there held in his right hand, loaded with gunpowder and a leaden bullet, and which he of his malice aforethought discharged at and against the said Edward Drummond, thereby giving him a certain mortal wound in and upon the left side of the back of the said Edward Drummond, a little below the bladebone of his left shoulder of the breadth of half an inch and the depth of twelve inches, and of which wound the said Edward Drummond did languish until the 25th of January, and languishing did live, on which said 25th of January he, of the said mortal wound so given in manner aforesaid by the said Daniel M'Naughton, died, and that he did wilfully kill and murder the said Edward Drummond.[9]

Having done this, Clarke then asked him whether he would plead "guilty" or "not guilty". M'Naghten, in a tolerably clear and firm tone of voice, answered "not guilty." He was given a chair to sit on in the dock and then appeared to go to sleep during the solicitor general's opening, but became more attentive when the prosecution's witnesses were brought in.

Sir William Follett QC MP

Solicitor General Follett led for the prosecution. He was aged 46 at the time of this trial and his health, which was usually fragile, was starting to show further signs of decline. Follett was very well-regarded by his peers and his powers as an advocate were highly rated, particularly on the Western Circuit. His performance in this trial, however, appears to be somewhat lacklustre. This could have possibly been due, at least in part, to the progress of his tuberculosis.

This disease would force him to give up legal practice in April the following year, before his death in June 1845.

Alternatively, his performance may simply have reflected his knowledge that he would lose the case (see later in this chapter). It would have been the usual practice for the attorney general to lead for the Crown in a murder trial of this importance, but Attorney General Sir Frederick Pollock was, at the time, leading for the Crown in the prosecution of 58 Chartists at Lancaster Assizes.[10]

Alexander Cockburn QC MP

The defence was to be led by Alexander Cockburn QC, and his performance provided a marked contrast to Follett's approach. Cockburn was aged 41 and he had rapidly developed a reputation with some stellar performances in court. By 1843 he was one of the leaders of the Western Circuit and he had recently been appointed Queen's Counsel. He was a noted orator who could capture, and hold, the attention of a courtroom. His trials were frequently reported in the press, and this drew yet more public attention to his performances – something that he always greatly enjoyed.

Lord Chief Justice Russell of Killowen[11] later wrote of Cockburn's "voice of great beauty"[12] and, on Cockburn's death in 1880, *The Spectator* wrote of his manner and voice being "as near perfection as such things can well be". Another described him as having:

> …a clear, sweet, penetrating voice, a fluency that seemed so easy as to make listeners sometimes fancy that it ought to cost no effort, and a grace of gestures such as it must be owned, the courts of law….do not often teach.[13]

In 1840, several West Country newspapers had published profiles of the leading barristers on the Western Circuit. The praise for Cockburn's work was most noticeable:

> There is about him no assumed air of solemn importance, no effort to look very keen and clever, no flurry, no fussiness, so noticeable in the little men trying to be grand. Self-possessed and easy, confident in his own powers, he sits in a careless attitude, making few notes and permitting his brief to lie unfumbled before him. But careless though he might appear to a dull observer, he is

> watching every word that falls from the witness or counsel on the other side; no point escapes him, no objection is overlooked …. In person Mr Cockburn is short and of rather slender frame, but active and agile. His face is sharp, his forehead broad and high, his eyes are bluish-grey, with a singular expression of quickness and keenness; his nose, mouth and chin are strongly marked and thin; his hair is of a reddish hue. . . . He is a lively speaker; his form is incessantly moving; he uses his arms freely, but appropriately, to add force to his energetic language, or we would rather say, to accord with it. In a fitting area, with a clear stage, we should expect to find him an exceedingly graceful speaker. It is evident from every sentence that falls from him, Mr Cockburn is a very accomplished man; he must have read much and thought deeply; he has mastered the graces of education, decorating the substantial temple of knowledge with the hues and forms of art. That such must be a gentleman, in every proper sense of the word, will be concluded; he is one of nature's gentlemen, perfected by training and education. That he is a universal favourite, beloved by all who know him, proves that he possesses the social virtues that win affection, as well as the talents that command admiration.
>
> – *Somerset County Gazette*

The Exeter and Plymouth Gazette called him "the Orator among the barristers of the Western Circuit".

Cockburn was a lover of music, the opera and the theatre, and he had friends in these professions. He was a captivating conversationalist and always attracted attentive listeners at social events. Alongside this, he had a formidable reputation as a lady's man, with several illegitimate children. His reputation was as the Buck of the Bar, and he was also well acquainted with the London *demi-monde*.

A modern judge, Lord Justice Ormrod, observed of Cockburn's performance in this trial:

> …from the whole tenor of his speech and the immense effort entailed, obviously took the most intense personal interest in the case.[14]

Ormrod also observed in the same essay:

> There is no doubt about the widespread concern at this period in the medical profession about the law's attitude to insanity as a defence to serious crimes, most of which at that period were capital offences. All the circumstances of the McNaughton case suggest that this most ably conducted offence was organized by what today would be called a "pressure group" of people, seriously concerned to bring about a much-needed reform of the law in insanity cases.

If Ormrod was correct in his surmise, and there is little reason to think he was wrong, it would explain a great deal. It would also be quite revealing if we knew who was within this group, how they managed their work and how it was financed, but it is unlikely that any papers relating to the group are still extant.

The difference in style between the two leaders in court would be very much between the old and the new. But there were other comparisons to be drawn, particularly between the lack of originality in the prosecution's approach to the evidence and the well-researched defence. Most crucial was the difference in their approach to insanity, and in this area, Cockburn's much greater understanding of the subject soon became clear when he began his defence of M'Naghten.

The Case for the Crown

In addition to Follett leading the prosecution, the prosecution team also included two more barristers, Adolphus Waddington and Russell Gurney. Gurney opened matters for the Crown by reading the indictment

> On the 20th January, at the parish of St Martin's-in-the-Fields, did feloniously assault Mr Edward Drummond with a certain pistol, which he then and there held in his right hand, loaded with gunpowder and a leaden bullet, and which he, of his malice aforethought, discharged at and against the said Edward Drummond, thereby giving him a certain mortal wound, in and upon the left side of the back of the said Drummond.

(The use of "giving him a certain mortal wound" was a standard phrase used when death was by shooting or stabbing but, given the very questionable medical treatment Drummond received after being shot, it does strike a rather false note.)

Follett's exposition of the facts of the killing of Drummond was clear and straightforward, relying on a description of M'Naghten's actions and the evidence of those actions being supported by unimpeachable witnesses. However, Follett was quite aware that such an approach by itself would fail unless he dealt with what all knew would be the main and probably sole line of defence – insanity. Follett stated his intention to the court and jury as:

> It has been the custom in these cases to refer to proceedings of authority, and to the dicta of judges who have tried similar questions; not that I mean to say for one moment that is a question of law; on the contrary, the question to be decided by you is a question of fact, a question of common sense and belief. The whole question will turn upon this:
>
> if you believe the prisoner at the bar, at the time he committed this act, was not a responsible agent;
>
> if you believe that when he fired the pistol he was incapable of distinguishing between right and wrong;
>
> if you believe that he was under the influence and control of some disease of the mind which prevented him from being conscious that he was committing a crime;
>
> if you believe that he did not know that he was violating the law both of God and man;
>
> then undoubtedly he is entitled to your acquittal.
>
> But it is my duty, subject to the correction of my Lord and to the observations of my learned friend, to tell you that nothing short of that will excuse him upon the principle of the English law.

Reliance on Ferrers' Case

Follett's speech then went on to refer to the requirement that partial insanity on any point was insufficient to acquit. For this proposition he relied on *Lord Ferrers' case*[15] – a case which, to say the least, was one of doubtful authority and it was decided over 80 years before M'Naghten's trial. The trial of Lord Ferrers was before his peers in the House of Lords. He was accused of murdering his steward, John Johnson. Ferrers' plea of insanity failed. After being found guilty, but before sentencing, Ferrers apologised for his defence of insanity, which he admitted to have used only because of family pressure.

He also expressed remorse for arguing for the claim of insanity – and was ashamed of having done so. He was the last peer of the realm to be hanged as a common criminal.[16]

The problem for the Crown, with reliance on *Ferrers*' case, was that there were more recent decided cases which did admit different definitions of partial insanity. Furthermore, Follett did not touch on any of the advances in the understanding of insanity, particularly in what was then known as monomania (in the nineteenth century this was partial insanity, usually connected to a single psychological obsession). The reliance on *Ferrers*' case would become a serious weakness in the prosecution's case, once Cockburn started on his defence.

R v Hadfield

There was one decision on insanity and attempted assassination that Follett had to deal with and that was *R v Hadfield,*[17] which involved an attack on King George III. As Hadfield had been acquitted, Follett knew that he could not ignore this decision and that he must comment to the jury on it. He did so by readily accepting that Hadfield was, as Lord Kenyon had found, unfit to plead and that the court fully recognised this. But matters could not be left there, as the outstanding event in that trial had been Thomas Erskine's[18] exposition, in defence of Hadfield, of what he understood was the correct position of English law on partial insanity.

Follett readily accepted the skill of Erskine's performance in *Hadfield.* However, although Erskine set out clear views on the short comings of the *Hadfield* decision, followed by his own views on partial insanity, the Bench did not consider, or comment on, Erskine's legal propositions. Instead, Lord Kenyon had heard enough and he stopped the trial and directed the jury to find Hadfield "Not Guilty: he being under the influence of insanity at the time the act was committed." None of Erskine's further comments on partial insanity had judicial comment or approval, as Kenyon had offered no discussion or judgment, he had simply terminated proceedings by his decision.

Follett, rightly, saw that he could not ignore the *Hadfield* decision, but he also knew that he must attack Erskine's proposition that the accused:

> …must be shown to labour under some delusion, and it must be shown that he committed the act in consequence of that delusion.

Follett pointed out that, when putting forward this proposition, Erskine was under no obligation to make any points against it, so that Lord Kenyon had heard no counter arguments against Erskine – a genuine point which in turn could weaken Erskine's proposition. Follett went on to posit some examples where he would argue against Erskine's view being valid.

Hadfield's acquittal had created an immediate problem for the court. It was obvious that Hadfield was a threat to himself and others and therefore could not be released into the community. He should be detained in custody, but the court had no power to order detention because of his acquittal. The Vagrancy Acts of 1714 and 1744 only permitted detention until a person recovered his mind. While this was not likely in Hadfield's case, there was the possibility that a period of calm and lucidity could allow for his release. He was held while the Criminal Lunatics Act 1800 was hurried through parliament and the terms of which then legalised Hadfield's detention.

R v Bellingham

Follett quickly moved on to deal with a far more contentious case – that of *R v Bellingham.*[19] Bellingham was an English merchant trading in Russia. His business there collapsed and Bellingham could not obtain any redress from the Russian state, which he regarded as primarily responsible for his losses. Lord Leveson Gower, the British ambassador in St Petersburg, would not accept that Britain was obliged to accept any liability for Bellingham's losses. Bellingham became deranged, as many people thought, through the scale of his financial loss, and the indignity of having been denied any legal redress. Then:

- On 11 May 1812, Bellingham shot and killed Spencer Perceval, the Conservative prime minister, in the lobby of the House of Commons.
- On 13 May, Bellingham was tried for murder.
- On 15 May, Bellingham was convicted.
- On 18 May, Bellingham was hanged.

The scandalously short time from crime to execution gives an idea of how little could be prepared for any effective defence of Bellingham. The more Bellingham's trial is looked at, the more unjust the proceedings and the verdict become. Bellingham was a hero to much of the English working class for shooting Perceval, who was deeply unpopular within that class.

Chief Justice Mansfield

Bellingham's trial was held before the dyspeptic Chief Justice of Common Pleas, Sir James Mansfield. Lord Melbourne wrote to Queen Victoria referring to some defects in Mansfield's approach to Bellingham's case. While his initial observations were quite reasonable:

> There were differences of opinion as to the manner in which Sir James Mansfield conducted the trial. Many thought that he ought to have given more time, which was asked for on the part of the prisoner, in order to search for evidence at Liverpool.

Unfortunately, he followed this by writing:

> But the law which he laid down in his charge is certainly sound, correct, and reasonable.[20]

Mansfield had been reasonably successful as a barrister, but he waited a long time to be appointed chief justice of Chester (1799) and then chief justice of common pleas (1804, aged 70). Mansfield had a notoriously bad temper that was coupled with a short fuse and both of these elements meant that he could easily be provoked in court.[21] His directions to the jury in this trial were quite extraordinary and thoroughly inappropriate, given his open and obvious bias against Bellingham.

Both Mansfield and Perceval had close ties to the Conservative party and both had held office in Conservative administrations. For the sake of transparency of justice, Mansfield ought really to have recused himself from sitting in this trial.

Mansfield's[22] address to the jury was a highly emotional display on his part:

> Gentlemen of the jury, you are now to try an indictment which charges the prisoner at the bar with the wilful murder (<u>here the learned judge was so hurt by his feelings, that he could not proceed for several seconds</u>) of Mr. Spencer Perceval, (in a faint voice) who was murdered with a pistol loaded with a bullet; when he mentioned the name of (<u>here again his lordship was sincerely affected, and burst into tears, in which he was joined by the greatest portion of the persons in court</u>) a man so dear, and

> so revered as that of Mr. Spencer Perceval, I find it difficult to suppress my feelings.[23]

This display of open emotion and prejudicial comment at the death of Perceval was, to say the very least, inappropriate for a judge of his seniority conducting a murder trial. The real damage was that his remarks would also have stirred up the emotions of the jury against Bellingham, thereby helping to prejudice the jury's consideration of the charge.

Mansfield continued by strongly praising Perceval's qualities to further add to his prejudice against Bellingham.

> As, however, to say anything of the distinguished talents and virtues of that excellent man, might tend to excite improper emotions in the minds of the jury, but I would withhold these feelings which pressed for utterance from my heart, and leave you, gentlemen, to form your judgment upon the evidence which has been adduced in support of the case, undressed by any unfair indignation which you might feel against his murderer, by any description, however faint, of the excellent qualities of the deceased.[24]

The use of "his murderer" was wholly inexcusable and prejudicial against Bellingham. At this stage of the proceedings he had not been found guilty of anything. The next passage of Mansfield's was less overtly partisan, but his remark to the jury about it being unnecessary to go minutely into the evidence did seem to be pushing the jury into the "right" direction. A twentieth century clinician writing of this trial referred to Mansfield's conduct in court as:

> The refusal to allow time for the arrival of witnesses, the prejudicial and emotional opening of the judge's charge to the jury and the complete exclusion of any reference to the precedents set in the trial of Hadfield were flagrant abuses of judicial function and prerogative.[25]

Mansfield's view of insanity as a defence

The chief justice moved on to the defence of insanity and showed little understanding of such a defence, let alone a question of partial insanity.

Emphasising, as he did, the old test of telling right from wrong, was unhelpful to the jury and he simply ignored the Hadfield case. Mansfield went on:

> There is a third species of insanity, in which the patient fancied the existence of injury, and sought an opportunity of gratifying revenge, by some hostile act; if such a person was capable, in other respects, of distinguishing right from wrong, there is no excuse for any act of atrocity which he might commit under this description of derangement. The witnesses who had been called to support this extraordinary defence, had given a very singular account, to shew that at the commission of the crime, the prisoner was insane. What might have been the state of his mind some time ago, was perfectly immaterial. The single question is, whether at the time this act was committed, he possessed a sufficient degree of understanding to distinguish good from evil, right from wrong, and whether murder was a crime not only against the law of God, but against the law of his country.[26]

Even in 1812, it would have been difficult to view that last sentence as an accurate definition of Bellingham's position before the law, or indeed an accurate definition of what the law was. The jury consulted for 2 minutes 30 seconds then withdrew for 14 minutes before returning and announcing that they found Bellingham guilty. In the course of the jury's deliberations, strong evidence about insanity appeared to have been ignored, quite possibly because of the manner of Mansfield's summing up.

Sentencing

Mansfield's sentencing of Bellingham to death was highly redolent of revenge:

> ….you have shed the blood of a man admired for every virtue which can adorn public or private life – a man, whose suavity and meekness of manner was calculated to disarm all political rancour, and to deprive violence of its asperity. By his death, charity has lost one of its greatest promoters; religion, one of its firmest supporters; domestic society, one of its happiest and sweetest examples; and the country, one of its brightest ornaments – a man, whose ability and worth was likely to

> produce lasting advantages to this empire, and ultimate benefit to the world. Your crime has this additional feature of atrocious guilt, that in the midst of civil society, unarmed, defenceless, in the fulfilment of his public duty, and within the very verge of the sanctuary of the law, your impure hand has deprived of existence a man as universally beloved, as preeminent for his talents and excellence of heart. To indulge in any conjecture as to the motive which could have led you to the commission of this atrocious deeds, would be to enquire into all that is base and perfidious in the human heart.

There was nothing about this trial that reflected well on English justice and certainly nothing that could have provided anything useful to the development of the legal concept of partial insanity. However, the *Bellingham* decision was later referred to by Lord Lyndhurst in *R v Offord*,[27] another trial where the defence to a murder charge was insanity. Lyndhurst approved of the *Bellingham* test for insanity, but despite this, the accused was acquitted.[28] Lyndhurst had expressed the test as "did he know that he was committing an offence against the laws of God and nature?" – A somewhat unusual way to define the law that was then applicable to homicide in England.[29]

Cross-examination of the Crown's Witnesses Against M'Naghten

The court continued by moving on to the cross-examination of the Crown's witnesses, but this yielded little of interest. Constable James Silver of A Division repeated his evidence of the shooting and his arrest of M'Naghten that had previously been given in the magistrates' court. No significant cross-examination was made. Further evidence was heard from Benjamin Weston, office porter; Richard Jackson, the apothecary who first treated Drummond; and Police Sergeant Shaw, who assisted in the search of M'Naghten's lodgings. Mr Guthrie, surgeon, gave evidence to the nature of the wound and was recorded as stating, somewhat contentiously, that the pistol ball had wounded the diaphragm "and that is a wound which never heals under such circumstances." This view would be challenged after M'Naghten was found to be insane.

More significant evidence was given by Inspector John M. Tierney of A Division, as he had spoken at great length with M'Naghten after his arrest. However, the defence team were clearly concerned at Tierney's inappropriate conduct in the way he did this. Tierney went to the Gardener's Lane Police Station sometime before 5 pm. He stated that between the hours of 5 pm and 11 pm he visited M'Naghten's cell several times "and conversed with him". He stated that when he first saw M'Naghten he cautioned him "that in any conversation we might have together he should say nothing to criminate [sic] himself, as it might be used to in evidence against him". He further claimed that he repeated this caution on several occasions later.

Tierney said "I suppose you will assign some reason to the magistrate this morning for the crime you have committed?" Tierney then claimed that M'Naghten said, "I shall give a reason – a sort of one." Tierney's rather curious response was "You might have stated anything you thought proper to me last night after the caution I gave you". This response must have been deliberately phrased to mislead M'Naghten, as it required him to be able to understand anything that was "proper", which in this context should not include anything that might incriminate him. As the interrogation continued, M'Naghten clearly did incriminate himself by admitting to the shooting.

Unsurprisingly, Tierney was cross-examined on his conduct by Cockburn:

*Is it your duty to put questions to the prisoner*s? –

As long as I do not interfere with the case in point I do not see any harm in putting questions to prisoners.

Did anyone direct you to put such questions? –

Certainly not.

What was your object in putting them? –

I wanted to get all of the information I could about his former life.

In order to give it in evidence against him? –

I never intended to give in evidence against him, anything he told me until he mentioned the name of Sir Robert Peel.

What was your motive for wishing to get information respecting his former life?

Nothing that I know of, but the anxiety of human nature, under such revolting circumstances, to know who and what he was.

Now, do you mean to swear that you ever intended to suppress the evidence you have given? –

Not to suppress it, but I had no intention to mention it till he mentioned the name of Sir Robert Peel. I cannot give you the precise conversation which took place at each interview, but I stated the substance of them all. A constable, of the name of Edwards, was present when the conversations took place, but he is not here today. As I did not intend to mention the conversations I did not make any notes of them, but I did make a memorandum of the conversation in which Sir Robert Peel's name was mentioned.

Why did you not have the morning conversation in the presence of the constable?

I wish he had been present. I had no motive for the conversation taking place in his absence. I first mentioned the conversation at Bow Street.

Do you mean to swear that you had no motive lurking in your mind when you asked him whether he intended to make any statement before the magistrate?

I had no particular motive, but I imagined the responsibility was off my shoulders after the caution I gave him on the previous night.

Was not the object of that interview to induce him to make that statement? –

I did it for the purpose of letting him know that I was ready to receive any communication he thought proper to make.

Now perhaps you will tell me on your solemn oath, whether, when you made that observation to him, you did not do so with the intention of extorting a confession from him? –

The remark was carelessly made. I wanted to turn the conversation, as I thought he was going to make a full confession, and I did not wish to hear it.

Quite what Tierney was trying to achieve is difficult to discern from the answers to the questions. It was certainly clear that Cockburn did not like the idea of multiple interviews without witnesses being present and Tierney became more than a little uncomfortable at the way that Cockburn pressed him. At least one part of the press felt as Cockburn did:

> This certainly was a specimen of 'entangling a man in his talk' for which Mr. John Tierney deserves, and we hope he will receive, a severe reprimand.[30]

The Defence's Case

To those who understood what was now happening in court, it was clear that the defence of M'Naghten would be founded on the medical evidence. The information produced by the defence's experts, and their analysis of his mental state, was going to be used to discredit the earlier decisions on partial insanity that were being relied on by the prosecution. The Crown's evidence had clearly already established that M'Naghten was the person who had shot Drummond and that act would not be contested, as it did not provide any proof of M'Naghten's sanity or insanity. It was obvious, from the outset, that the sanity/insanity question was the key element in the trial, and yet the prosecution would not provide a single medical witness to give any evidence of sanity.

Although there was much speculation that Peel was the original target, this trial was about the killing of Drummond and the prosecution correctly concentrated on the actions of M'Naghten, without being side-tracked into speculation about Peel.

There was some evidence that Peel was the intended victim, but as the only evidence that this might be so came from Inspector Tierney there was no point in following this. Tierney's interviews, with no other witnesses present, would be insufficient in the absence of any corroboration.

A difficulty for Follett was that those who were well acquainted with M'Naghten were all firmly of the view that he had seen, and heard, Peel in the chamber of the House of Commons and that M'Naghten could not have made a mistake as to Peel's identity. M'Naghten had listened to Peel well enough to pass an opinion to his acquaintances in Glasgow as to his qualities as a speaker.[31] There was also evidence that M'Naghten had asked others in Whitehall to point out Peel to him, and this militates against M'Naghten being able to identify Peel from his visit to the Commons to hear Peel speak. But, against this should be added the evidence of Dr E.T. Monro. He gave evidence that M'Naghten had said to the doctors who examined him in Tothill Prison that:

> …the person whom he fired at gave him, as he passed, a scowling look. At that moment all the excitings of months and years rushed into his mind, and he thought that he could only obtain peace by shooting him.

Follett was still left with no proof that M'Naghten intended to shoot Peel, whatever the suspicions that were held on this point.

When the Crown had concluded its case, Cockburn had immediately asked the Bench that he be allowed to commence the defence at the start of the following day, rather than in the relatively small amount of time still left in the Friday session. He explained to the Bench that he was indisposed and spoke only with "great pain" and this could limit him in his address to the jury. The court agreed to his request and adjourned until the following day. It is a little doubtful that Cockburn was genuinely ill. He had cross-examined during the first day and the court reporters had managed perfectly well to hear what was said, although some said they could detect a cold in his speech. But when it came to his application for adjournment, *The Times* reporter could not hear the exchange. The Bench had made it clear, in agreeing to Cockburn's request, that they expected the case to be concluded on the following date.

Cockburn's indisposition, if not real, came from his determination not to have his presentation of evidence interrupted by the overnight break between Friday and Saturday. Having obtained the adjournment, his defence the following day could be put forward in one continuous argument, which would make the presentation more effective and more easily followed by the jury and the Bench. The adjournment also meant that the prosecution team would not gain any advantage by being able to analyse Cockburn's opening overnight. In fairness to Cockburn, he was prone to coughs and colds but, this time, it seems to have been unduly opportune.

The Defence

In his defence of M'Naghten, Cockburn's approach provided a marked contrast to Follett's more predictable, even pedestrian, opening. Cockburn's address to the court and jury still reads well over 180 years later. Cockburn was rightly proud of his written and spoken English and throughout his professional life he devoted considerable time to the clarity and logical construction of his speeches. His style was undoubtedly very much of its time, but it is not hard to understand the words, and their effect, when delivered with fluency in Cockburn's mellifluous and clear voice.

Cockburn first dealt with the weight that was imposed on him (and by extension on the jury) when defending in a capital case, and the difficulty of preconceived ideas of guilt when someone as well-known and liked as Drummond had been murdered.

> I believe that you – I know that the numerous professional brethren by whom I see myself surrounded – will understand

> me when I say that of all the positions in which, in the discharge of our various duties in the different relations of life, a man may be placed, none can be more painful or paralysing to the energies of the mind than that of an advocate to whom is committed the defence of a fellow being in a matter involving life and death, and who, while deeply convinced that the defence which he has to offer is founded on truth and justice, yet sees in the circumstances by which the case is surrounded, that which makes him look forward with apprehension and trembling to the result.

An excellent explanation of his position that also, without saying so, explained the onerous position that the jury was in.

Cockburn continued:

> …in all classes of this great community – in every corner of this great metropolis – from end to end, even to the remotest confines of this extensive empire – has this case been already canvassed, discussed, determined – and that, with reference only to the worth of victim, and the nature of the crime – not with reference to the state or condition of him by whom that crime has been committed; and hence there has arisen in men's minds an insatiate desire of vengeance – there has gone forth a wild and merciless cry for blood, to which you are called upon this day to minister! Yet I do not complain. When I bear in mind how deeply the horror of assassination is stamped upon the hearts of men, above all on the characters of Englishmen – and believe me, there breathes no one on God's earth by whom that crime is more abhorred than by him who now addresses you, and who, deeply deploring the loss, and acknowledging the goodness – dwelt upon with such touching eloquence by my learned friend – of him who in this instance has been its victim would fain add….an humble tribute to the memory of him who has been taken from us.

This was a little flowery by today's standards, but that does not detract from its clarity, which was such that no juryman could fail to be impressed.

But, Cockburn claimed, he would not give way to despair or despondency when dealing with such a grave matter, as he was appearing in a British court, before British judges and a British jury. This was a flattering approach, that sounds rather hackneyed today, but it does appear to have made an impression in that courtroom – Cockburn's words were not obsequious, nor mere braggadocio, but a firm statement of his belief in British justice – something which was probably shared by the jurymen.

To complement his usual eloquence, Cockburn was far better read on the subject of insanity when compared with Follett;

> …I am enabled to understand how it was that crude maxims and singular propositions founded upon the hitherto partial knowledge of this disease, have been put forward and received as authority, although utterly inapplicable to many of the cases arising under the varied forms of insanity. Science is ever on the advance, and no doubt, science of this kind, like all other, is in advance of the generality of mankind.

This passage made the important point, for both judges and jurymen, that the science of insanity was then in its infancy, but it was developing and was not frozen in time, such as *Ferrers*' case now was. By implication he was also making the point that old theories about insanity no longer applied. He followed this up with promising to turn:

> …to the doctrines of matured science rather than to the maxims put forth at times when neither knowledge, nor philanthropy, nor philosophy, nor common justice, had their full operations in discussions of this nature.

Next, a touch of theatre came in this address when Cockburn referred to the prosecution having cited Lord Hale's views on insanity from the seventeenth century:

> My learned friend, the Solicitor General, has read to you the authority of Lord Hale upon the subject matter of this inquiry. I hold in my hand perhaps the most scientific treatise that the age has produced upon the subject of insanity in relation to jurisprudence – it is the work of Dr Ray, an American writer on medical jurisprudence, and a professor in one of the great national establishments of that country.[32]

Lord Hale had held the view that a mentally ill person, who had the understanding of a 14-year-old, would be guilty if he committed a felony or treason. Ray's book firmly rejected that view due to the lack of knowledge of insanity in Hale's time, 160 years before. Ray's challenge was:

> Could Lord Hale have contemplated the scenes presented by the lunatic asylums of our own times, we should undoubtedly have received a very different doctrine from him.

Cockburn followed with an extract from the speech of Erskine in his defence in *Hadfield*, praising it as the only true application of the law and insanity and added

> Upon that argument I take my stand this day. I will bring this case within the scope of the incontrovertible and unanswerable reasoning which it comprises....

This was a very bold statement by Cockburn in M'Naghten's defence, as Erskine had made it clear that, in his defence of Hadfield, he was putting forward his own view of the law:

> I must convince you, not only that the unhappy prisoner was a lunatic within my own definition of lunacy, but that the act in question was the immediate, unqualified offspring of the disease.[33]

The solicitor general had put forward two decisions in support of his case in his opening address. These were the trials of Earl Ferrers and Sergeant Hadfield. Cockburn was unperturbed by either decision being cited for, as he said, he intended to use more of Erskine's observations in *Hadfield* to support M'Naghten's acquittal. In the case of *Ferrers*, in Erskine's words, "there could not be a shadow of doubt" as to Ferrers' guilt. Erskine had then carefully described Ferrers' behaviour and how it was not comparable to Hadfield's deed.

Cockburn made a head-on challenge to the prosecution's use of old precedents in an area where scientific thinking had manifestly moved on:

> I think it will be quite impossible for any person who brings a sound judgment to bear upon this judgment, when viewed with the aid of the light which science has thrown upon it, to come to

> the opinion that the ancient maxims, which, in times gone by, have been laid down for our guidance, can still be taken to obtain in the full force of the terms in which they were laid down. It must not be forgotten that the knowledge of this disease in all its various forms is a matter of very recent growth.

For all that Cockburn had presented in his address, the key to the outcome of this trial lay in what was a relatively new practice for trials – the presentation of expert medical practitioners on the nature of insanity. This was, without doubt, an area that was in its infancy, but Cockburn had a greater familiarity with its development than either the prosecution's team or the Bench.

Evidence From Those Who Had Known M'Naghten

Evidence was initially taken from M'Naghten senior, who spoke of his son's gradual estrangement. More tellingly he gave first-hand evidence as to his son's mental state:

> …he then told me that various prosecutions had been raised against him, begged that I would speak to the authorities of the town [Glasgow] upon the subject, in order to have a stop put to them. He particularly mentioned the name of Sheriff Alison, as one of the people I must speak to. I asked who the persons were that persecuted him, and he told me that Mr Sheriff Alison knew all about it…
>
> [Later] he then said that the persecution still continued, and he was followed day and night by spies; wherever he went they followed him.

There was more in the same vein.

William Carlo, a turner, gave further evidence and in this he explained that he did not believe that M'Naghten was mentally ill and so he visited him. During a walk he spoke of his visit to France:

> he told me he was very much persecuted by certain parties, who always followed him about wherever he went and he could get no rest for them night or day……they were sure to send their emissaries before him and he was known wherever he went.

Mrs Jane Patterson was M'Naghten's landlady occasionally in Glasgow, this arrangement ending two years before the shooting:

> …I observed something very peculiar in his manner. His eyes presented a very strange appearance, he looked wild and very different from what he used to……he could not stop in London or in France, as he was constantly haunted by a pack of devils following him….

Henry C. Bell one of the sheriff's deputes:

> …[he] called upon me about nine or ten months ago and complained that he was harassed to death by a system of persecution which had for some time been adopted towards , and for which he could obtain no redress whatever…. That he was constantly beset by spies and that he considered his life and property in danger…

Alexander Johnston MP:

> The prisoner called upon me about a twelvemonth ago and complained of being subjected to an extraordinary system of persecution……On subjects of general business he talked very rationally, but with respect to this particular business he said that he had for a considerable time been persecuted by the emissaries of a political party, whom he had offended by interfering in politics. He also complained of being attacked through the newspapers, and said the persons of whom he complained followed him night and day; that he could get no rest for them; that they destroyed his peace of mind……He then said that he thought his persecutors would be satisfied with nothing but his life….

Sir James Campbell, lord provost of Glasgow met with M'Naughten in May 1842:

> …he said he wanted my advice and protection. He said that he was the victim of extraordinary persecution; that he was followed and beset by spies day and night and he could not get rid of them; they dogged him wherever he went and he could not in

> consequence get any rest, day or night; that he was afraid to go home and therefore been compelled to sleep in the fields in the suburbs of the town....

Hugh Wilson, commissioner of police at Glasgow:

> ...I recollect his calling upon me, about eighteen months ago, to make a complaint. He said he had come to consult me on a very delicate matter and .....said that he was the object of some persecution....that he thought it proceeded from the priests at the Catholic chapel in Clyde Street, who were assisted by a parcel of Jesuits....that they followed him wherever he went and were never out of his sight and when he went to his bedroom he still found them with him........In two or three days he again called, and on alluding to the subject said the Tories had joined with the Catholics, that he could get no rest either day or night through their persecuting conduct....

It is more than a little surprising that the above evidence from Glasgow officials was so readily discounted by those in London. Perhaps this was a superior attitude when it came to matters outside London, but the Bench quite clearly had a more rational approach to this evidence.

The Expert Evidence for the Defence

As noted earlier in this chapter, the unusual feature of this trial was the absence of medical experts on behalf of the Crown. Given the importance of the plea of insanity, this lack of medical evidence from the prosecution was not only a startling omission, but it was one which was potentially fatal for the prosecution's case. Quite why the prosecution team took the decision not to put forward medical experts was unclear, although it would become so once the defence forcefully went at the prosecution's inadequate case. Facing counsel who had already established a reputation for winning important cases and not having any sound medical evidence of sanity to support the prosecution's case was to be a major error. However, it could have been that it was simply too difficult to find any doctors of repute who were prepared to support the prosecution case, given that it was so reliant on antiquated findings and precedents.

It was also the case that doctors who practised in this area of medicine increasingly mistrusted, with good reason, the old legal decisions on insanity. But, whatever the reasons, this was a significant weakness in the prosecution's case and it was most unlikely that Cockburn would fail to attack it. If the prosecution had tried and failed to find doctors prepared to give evidence as to M'Naghten's sanity, then the weakness of the case for the Crown was bound to be fully exposed.

The Prosecution's Medical Experts

It was known that Mr Lavies, the surgeon to Tothill Fields Prison, went to see M'Naghten[34] soon after M'Naghten arrived there on 22 January. The answers that M'Naghten gave to his questions convinced Lavies that he was not insane. However, the view of a prison surgeon on a question of insanity would have been worth little, given that his usual practice would have had little to do with the treatment of the insane.

Lavies was accompanied to the prison by Mr Amyoto, chairman of the visiting magistrates at Tothill Fields Prison. He was also convinced that M'Naghten was sane, though his utter lack of qualifications to give a professional view on insanity meant his opinion was worth even less. In any event, neither man would be put forward to give evidence for the prosecution. It is possible that other doctors, instructed by the prosecution team, did not give evidence because either they too considered M'Naghten to be insane or their views were not regarded as strong enough to stand up to cross-examination.

On 24 January, the *Morning Post* reported that Mr Lavies had again visited M'Naghten and that he had come away from the meeting "convinced of M'Naghten's sanity". On the same day, there was another visit by doctors reported in the *Morning Post*:

> ...several physicians of eminence connected with the various lunatic asylums of the metropolis (amongst whom were Doctors Monro and Sutherland) visited M'Naughten at Tothill-fields Bridewell. The usual course pursued on these occasions towards suspected lunatics was not deviated from in the present instance. ...The result of the interviews of the various medical gentlemen with the prisoner, was in each case the same – namely, a conviction that M'Naughten is perfectly sane, and that the statement made by him before Mr. Hall, at Bow-street, was a premeditated one.

It is not known who provided this information to the *Morning Post*, as it was either fabricated or merely wishful thinking, which the press would discover later when Monro and Sutherland gave evidence for the defence.

Dr E.T. Monro's Expert Evidence for the Defence

Dr Monro[35] was the first medical witness called by the defence. He told the court that he had thirty years' experience of treating the insane. He had been asked "by friends of the prisoner" to examine M'Naghten. It was unusual for an expert witness to be instructed other than by the legal team defending, or prosecuting, the accused. This unusual manner of instructing experts does seem to suggest that those experts who gave evidence in M'Naghten's defence were anxious, not only to see justice done, but to move matters forward from the injustice of the likes of the Bellingham trial. Clearly, Cockburn was not going to pass on Monro's evidence, even though he was not, apparently, instructed by the defence team.

At the visit to examine M'Naghten, on 18 February, Monro was accompanied by Sir A. Morison, Mr M'Clure and other, unnamed, professional gentlemen who would be known when they took the stand to give their opinions. Also present were Dr Sutherland jnr. and Dr Bright, both instructed by the Crown, but, although they had observed M'Naghten, they did not ask any questions of him. All of the doctors appearing for the defence asked questions of M'Naghten in the presence of all the others, so that all present were aware of all the questions and M'Naghten's answers.

Dr Monro's Summary of M'Naghten's Delusions

Monro's evidence on M'Naghten's delusions was clear and detailed and it would wreck the prosecution's case, such as it was.

Monro gave evidence that during his meetings with the accused, he had established M'Naghten believed that:

1. He had been persecuted in Glasgow, Edinburgh, Liverpool, London and Boulogne, by a "crew" that had followed him wherever he went, and that his persecutors had given him no peace. M'Naghten had become certain that this persecution would kill him – he said, "it was grinding of the mind".
2. He had taken no medical advice on his mental state. He said that "if he had taken a ton of drugs it would be of no service to him."

3. He said that people had stared at him and talked about him in Glasgow. They said he was a murderer and "the worst of characters". They also tried to associate him with the "dirtiest of crimes".
4. Wherever he went, "he was tossed like a cork on the sea, that wherever he went, whether in town or country, or by the sea shore, he was perpetually watched, and followed".
5. In Edinburgh, a man on horseback watched him and, in the same city, a man nodded to him and said, "that's he."
6. He maintained that the city authorities in Glasgow would not help him and that his complaints were sneered at. He claimed that Sheriff Bell "had it in his power" to stop his persecution, but he would not do so.
7. If he had a pistol then, he said, he would have shot Sheriff Bell dead as he sat in his courthouse.
8. He maintained that Mr Salmon, the procurator-fiscal, Mr Sheriff Bell, Sheriff Alison and Sir Robert Peel might have put a stop to his persecution, if they had cared to.
9. On leaving the Glasgow courthouse, he once saw a man with a bundle of straw under his arm who scowled at him and he knew well enough what was meant by this "as everything was done by signs." He was represented to be under a delusion; but he knew that the straw denoted that he should lie upon straw in an asylum.
10. When he set off for England on the Glasgow-Liverpool steamboat,[36] he was watched and examined closely by all the people nearby him.
11. People had followed him when he went to Boulogne, twice, and while there:
    - they would never allow him to learn French,
    - they wanted to murder him,
    - individuals were made to appear before him like those he had seen in Glasgow and
    - as a consequence, he could not go out after dark for fear of assassination.
12. When he sought the protection of Mr Johnson, MP for Kilmarnock, he was told that he was labouring under a delusion, but M'Naghten was sure this was wrong, and he claimed that he was not insane.
13. He had seen paragraphs in the press:
    - *The Times* contained allusions which he was satisfied were aimed at him.
    - The *Glasgow Herald* also carried "beastly and atrocious, insinuating things, untrue and insufferable" to him.

14. On one or two occasions something "pernicious" had been put in his food.
15. He had turned to the study of anatomy to seek peace of mind from his persecution, but he had not found any mental peace at all.
16. He believed that the person he had shot at in Charing Cross was part of the system that was destroying his health. Therefore, after he fired, "every feeling of suffering which he had endured for months and years rose up at once in his mind and that he conceived he should obtain peace by killing him". This is significant, in that Drummond, on leaving the bank, walked towards M'Naghten, who was standing in a doorway looking up Charing Cross watching Drummond walk towards him. This is the only occasion where we know that M'Naghten and Drummond faced each other, although neither knew who the other was.

Cockburn asked Dr Monro if he considered that these delusions were genuine or assumed. Monro replied that they were real "beyond a shadow of a doubt". Monro added:

> The act with which he is charged, coupled with the history of his past life, leaves not the remotest doubt in my mind of the presence of insanity sufficient to deprive the prisoner of all self-control. I consider the act of the prisoner in killing Mr Drummond to have been committed whilst under a delusion: the act itself I look upon as the crowning act of the whole matter – as a carrying out of the pre-existing idea which had haunted him for years

Cockburn asked if M'Naghten's actions were consistent with a partial delusion that deprived him all self-control. Monro answered:

> Certainly; monomania may exist with general sanity…An insane person may commit an act similar to the one with which the prisoner is charged and yet be aware of the consequences….

Cross-examination by Follett did not yield anything at all that weakened the effect of Monro's forceful testimony.

There is one aspect of Monro's testimony that is worth considering more closely and that is point 16 above and the question of who M'Naghten thought he was firing at.

The Old Bailey Online transcript of the trial shows that Dr Monro said, to the best of his recollection, that:

> …. [M'Naghten] imagined the person at whom he fired at Charing-cross to be one of the crew – one of the system destroying his health.
>
> Q. When you say "the person," do you mean that he used the expression, or did you put any name to him?
>
> A. I did not put a name to him – I think I called him "the person" – I cannot recollect the form of the question I put to him – I have no doubt I must have asked him who he conceived the person to be at Charing-cross. <u>He [M'Naghten] said he [the person he shot] was one of the system, one of the crew destroying his health</u> and that when he saw this person, every feeling and every suffering he had endured for months and years rose up in his mind at once, and that he thought he should obtain peace by shooting him.

Taken at face value, what M'Naghten said is that he saw the person at Charing Cross as being one of the number who were constantly harassing and threatening him. If this is correctly recorded, M'Naghten cannot have meant that Peel was his target, as he was regarded by M'Naghten as the chief Tory and one that M'Naghten had seen in Parliament. He did not think Peel to be "one of the crew".

In answer to a question from the prosecution's cross-examination, Monro said:

> I think one of the gentlemen [examining doctors] asked him whether he considered he had fired at Sir Robert Peel, he hesitated about that, and at length he said he was not sure whether it was Sir Robert Peel or not. I do not think I put any question to him to ascertain if he knew who the person was he had fired at; but certainly in my presence it was asked of him if he knew, and it was asked him more than once. He hesitated and paused, and at last stated, to the best of my recollection, that <u>he did not know whether it was Sir Robert Peel or not</u>. He did not say, to the best of my memory that he should not have fired if he had not believed it was Sir Robert Peel. I have no note of that sort….

> I do not remember his saying that he should not have fired if he had not thought it was Sir Robert Peel. I do not think he said that, he said the person at whom he fired scowled at him, gave a scowling look as he passed him, and all his feelings rushed into his mind at once – all he had suffered for years, and he thought it would give him peace if he shot him, and he thought him one of the system – that was in answer to questions put – I did not say, "Did you think it would give you peace of mind if you had fired at him?" – I certainly avoided all leading questions. I should have said, "Do you know at whom you fired?" – I do not think I put the question at all myself – I think it was, "Did you know at whom you were firing?" and he stated he believed it was one of the system that was destroying his health – that was not at the same time that he hesitated, and said he did not know whether it was Sir Robert Peel – he said that in reply to another question – there was a good deal of repetition – perhaps it was difficult to avoid it; and the gentlemen who came from Scotland put the same questions, not knowing what we had asked before.

No doubt the recording of what was said in court was not as rigorous then as it would be today. However, it is difficult to read Monro's answers as providing a positive answer as to who he understood M'Naghten intended to shoot. Further, Hugh Wilson, commissioner of police at Glasgow, was cross-examined by Follett and the final part of his evidence was revealing:

> I observed a change in him when he called on me the other day, a restlessness in his manner, looking about, and staring with his eyes – he was very bad, very much excited, the last time I saw him, which was last Aug., he then complained to me in the same way, and said that he was not able to suffer longer – something must be done for him. Without his speaking of any particular party at that time, I understood him to mean the same party he had before spoken of the Catholic priests, and the police were the parties he had spoken of before, and spies. He said the police were at the bottom of it, in fact that it was a combined system, the whole were leagued against him, the police, the Jesuits, the Catholic priests, and the Tories – he mentioned the Tories – I

> believe he described them – I did not understand him to mean any person, but just the Tories as a body – that was what he repeated to me on several occasions.

Wilson had clearly listened to M'Naghten's disturbing tale carefully. It is telling that, in explaining his persecution, he mentioned the Tories, but he did not mention the Chief Tory – Sir Robert Peel. If Peel had been the intended victim one would have expected M'Naghten to have referenced this as his motive. It must be admitted that the recording of what was said in court is not without problems, but the absence of any statement in court that Peel was M'Naghten's target is fairly clear. It is apparently the case that he did name Peel when Inspector Tierney conducted his irregular examination of M'Naghten (according to Tierney), but that interrogation was not in the presence of witnesses and therefore it could not have been given in court by the prosecution.

The Other Defence Experts

Sir A. Morrison MD was the next witness and he confirmed his agreement with Monro's evidence. This was followed by further confirmation of insanity from:

- Mr William M'Clure, surgeon,
- Dr W. Hutcheson, physician to the Royal Lunatic Asylum, Glasgow,
- Dr P.J. Crawford, Glasgow and
- Mr Aston Key of Guy's Hospital.

The Reaction to the Experts' Opinions

At this point, the trial took a most unusual course. The defence called Mr Forbes Winslow, surgeon of Guildford Street, who was the author of several works on insanity, including the recently published *Plea of Insanity in Criminal Cases*. He had not been summoned to court by either the prosecution or the defence, but he had attended both days of the trial and had listened intently to the entire proceedings. He was asked by Mr Clarkson for the defence:

> Judging from the evidence which you have heard, what is your opinion as to the prisoner's state of mind?

To this question Winslow replied:

> I have not the slightest hesitation in saying that he is insane, and that he committed the offence in question whilst afflicted with a delusion, under which he appears to have been labouring for a considerable length of time.

This comment prompted Chief Justice Tindal to intervene, and he asked Winslow to repeat what he had said, which Winslow did. Winslow's evidence was quite extraordinary in that he was apparently only there as a spectator in the court and had not been instructed by either side. The alacrity with which the Bench allowed him to give evidence almost seems to suggest that the Bench was struggling with the overwhelming evidence given on behalf of the defence and that they were looking for some other independent corroboration. However, it seems more than a little fortuitous that Winslow was there (and in a good seat). Was his presence really by chance?

While the next defence witness, Dr Phillips, was being called, the three judges conferred and, before Phillips could take the oath, Tindal CJ again intervened and asked Follett:

> Mr Solicitor General, are you prepared, on the part of the Crown, with any evidence to combat this testimony of the medical witnesses who have now been examined, because we think that if you have not, we must be under the necessity of stopping the case? Is there any medical evidence on the other side?

Follett admitted that he had no medical evidence to answer that which was presented by the defence. As Follett explicitly said that he had not any medical advice of M'Naghten's sanity, this must be confirmation that the prosecution had not had any advice that M'Naghten was considered to be sane.

Tindal CJ thereupon stopped the proceedings with the following:

> We feel the evidence, especially that of the last two medical gentlemen[37] who have been examined, and who are strangers to both sides and only observers of the case, to be very strong, and sufficient to induce my learned brothers and myself to stop the case.

Follett, with good grace, conceded that in view of the comments from the Bench, and he not being able to counter the defence's evidence, he could not reasonably press further for a conviction. This only left Tindal CJ to explain matters to the jury. His remarks stressed the evidence of the doctors:

> …I have undoubtedly been very much struck, and so have my learned brethren, by the evidence we have heard during the evening from the medical persons who have been examined as to the state of mind of the unhappy prisoner, for unhappy I must call him in reference to his state of mind.

The jury required no more evidence and quickly returned a verdict of not guilty on the grounds of insanity.

For such a *cause célèbre*, the collapse of the trial provided something of an anti-climax for the public. The death sentence – widely expected, and hoped for by many – was not pronounced and M'Naghten was not guilty and would therefore survive – a survival that was detested by many who had ardently expected a guilty verdict and swift execution.

Why Was the Crown's Case Apparently So Weak?

The lacklustre prosecution case becomes more understandable when the lack of medical evidence on the part of the prosecution is looked at more closely. The prosecution had instructed at least two doctors to attend the first examination of M'Naghten. The doctors instructed by both the prosecution and the defence were together during the examination. Cockburn, in his opening for the defence, had made much of the conduct of the prosecution towards their expert witnesses:

> [M'Naghten] has been visited by members of the medical profession, of the highest intelligence and the greatest skill, not chosen by the prisoner himself, but some of them selected by his friends, and others deputed by the Government…. They visited the prisoner together several times: they together heard the questions put to him, and noted the answers he gave. My learned friend has accurately told you the nature of the defence I have to offer; he has sought to anticipate it by evidence to establish the prisoner's sanity.

Then came Cockburn's taunting question for the prosecution:

> How is it then, that, the medical team employed by the Crown have not been called?
>
> Why, my learned friend has now beside him, within his arm's reach, two of the medical gentlemen sent by the Government,[38] and he has not dared to call them. My learned friend knew (because their opinions have been communicated to the Government and to my learned friend) that the man was mad, and in justice to the public and to the prisoner, those gentlemen ought to have been brought forward.
>
> I was astonished when the case for the prosecution was closed without those two witnesses being called. They sat within my learned friend's call, and yet my learned friend, in the exercise of the discretion which is his characteristic, dared not put them in the witness box.
>
> Their testimony is, however, upon record; it requires not their delivery by their own mouths of the opinions I know them to entertain; their absence from the witness box speaks trumpet-tongued as to the opinions they were ready to pronounce; and when I call before you the medical gentlemen who have attended at the request of the friends of the prisoner, and have communicated with this poor deluded maniac, and it is found that their opinions correspond in all particulars, there will not be a shadow of doubt that this was no simulated insanity.

The only reasonable explanation for the failure of the Crown's experts to be called must be as Cockburn suspected. However, having two of the Crown's experts clearly present in court, sitting there as quiet as church mice, only served to highlight to all those present in court, including the Bench and jury, the prosecution's inability to counter the evidence that Cockburn was about to bring forward.

Why Then Did This Matter Even Come to Trial?

There were many, from the queen downwards, who wanted, and expected, the jury to deliver a guilty verdict. If the prosecution had declined to prosecute M'Naghten for murder, and the judges directed that M'Naghten be taken straight to Bethlem Hospital for being a lunatic, it would have probably brought down the royal wrath upon their heads – and a large proportion of both Houses of Parliament would have held the same view. It was most likely that public opinion was only going to be satisfied by a public trial taking place and both legal teams knew it. A finding of insanity would then be the act of the jury, after a trial, and the government could say, rightly, that due process had then been seen to have been followed.

When looked at from this point of view, most of the principal legal figures in court would have known what was likely to happen before the trial opened. This was, of course, provided that the defence was conducted adequately and that the prosecution was much more than adequate. If this is a correct analysis of the circumstances, one cannot help but have sympathy for the position Follett had been placed in.

There was another aspect of the trial that was commented on by the *Times*[39] and that was participation of the jury:

> … It ought to have been left to the jury to determine from the facts of the case whether M'Naghten's delusion, proved by the doctors, was or was not such as to render him incapable of telling right from wrong when he shot Mr Drummond. This important point ought not to have been assumed from mere a priori probability. The fact of his madness or delusion is one thing, but its effect upon his moral perception is quite another; and the importance of keeping the questions distinct is now clear from the answers of the Judges. This was <u>not</u> done in the late trial.

It was not an ending to the trial that was expected, with the prosecution effectively surrendering their position and Follett admitting that he could not "press for a verdict against the prisoner". This really left the jury with nothing to decide, particularly after Tindall had clearly indicated that there was no doubt in his mind of M'Naghten's insanity.

Follett's Explanation

Before Chief Justice Tindal addressed the jury, Follett spoke on behalf of the prosecution, and his own words explained the position that he had been placed in:

> I was anxious, however, to say, on the part of the Crown, that they have no object whatever but the attainment of public justice, and I believe I am right in saying that, on the part of

> the prosecution, every facility has been given to the defence. There is no wish, there can be no wish on the part of the public prosecutor, but that the ends of public justice shall be attained; and, certainly, when in the streets of this metropolis a crime of this sort was committed, it was incumbent on those who have the care of public peace and safety to have the case properly investigated.

This was a clear and accurate summary of his duty to the Crown and the court in this trial. It is unfortunate that more commentators did not take the time to read and understand the position of the defence.

Cockburn is Acclaimed

It should be noted that, after the end of the trial, Cockburn's skill in saving M'Naghten from the gallows was praised, and there is no doubt that his defence thoroughly dismantled the prosecution's case, such as it was. As time passed, and Cockburn's star shone brighter, some lost sight of what had actually happened in this court. In the 9th volume of Foss's *Judges of England* the following was written about the trial:

> Among other cases in which he distinguished himself as a leader was the eloquent and impressive defence in 1843 of M'Naughton, who had shot Mr Drummond, in which he satisfied the jury that the client was not a responsible being.

The defence's expert evidence was overwhelming and the strength of Tindal CJ's direction to the jury left them with little choice but to find M'Naghten not guilty, but insane. There were several factors contributing to this acquittal – the expert evidence, the weakness of the prosecution and the intervention of Tindal all had played their part.

In the Appendix to this book there is a summary of how, following this verdict, the House of Lords and the English judges constructed a code in regard to pleas of partial insanity. Unfortunately, the House of Lords did not appear to notice that the Code they eventually adopted was such that it was most unlikely that M'Naghten would have been found not guilty if this code had been applied to his trial, which is rather ironic as the code was named after him.

The Lancet's Last Word

The *Lancet*'s editor had not quite finished his criticism of the manner in which M'Naghten's trial was constructed. At the end of the issue of 18 March 1843, the editor expressed the view that it was his:

> firmly established conviction that at the late trial of M'NAUGHTEN evidence was received which was not strictly admissible –
>
> that in the opening speech of the counsel for the prosecution no reference to the insanity of the accused ought to have been made, that the opinions of medical men who had only heard the trial ought not to have been received, –
>
> that the counsel for the prosecution should have replied to the arguments and pernicious statements of the counsel for the prisoner –
>
> that the judge should have summed up on the whole case leaving it fairly to the jury to found their verdict upon the belief which they consciously entertained, after hearing the evidence, whether M'NAUGHTEN did or did not know that he was doing wrong when he levelled the pistol at the back of his unfortunate victim.

The Costs for this Trial

Another important area of uncertainty in this trial is the costs. M'Naghten had £750 in his bank account when he was arrested. This was a substantial sum in 1843, and is equivalent to roughly £83,000 in 2026. It was far more than the average woodturner would have earned at that time. However, three points should be made with regard to this amount:

1. The contemporary reports of his arrest and trial do not show any particular astonishment at the amount of M'Naghten's wealth. Equally, none of those interviewed by police, or those who gave evidence in court, seemed unduly surprised at the amount of M'Naghten's savings.
2. While working as a woodturner, there was evidence of the speed at which M'Naghten worked (he claimed to be able to do the work of three men in one day) and the long shifts he could put in in his workshop. He often had other woodturners working for him which, despite their wages, would still have increased his profit.

3. He was not a man of extravagant tastes and he lived very simply:
   i. He was not noted as a drinker or a glutton, in fact he dined frugally on very basic fare.
   ii. He lodged in very Spartan lodgings to avoid unnecessary expense, often sharing a bed with other lodgers in order to save money. At times he lived and ate in his workshop, thus saving more.
   iii. He did not spend significantly on clothes, furnishings or entertainment, although he liked to be smart in his youth.
   iv. He was not a womaniser. Nowhere in the press reports of the evidence given in court, and the research of the press into his life, is there any mention of connections of any sort, even just friendships, with women.
   v. He was not known as a gambler, either at cards or on the turf.
   vi. He had no wife or other dependants to support.

In the press reports of 1843, there was no astonishment at the amount of money in M'Naghten's possession, which seemed to imply an acceptance that a single-minded work ethic could bring such rewards. There was also no surprise or disbelief from those in his home area in Glasgow.

The £750 was released by the court to assist in meeting M'Naghten's defence costs, but the court does not appear to have had any concerns as to the provenance of the savings or the amount. It is also important to note that the contemporary press reporting did not seem to regard the amount as worthy of any significant comment. It appears to have been looked on as the amount that could be saved if a person worked and lived as M'Naghten had chosen to live and work.

The expenditure on defence costs for his trial was going to be significant. There would have been no reason for the defence team (barristers and solicitors) to have waived their fees, particularly given the shortage of time and the amount of preparatory work that would have been required before the trial. Several witnesses were in Scotland and this would have meant greater expense in getting them to and from London for the trial.

All of the medical witnesses would usually have charged for their appearances in court. We know that two of the witnesses, Crawford and Hutcheson, were "present at the request of friends of the prisoner".[40] Therefore any fees for their appearances would appear to have been the responsibility of those who instructed them. However, given the short period of time for instructions, it could well be that there was an understanding for later reimbursement for these witnesses. Forbes Winslow fell into a different category as he did not attend at anyone's behest (as far as is known).

It seems that there would have been sufficient to meet the costs of:

- One silk (Cockburn)[41]
- Three juniors (Clarkson, Bodkin and Monteith)
- Two solicitors (one firm in Scotland and one in London)
- Scottish witnesses' travel expenses and accommodation[42]
- Professional fees and expenses of other medical experts attending (but not Forbes Winslow) if they were reimbursed for their opinions and appearances.
- Court costs

There is no record of whether or not there was any of the £750 left to assist M'Naghten once he was in Bethlem asylum. If there was, it would seem unlikely that there could have been very much.

In an essay on this trial, Sir Roger Ormrod, a retired Lord Justice of Appeal, made a very pertinent analysis of time in this trial.[43]

1. M'Naghten was brought before a magistrate on the day of the shooting.
2. On the following day M'Naghten was committed for trial at the Old Bailey and the trial was listed for 2 February, a mere thirteen days after the shooting and only eight days after Drummond's death.
3. By 2 February, both counsel (Mr Clarkson) and solicitors had been engaged. Mr Clarkson requested an adjournment to permit the defence to be prepared.
4. The court only allowed a month's adjournment and listed the trial for 3 March.
5. By the 3rd M'Naghten had a defence team, described by Ormrod as "four eminent counsels", and a solicitor was also instructed.
6. Further, in only six weeks, the defence was ready and nine medical witnesses were available to give evidence, in addition to non-medical evidence.

This amount of work by the legal team would not have been prepared without a great deal of urgent work. Given the short amount of time available for this work, it could not have been prepared without long hours by the legal team.

A Last Word from Ormrod

> …how this was organized and by whom is an intriguing question which can only be answered in part. Obviously the costs of such a defence must have been very heavy, and some person or persons must have been strongly motivated to undertake and carry out so much work in such a short a time…the intensity of the interest and concern of those in the case seems to suggest that they were activated by something more than the fate of an obscure Scotsman who had murdered an innocent victim by mistake…Cockburn himself, from the whole tenor of his speech and the immense effort entailed, obviously took the most personal interest in the case.

It has been suggested that M'Naghten was paid the £750 to assassinate Sir Robert Peel.[44] This seems to me to be inherently unlikely.

- Firstly, if an assassination was being planned, would a mentally unstable woodturner be the choice of assassin?
- Secondly, would someone who paid an assassin choose to engage one who knew little of the geography of Central London and could not recognise his target? To do so would assuredly jeopardise the whole plan.
- Thirdly, the amateurish behaviour of M'Naghten in repeatedly walking up and down a crowded Whitehall, asking people to point out Peel, would hardly be the behaviour of a paid assassin.
- Fourthly, asking people to point out Peel merely drew attention to M'Naghten for asking questions, which in turn should have ensured that M'Naghten would be caught by bystanders or the police. That he was not found out early-on in his repeated reconnaissance is solely down to the incompetence of both the police and civil servants – aided by M'Naghten's poor choice of where to shoot Drummond.

If an assassin was required, one with better attributes would surely have been selected.

PART II

Chapter 9

THE SURGEONS AND DRUMMOND'S TREATMENT

This chapter was written 180 years after the events that are the subject of the book. Therefore the lack of some contemporary details is, to a degree, filled by the insights offered by modern medicine. I have been fortunate to have been able to seek the advice of a modern practitioner in emergency medicine – Colin Holburn, MB ChB FRCS(Ed) FRCEM. His help and advice have both been generously given and both have been invaluable in writing this chapter. However, as the author, any errors found must remain my responsibility alone.

"Operating theatres were gateways to death."[1]

It is stating the obvious that Mr Drummond was, after the shooting, facing emergency medical treatment, but that this treatment would be without:

1. *the benefit of anaesthetics* – these first came into practice later in the 1840s and,
2. *the ability to treat any infection with antiseptics* or *antibiotics* – antiseptics came into practice in the 1870s and antibiotics were an invention of the twentieth century and,
3. *control of pain for surgical operations*, or as part of post-operative care,
4. *Modern techniques*, such as scanners (MRI, CT, X-ray).

The absence of these fundamentals of modern medicine meant that any patient faced with surgery for a gunshot wound was going to suffer serious pain and have a substantial risk of infections from the injury, surgery and any subsequent treatment. In 1843, post-operative infections meant that there was a far higher chance of death, both during and after surgery, than would be the case today.

Surgery in 1843

Operating theatres of the 1840s were quite literally that, theatres. These theatres contained tiered rows of seating in an attempt to give all spectators a view of the proceedings. There were no partitions or glass screens between the spectators and the patient. Nor was there any attempt to reduce infection risk (no gowns, masks or gloves). The spectators would have been a mixture of students, doctors, surgeons and any other individuals who were interested in, or merely curious about, surgery. Surgery then was also exclusively a male preserve.

An operating table of the 1840s was just a wooden table that would have become stained, from previous operations, by blood, and other miscellaneous bodily fluids. The table might have been scrubbed with water between operations, but that would have been all, meaning it carried considerable potential to infect the next patient that was operated on it.

During the 'performance' in the theatre, there would have been explanations and commentary from the surgeon and his assistant about the surgical procedure, and questions could be asked by interested spectators while the patient was being operated on. Conversation within the audience, street noise from outside and screams of agony from the patient on the table would all have made the operating theatre a far cry from today's operating theatres.

There was no standardisation of the surgical instruments used in 1843. Each surgeon would have had his own preferences for particular knives, probes etc. A surgeon's knives were often embellished with purely decorative motifs that had been etched into the steel blades, something which easily retained dried blood from previous operations. The same applied to a surgeon's instrument case with its fabric linings. It was only a minority of surgeons who actually cleaned their instruments and when this was done, it was usually only for appearance's sake – the majority of surgeons did not bother. As sterilisation of surgical instruments was not understood or practised, so were hands inadequately cleaned (or not cleaned at all). There was not, as yet, any understanding of the transmission of infection by physicians' hands or clothes.[2] This lack of knowledge also contributed to the high incidence of deaths in childbirth.

There was no use of surgical gloves. A surgeon would have used his fingers as auxiliary instruments, particularly to explore wounds, feel for stones or extract pistol balls. This was regardless of where the fingers had been before and how contaminated they might have become. Surgeons usually operated in their everyday clothes and merely donned an apron when operating to try to protect their clothes from blood etc. The surgeon's apron was unlikely to be clean and would generally be stained from previous operations. The apron was therefore, an additional source of transmission of infections from surgeon to the patient.

The Surgeons Arrive

Drummond had been shot in the back, just below his left shoulder blade and close to his spine. He was able to walk a few yards, with some difficulty, from the scene of the shooting back to Drummond's Bank, where he was accommodated in a private room. There he was examined by Richard Jackson, an apothecary and surgeon,[3] who had been called to the bank. Jackson had known Drummond since Drummond was a child. His examination was fairly cursory and Jackson decided that Drummond was well enough to be taken by his own carriage to his home in Lower Grosvenor Street. Jackson accompanied him there, arriving at 5 pm. Sir Robert Peel rushed to see his friend as soon as he heard of the shooting and he was most shaken by his friend's condition.

At Drummond's house, a medical team was being assembled. One of the unknown, but nonetheless important issues, was how this team was engaged and assembled. The team was composed of

- Mr George James Guthrie senior,[4] a surgeon,
- Mr Bransby Cooper, a surgeon,
- Richard Jackson, an apothecary and surgeon,
- Mr Hume, a surgeon
- Mr Chambers and Mr Guthrie junior, who were added to the team later; both were junior surgeons.

This looks to be an unusually large team of surgeons (and six separate fees). There were also nurses present, but press reports do not specify how many. The coverage in the press centred on Guthrie senior and Bransby Cooper, to the extent that it is difficult to know what work the other surgeons were contributing to. Guthrie appears to have been more to the fore, being the more forceful of the two. It is odd that the team was exclusively surgeons and lacked even a single physician – a point that would later be highlighted by *The Lancet*.

The time of the shooting was approximately 3.40 pm (the time Drummond left the bank) and it took at least 80 minutes to get Drummond to his house from the scene of the shooting.[5] Meanwhile, Bransby Cooper arrived at his own home in Spring Gardens, which backs on to Charing Cross, at 4 pm. Given the close proximity of his house to the scene of the shooting it would be astonishing if he was not told of the events as soon as he reached his home, but Cooper did not arrive at Drummond's house until 5 pm. In fact, none of the medical team, apart from Jackson, were there until 5 pm.

Guthrie also arrived at 5 pm, having been collected by Drummond's sister in a carriage. A modern-day map of that area of London shows the route from Charing Cross to Lower Grosvenor Street would take 25 minutes at walking pace. It is probably reasonable that a horse-drawn vehicle would not be any quicker, given the congestion of horse-drawn traffic and little by way of traffic management in central London. While the medical concept of the Golden Hour after serious trauma is a modern concept, taking 80 minutes to deliver Drummond's first treatment cannot have improved his chances of survival.

The First Medical Examination

Jackson's initial view was that Drummond had lost only a minimal amount of blood from the wound. He had not attempted to trace the path of the pistol ball in order to assess any internal damage that it might have caused. Immediately on their arrival, Guthrie and Bransby Cooper set about their own examination of the wound. They confirmed that a small calibre pistol ball had entered the left side of Drummond's back, close to his spine and left shoulder blade.

They then followed the standard procedure for that time and attempted to trace the pistol-ball's path by inserting their (unsterilised) fingers into the wound and feeling for the path of the ball. They could not trace the path of the ball very far. Although the use of fingers in this way was fairly common practice, we now know that the manner, and frequency, with which this exploration was made will have increased the likelihood of Drummond's death from infection, leading to sepsis.

President James A. Garfield, twentieth president of the USA, was assassinated in 1881. The physicians attending him could not find the fatal bullet and they repeatedly probed the wound. Their hands and instruments were not sterile and the president died of a ruptured splenic artery aneurysm, following sepsis and pneumonia. It is generally accepted that the repeated probing by the physicians introduced the infection into his body.

Guthrie and Bransby Cooper decided that the pistol ball had either passed over the left hipbone or under the lower left rib. The ball had then been deflected upwards and ended its travel at the front of Drummond's body at the pit of the stomach, very close to the surface of his flesh (later described by Bransby Cooper as "lying on the cartilage of the 8th rib"). In order to try to establish the course of the ball, it had been necessary for the surgeons to widen the entry wound with their fingers. Their further attempts to identify the path of the ball had all failed and the surgeons could therefore only guess at what damage had actually been done. [6]

The pistol ball was eventually found when Drummond was turned to lie on his back. The ball could then easily be identified as a visible lump that was lying very near the surface of Drummond's abdominal skin. Guthrie made a small incision and the ball was easily removed by Bransby Cooper using his fingers. The *Morning Post* reported this as Bransby Cooper making the incision and Guthrie removing the ball. (Whoever did it, the ball was removed by fingers, which is probably very relevant as a few days later there is reference to this abdominal wound becoming inflamed).

An element of low farce then entered these proceedings when the surgeons offered the extracted pistol ball to Drummond's sister. Understandably, she recoiled from holding the object that had wounded her brother, and she refused to touch it. It seems the surgeons had the odd notion that she would welcome holding the pistol ball, still warm from her brother's chest. The ball was taken away by her maid. Later, at the committal proceedings, the ball was produced by Mr Maule, the treasury solicitor who, on oath, stated that the ball then produced was the fatal ball. He recognised it, as it had been marked before being passed to the maid. Curiously, at M'Naghten's trial, the ball was this time produced by PC Silver, who, on oath, stated that he had received the ball from Colonel Drummond.

The modern concept of the chain of evidence had not been developed at this time….

The First Bulletins

The *Morning Post* of Monday the 23rd reported that:

> On making inquiries in Grosvenor-street, we were informed that a consultation had taken place at 10 o'clock (evening), at which hour Mr Drummond was going on so favourably, that the surgeons did not deem it necessary to issue any further bulletin.

This early bulletin now seems absurdly optimistic. Whether this was the product of the surgeons', or the reporters', wishful thinking is impossible to tell. When Bransby Cooper first gave evidence at M'Naghten's appearance in the Magistrates' Court, he was asked if Drummond was in any danger from his wound. He replied that Drummond was in no immediate danger,

> …although it would not be true to state there is no danger, for it is very possible that inflammation may ensue.

PORTRAIT OF DANIEL M'NAUGHTEN.

THE MARKETS.

Right: Daniel M'Naghten, from the *Illustrated London News*. (Wellcome Collection)

Below: A Map of Charing Cross and Whitehall from 1833, showing the scene of the shooting. Drummond's Bank was to the left of the marker for Charing Cross, and the shooting took place between there and the Admirality Building.

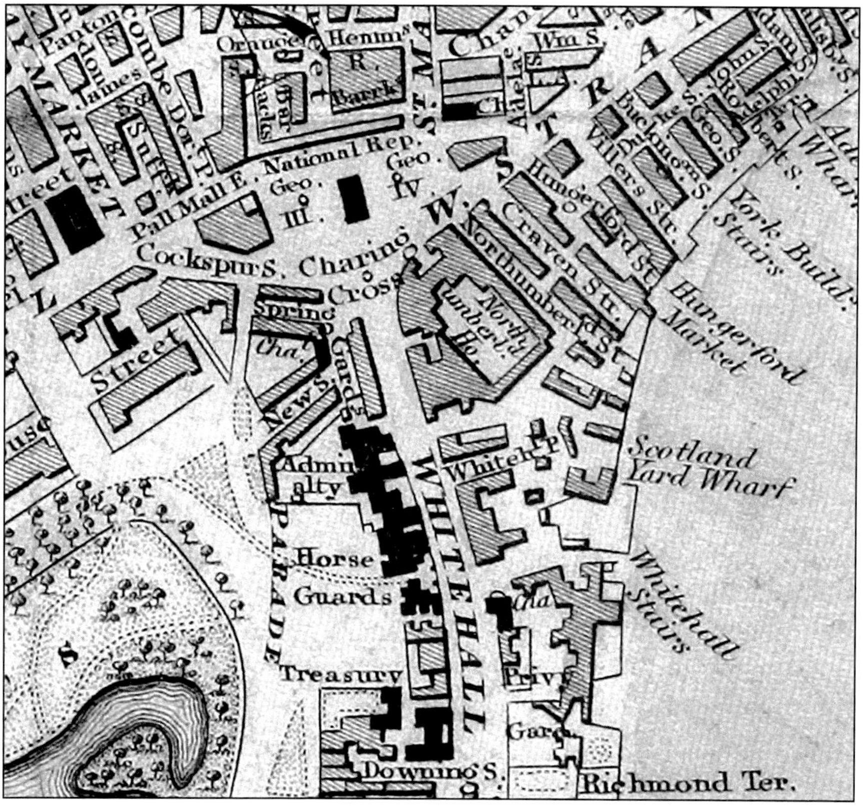

Prime Minister Sir Robert Peel, the intended target. (Catholic University of Leuven, Belgium, public domain)

Right: Drummond's Bank, as the building stands today.

Below: The prison yard of Tothill Fields Prison where M'Naghten was held during his trial at Bow Street Magistrates' Court. (Wellcome Collection)

BOYS EXERCISING AT TOTHILL FIELDS PRISON.

Above: Newgate Gaol, where M'Naghten was held, pending his trial. (Wellcome Collection)

Left: The Old Bailey in 2004. (Photo by Nevilley, CC-BYSA 3.0)

Above: The trial at the Central Criminal Court in the Old Bailey. (Alvin, public domain)

Right: Dr E.T. Monro, 1851. (Wellcome Collection)

George James Guthrie, surgeon. Wood engraving by F.S., 1856, after J. Mayall. (Wellcome Collection)

Bransby Blake Cooper, surgeon, illustrated here as being attacked by a man holding a giant lancet, representing the *Lancet* (medical journal). Coloured etching by "Dicky Fubs" [H. Heath?], 1828. (Wellcome Collection)

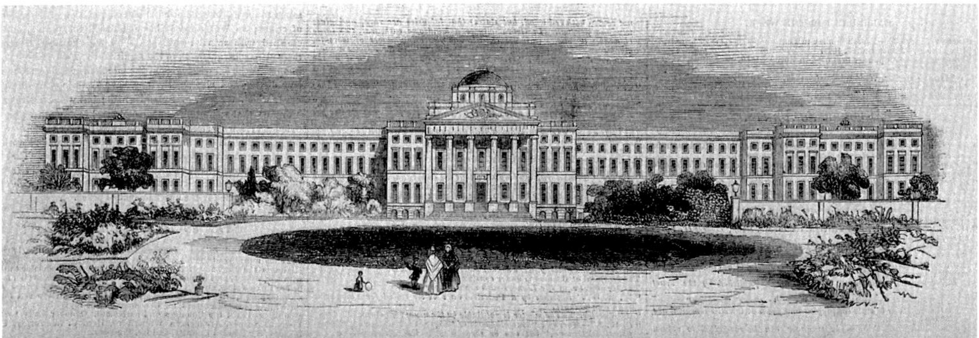

BETHLEM HOSPITAL.

Above: Bethlem Hospital, St. George's Fields, Lambeth, where M'Naghten was sent following the conclusion of the trial. (Wood engraving, 1848, Wellcome Collection)

Below: Broadmoor Asylum for Criminal Lunatics, Broadmoor, where M'Naghten was transferred in 1864. (Wellcome Collection)

ASYLUM FOR CRIMINAL LUNATICS, BROADMOOR, SANDHURST, BERKSHIRE.

Above: Day room for patients at Broadmoor. (Wellcome Collection)

Below: Edward Oxford's attempt at the assassination of Queen Victoria. (Public domain, Library of Congress)

A Seriously Misunderstood Discovery

Bransby Cooper also mentioned that Jackson, the apothecary, had drawn his attention to the location of the wound in Drummond's back and he pointed out that it matched with corresponding holes in Drummond's shirt and waistcoat. This, we now know, was potentially a very serious issue, in that if the pieces of material had been carried into the wound by the ball, and then left in Drummond's body, they could be a source of a serious, potentially fatal, infection. This was not a risk that was generally recognised at that time. There were no further comments from the medical team on this point, which suggests that no attempt was made to find and extract any bits of the material that might have been taken into the wound.

The *Morning Post*[7] reported that:

> …a portion of Drummond's flannel vest and shirt remained in the wound and caused some irritation, <u>but no danger was apprehended</u>.[8]

Although this was published on 21 January 1843, the information was made known to the press by the medical team on the previous day. That "no danger was apprehended" from the clothing fragments remaining in the body illustrates how little was then understood about the sources of infection. It would not be unfair to speculate that this could have been the source of the fatal infection.[9]

The Press and the Surgeons

There was a great demand for bulletins, and therefore regular updates of Drummond's condition were given frequently to the press by the surgeons. These were almost the only source of information as to Drummond's state of health that was available to readers of the press. The press reported the progress of the treatment as set out in the following paragraphs:

1. The surgeons had encountered some difficulty in locating the pistol ball "as it had followed" an eccentric path through the body. This was reported[10] as:

> The ball had entered [the back] near the spine and that it had made a circuit either over the hip bone or under the lower rib, and then lodged near the pit of the stomach under the breast: thence

> the ball was extracted by Mr Guthrie without any difficulty, as it lay near the surface.

Two things stand out in this paragraph. As the path of the ball had not been traced, the eccentric path suggestion was no more than that, a suggestion. Also, the surgeons did not know how the ball had ended up in the pit of the stomach or how much damage it had caused during whatever path it may have followed.

2. Later the same day, there was a further announcement from Guthrie and Bransby Cooper:

> The ball has been extracted. No vital part is injured and Mr Guthrie and Mr Bransby Cooper have every reason to believe that Mr Drummond is doing very well.

This was an astonishing statement, given that the surgeons had not established that no vital part had been damaged, again because they had not established the path of the ball. As to having "every reason to believe that Mr Drummond is doing well", there was no reason known to the surgeons to substantiate this claim.

It is also to be noted that there is no mention of the other surgeons in this bulletin. As mentioned, the press reporting focussed on Guthrie and Bransby Cooper and this makes it difficult to understand the parts played by the other surgeons.

3. On the same day, Queen Victoria's *Journal*[11] recorded a more realistic view:

> …[Prince Albert] received a letter from Sir Robert Peel, giving on the whole a good account of poor Mr Drummond, though there were some uncomfortable symptoms.

Encouraging though the surgeons' opinion may have seemed, on the next day the entry in Queen Victoria's *Journal*[12] referred to alarm in the night, but now the surgeons thought Drummond was almost safe.

> Colonel Drummond has returned & Albert saw him: his brother was much better, but they had been alarmed about him last night. Now the doctors thought they could almost pronounce him safe.

This information was from someone present and he had been given information of concern about Drummond the night before – something that the surgeons' statements omitted. The surgeons then swung from alarm in the night to Drummond being almost safe.

4. There is a further comment in the Queen's *Journal*[13] that covers a meeting after Drummond's death with Peel, in which he spoke of Guthrie: "…but it seems that Mr Guthrie, one of the surgeons who attended him, most skilful about gunshot wounds – had but little hope from the 1st."

This comment from Guthrie is strange indeed. Peel was now being told that, in Guthrie's view, there had been little hope from the outset. This view was not reflected in the surgeons' press releases and therefore it appears to be no more than Guthrie trying to protect his professional reputation.

5. The *Spectator*[14] commented: "At half past twelve o'clock last night [Drummond] was doing well." On the same day, Bransby Cooper gave evidence at the Bow Street Police Court. He described

> …the circuitous course taken by the ball: which was first sought in the back, but was ultimately found slightly protruding just under the skin on the front: having traversed round the left side of the patient's body. [It was added] that Mr Drummond's would be a protracted confinement, for the danger was yet to come in the process of suppuration.[15]

Bransby Cooper does not appear to have been asked to give any more details of the path followed by the pistol ball. The path was still unknown, other than where the ball entered the body and where it came to rest, but it was a more reasonable comment than Guthrie's.

The Times of 21 January 1843, had obtained a view, presumably from the surgeons:

> It was thought at first that the wound was of a dangerous character, on the supposition that the ball had taken serious effect internally: but on further consideration it did not appear that any vital part was injured. The symptoms exhibited by the patient, after the ball was extracted, were found to be favourable, and there seemed to

> be no reason then to apprehend that the event would be attended with fatal effects.

There is no source quoted by the paper for this description of Drummond's situation. The surgeons' earlier bulletin on the 21st said that no vital part had been injured, as did this bulletin. The statement above that there was "no reason then to apprehend that the event would be attended with fatal effects", seems very rash, given how little the surgeons knew about the path of the ball and what damage it had done. The statement also omitted the substantial risk of infection. It was also flatly contradicted by the evidence that would later be given at M'Naghten's trial.

Bransby Cooper's Evidence at M'Naghten's Remand Hearing

On 23 January Bransby Cooper gave evidence at M'Naghten's remand hearing. He gave the following details of Drummond's injury:

> My attention was called by Mr Jackson to a wound in Mr Drummond's side, which upon examination I found to correspond with openings in his shirt and flannel waistcoat. I then searched the course of the wound for the ball, and, in order to do so, was compelled to enlarge the opening made by the ball in the skin. I could not, however, during this period of the examination, find the ball. In the course of a short time Mr Guthrie, who had also been sent for, arrived, when the wound was again examined, but we were still unable to find the ball. We then directed Mr Drummond to be turned upon his back, in order that we might examine the anterior part of his body, when a small projecting lump was observed, which, upon examination, was found to be the ball immediately under the skin, so that a mere incision of the lancet lead to its extraction. The opening made showed that the ball had traversed round the left half of the wounded gentleman's body…
>
> I do not consider that any immediate danger is to be apprehended, although I cannot say that there is no danger as it is very possible inflammation may take place.
>
> In my opinion his confinement will be very protracted, as all the danger is still to come.

It seems odd that his evidence should describe the pistol ball as wounding the "side" of the victim, when all other statements refer to the entry wound as being in Drummond's back, close to the left edge of the spine.

Drummond's Decline

Queen Victoria recorded in her *Journal*: "The accounts of poor Mr Drummond not so good today."[16]

On the same day, *The Times* reported:

> *State of Mr Drummond's Health*:
> It is with extreme regret we have to announce that a very unfavourable change in Mr Drummond's symptoms took place on Saturday morning. The favourable state in which we described the unfortunate gentleman to be in our latest accounts published on Saturday morning, continued throughout Friday night, and the most sanguine hopes were entertained by his eminent medical attendants that, severe as the wound was, no vital part had been injured (A), early in the forenoon of Saturday however, Mr Drummond showed symptoms of considerable uneasiness, and felt much pain as induced his friends to believe that inflammation had taken place.
>
> A consultation between the medical gentlemen was immediately held, when another examination of the wound was determined on, and it was then discovered that the lowest of the ribs, had been seriously injured by the ball, that inflammation had made its appearance (B) and that the danger which was now to be apprehended, under the circumstances, had greatly increased. In order to subdue the inflammation, it was arranged that a quantity of blood should instantly be taken from the sufferer (C), and Mr Guthrie accordingly proceeded to open a vein in the left arm, but the operation proved fruitless. An attempt was then made to obtain blood from the right arm, but still without success, and it was then determined that the temporal artery should be opened. The operation was forthwith performed and a considerable quantity of blood was taken from the patient, which for a time lessened the dangerous symptoms that had appeared. Towards evening, however, another consultation was held, at which time the inflammation had but very slightly subsided, notwithstanding the

> application of a great number of leeches to the back of the patient, in addition to general bleeding; it was then determined that unless a favourable change took place by 10 o'clock, the bleeding should be repeated. The unfortunate gentleman experiences great pain and difficulty in breathing." [Author's added emphasis]

(A) This comment admits the seriousness of the wound, but adds that no vital part had been wounded. As the path of the bullet had not been identified it is difficult to understand what basis there was for the surgeons' claim.

(B) "…it was then discovered…." But no explanation was offered as to why this was discovered at this late stage or why they did not find it on the first examination.

(C) Bloodletting would not have helped the patient in any way and opening a vein would have offered another place of possible infection.

"Eminent" was certainly an unusual term to apply to Bransby Cooper, as his contemporaries did not seem to regard him as such.

Bleeding

Leeches, as mentioned in the extract from *The Times* (above), had been used for bloodletting since antiquity. Their use was based on the theory of humours (which itself dates from at least the fifth century BC) which held that the four so-called humours of a person (blood, black bile, yellow bile and phlegm) must be maintained in balance for a person to have good health.[17] There was, and still is, no medical benefit in bloodletting to treat a pistol wound, no matter how much the surgeons might like to have believed that bleeding was beneficial. All that bloodletting did was weaken the patient. It is rather surprising that the belief in bleeding helped a patient's recovery was so rooted in medical lore when there was no empirical evidence to support this belief. In 1747, a book was published called *Primitive Physick*. It was written by John Wesley, the Methodist. Wesley was not a doctor, but his advice on living well probably added more to the wellbeing of the public than bloodletting ever did.

The *Lancet* of 18 March 1843 was not aware of the exact amount of blood that was removed from Drummond, but:

> …from the repeated venesections[18] and the applications of a great many leeches, we are led to infer that a large quantity of blood

> must have been abstracted. Now considering the extent of the injury and the consequent severe call on the vital powers for its reparation, it is evident that nothing but the presence of acute inflammation in a vital organ could have justified depletion to any great extent. But the surgeons, it appears, considered that inflammation had come on. Inflammation of what?

Although the full extent of the bleeding was not recorded, it appeared to *The Lancet* that it was carried "a great deal too far". *The Lancet* admitted that it seemed likely that Drummond's wound would prove fatal, but having said that, "there is nothing like accurate diagnosis, or scientific practice". That there appears to have been no record of the amount of blood taken is striking. Surely a record of what was taken and when was important for the surgeons to be aware of the total amount removed? Was it possible that a record was kept but not disclosed?

Some of those in surgical practice had already started to doubt and question the validity of bleeding as a treatment in the absence of any scientific proof of the manner in which bloodletting produced any verifiable benefit to the patient.

Midnight, Sunday Night[19]

> It gives us much pleasure to state that on the arrival of Mr Guthrie and Mr Cooper at 10 o'clock last night, they were of the opinion that the unfavourable symptoms which had presented themselves during the day had somewhat subsided. At [12 o'clock] they considered Mr Drummond better; he experienced considerable difficulty in breathing from 1 o'clock till 4; but <u>the bleeding had proved beneficial</u>.

The notion that bleeding the patient had proved to be beneficial was only in the surgeons' imagination. If there really was any easing of Drummond's symptoms it could only be from his body trying to fight the infection. Before leaving, Mr Guthrie and Mr Cooper issued the following bulletin:

> "The difficulty of breathing has diminished since midday and Mr Drummond is so much better.
>
> Mr Guthrie jnr. remained in attendance all last night and will do so again tonight.

A consultation of the medical gentlemen was held at 9 o'clock this morning, but no further bleeding was then deemed necessary, and the following announcement was left for the information of visitors:

"Mr Drummond is as well as can be expected and his wound is going on favourably."

During the day, the medical gentlemen frequently visited their patient, and at half past 10 o'clock this evening another consultation was held, after which the following document was issued:

"Mr Drummond is going on favourably and is rather better this evening."

This last sentence is simply not credible, as the surgeons were already aware of inflammation having set in.

Further Deterioration in Drummond's Condition

The Times, 24 January 1843

A messenger from Grosvenor Street arrived this afternoon with the painful intelligence that an unfavourable change had taken place in the course of the morning and that the symptoms which had since manifested themselves had caused very serious alarm in the minds of the friends of the unfortunate relative of the Colonel. Indeed they have assumed such an alarming a character that the return of Colonel Drummond to the [Windsor] Castle has been postponed until tomorrow.

In announcing that a deterioration of Drummond's condition had occurred, it is curious that the announcement dealt only with the serious alarm "in the minds of the friends of the relative". At this crucial point in Drummond's struggle, there is apparently only silence from the medical team. Further, there is no explanation of what the deterioration actually was.

Queen Victoria noted in her *Journal*:

Col. Drummond wrote a very indifferent account of his poor brother, I am sorry to say. It is very sad, for everyone says he

> is such a good sensible man & universally liked. The family are greatly distressed.[20]

The Times, 24 January 1843

> It is with extreme regret we have to announce that another unfavourable change has taken place in Mr Drummond's health ... towards morning he became very restless. It soon became evident that the inflammation was increasing: and at 10 o'clock a consultation of the medical gentlemen took place, when it was determined that the patient should again be bled, which operation was immediately performed by Mr Guthrie.

The following announcement was then issued for the information of visitors: "Mr Drummond is going on rather favourably than otherwise."

It is difficult, considering the previous bulletin, to accept that this view can possibly be justified. To print that the inflammation was increasing and then announce that the patient was going on rather favourably than otherwise appears to be nonsense.

> Throughout the day the unfavourable symptoms did not in the least decrease.... In the course of the afternoon it was seen that Mr Drummond was not so well, and in consequence, another consultation was held at five o'clock, when it was deemed necessary to take more blood from the sufferer, which was at once accomplished.
>
> The medical gentlemen remained in attendance a considerable time and subsequently issued the following announcement – "Mr Drummond still continues in a critical state."
>
> Before separating, however, it was considered necessary that another consultation should be held in the course of the evening and 9 o'clock was appointed for that purpose. Upon them assembling, Mr Drummond was found to be in much the same state, but if anything rather improved.

The improvement was ascribed to the benefits of bleeding the patient. Again, there are no benefits from bleeding, particularly for a patient in Drummond's weakened condition. Indeed, by this time, the amount of blood removed from Drummond's system must have been threatening his health and life. Nonetheless, the surgeons noted that although Drummond's adverse symptoms had not decreased: "Drummond was found to be in much the same state, but if anything rather improved."

This is further nonsense – how can a person be in the same state of health and at the same time be "rather improved"? Unfortunately this was repeated at 10 pm, when the surgeons left, the following bulletin was given, "Mr Drummond is in much the same state, but if anything has gained a point."

The Death of Drummond

The Times, 25 January 1843

> THE COURT – WINDSOR
> A messenger was despatched from the Castle this morning to the residence of Mr Drummond, in Grosvenor Street, who returned shortly after 2 o'clock with a very unfavourable account of the symptoms which had manifested themselves in the course of the night. Another messenger arrived at Windsor this evening from town and at the time of leaving Grosvenor Street, Mr Drummond was considered to be in considerable danger.

Queen Victoria recorded:

> On returning from our walk, Ld Morton gave Albert a letter from Colonel Drummond, saying that since 7 yesterday evening all their hope has vanished & that probably his poor brother would no longer be alive, when this letter reached us. How very sad!... When Albert returned from shooting, he found a note, written by Ld Morton (but which had been opened by Anson, Ld Morton having gone up to Town, to see Col. Drummond). The contents were the following: "my poor dear Brother expired at ½ past 10 o'clock." How too shocking! We had so hoped poor Mr Drummond would recover & can both hardly think of anything else, particularly these last 2 days & since the sad accident occurred).[21]

The Times, 25 January 1843

> …it is with the most unfeigned regret that we are compelled to announce that the very unfavourable symptoms under which we described Mr Drummond as suffering in our last publication, very materially increased in intensity during yesterday: indeed, in such a an alarming state is the unfortunate gentleman, that scarcely any hope remains of his recovery.
>
> At 10 o'clock, a consultation took place, at which, as usual, all the medical men attended, and shortly afterwards the following bulletin was issued: "Mr Drummond still continues in a very precarious state."

Between that period and 4 pm, the visits of one or other of the surgeons were very frequent, and at the last mentioned hour another consultation was held, when the announcement as to the state of the patient was as follows: "Mr Drummond is in a very unsatisfactory state, but if anything, his symptoms are one shade more favourable."

Given the continual decline in Drummond's health, it is hard to understand how the above announcement could say there was a slight improvement. In the course of the evening, it became apparent to those in attendance that Mr Drummond was getting worse and at 10 pm the surgeons again met, and remained in consultation for some time, at the close of which the very alarming announcement as follows was made: "A change considerably for the worse has taken place."

12.30 am:

> Upon inquiry being made at the above hour we were informed that Mr Drummond's symptoms had not at all improved and great fears were entertained that he would not survive the night.

The Times, 26 January 1843:

> It now has become our very painful duty to announce that Mr Edward Drummond died yesterday morning about half-past 10 o'clock.

The *Morning Post* recorded:

> At nine o'clock on Wednesday morning, when a pulse could be felt nowhere, and a slight fluttering of the heart was alone perceptible, he retained the power of moving his limbs, pressed Mr. Guthrie's hand, and with that sweet smile on his countenance which was so endearing, asked if all hope was past?
>
> On Mr. Guthrie's replying that all hope in this world was over, and that he must put his trust in God, he said, "Well, I have endeavoured to live honestly, doing as much good as I could, and I place my hope in God's mercy for my redemption." Turning to his sister, whose self-devotion had been unequalled, and who was crying by his side, he said, "We have lived long and happily together, and my only regret is in parting with you." He then asked if he should live much longer, and on being told perhaps an hour or two, he said, "The sooner the better – I don't feel pain"; and added, with a smile, "That ugly French word malaise expresses most fully my burden." Shortly after he said, "Will it be presumptuous in a man in my situation to ask for a little wine and water, with soda or potass [sic] water?"; and on its being given to him, conveyed it to his mouth, and drank. He lingered until half-past ten o'clock; when he expired, surrounded by his relatives.

Queen Victoria recorded in her *Journal*[22] that Prince Albert had heard from Lord Morton that the Drummond family were most distressed by Edward Drummond's death, although Edward remained calm and resigned to his fate. The family had spent the greater part of the night in prayer with Edward. Lord Morton also reported that Charlotte Drummond, Edward's sister, was inconsolable at his death. Morton also told the queen at dinner that Colonel Drummond was much distressed at his brother's death.

The Inquest

As well as the above information, *The Times* contained evidence given at the coroner's inquest on Drummond's death.

> The body of the late E Drummond was opened by Mr C Gardiner Guthrie[23] on Thursday 26th January at 1 o'clock in the presence of Mr Chambers, Mr Hume, Mr Guthrie, Mr Bransby Cooper and

Mr Jackson. The ball entered behind, two inches from the spinal process or ridge of the backbone, between the 11th and 13th ribs and three inches from the inferior angle of the shoulder blade. It was extracted in front, between the cartilages of the 7th and 8th ribs about ten inches distant from that part which is commonly known as the pit of the stomach. The ball after entering the cavity of the chest slightly abraded the left lung at its lower and inferior, which was part covered by recent lymph, the lung being internally sound. The left side of the chest contained nearly a pint of red coloured serum. The ball perforated the diaphragm, or muscular partition dividing the chest from the abdomen: it grazed the fat of the left kidney and passed through the great omentum below the stomach to the part where it was extracted, but giving rise to an effusion of blood, which was found coagulated and diffused, to the amount of perhaps 10 ounces. The absence of all that shock and alarm which almost invariably follows the opening into either of the gross natural cavities of the body, together with the great difficulty of ascertaining the spot at which the ball had entered, from its small size, gave rise, during the first 12 hours to the anxious hope that it had not passed directly across. We consider such a wound to be inevitably fatal.

W F Chambers
J R Hume
G J Guthrie
Bransby B Cooper
Richard Jackson

(Also present were two "young gentlemen", Mr Cocks and Mr Johnson, who were brought there by Bransby Cooper and Guthrie senior, respectively. The reason for these two young men being there is not known.)

There are several serious questions that arise from the evidence given to the coroner.

1. There was no independence in the preparation of this report. The signatories were from all those involved in the treatment of the deceased when he was alive and therefore the objectivity of their evidence, given in the coroner's court, should not have been relied upon. Any errors in their analysis of the injuries, or the treatment given to the patient, were highly unlikely to be revealed by the surgeons at this stage.

2. It is curious, and a little worrying, that the team of surgeons appointed Guthrie's son to carry out the autopsy. As his father appears to have been the dominant figure among the surgeons, there was even less likelihood of there being any criticism of Guthrie senior's role by his son. But why would the most famous of these surgeons, who had been at the centre of the treatment throughout, eschew the limelight and put his far less experienced son in that position? Could they possibly have been relying on Guthrie junior not to raise any issues?
3. After all the optimism of the regular health bulletins while Drummond was still alive, this report now describes the wound as "inevitably fatal"; a finding that neatly concludes the issue with no criticism of any part of the treatment, particularly the amount of bloodletting. That no questions were asked by the coroner about the conflict between the information that was given out while Drummond was alive and the sworn information given to the coroner is very surprising indeed. If the coroner had asked more of the surgeons, he would probably have been told that the surgeons didn't know the extent of the wounding until the autopsy. Which may have been correct, but hardly reflected well on Guthrie and Bransby Cooper, who both were said to have had considerable experience of weapon injuries – both had earned good reputations during the Napoleonic Wars.
4. This report puts the extraction of the ball 10 inches away from the pit of the stomach, whereas the earlier description, when the ball was actually extracted, was that it was "adjacent" to the pit of the stomach. By the time that the post-mortem was carried out, the pistol ball had long been removed from Drummond's abdomen. Which description was correct?
5. The surgeons' evidence on Drummond's death, as given to the coroner, referred to the great difficulty in identifying the entry wound. This conflicts with the clear information that the entry wound had been identified. It was almost the first thing that the surgeons did when examining Drummond's wounds, after the surgeons' arrival, on the same day as the shooting. Drummond was lying on his front when Guthrie and Bransby Cooper first examined the entry wound. Only after this, they turned Drummond on to his back and found where the ball was lodged near the pit of the stomach.
6. Later, at M'Naghten's trial, Mr Guthrie gave evidence, on oath, about the wound suffered by Drummond:
   - Guthrie said that he had "no hesitation whatever in saying that his death was occasioned by the wound."

- He added that it was "quite impossible that any person could have survived such a wound."
- Again, he stated that the bullet "wounded the diaphragm and that is a wound which does not heal under any circumstances. It is certainly a mortal wound. I never knew a person to recover from such a wound made by a ball, but when occasioned by a lance, sword or spear, I have seen it healed."
- Mr Bransby Cooper, on oath, said "I perfectly agree with Mr Guthrie with respect to the nature of the wound and have no doubt whatever that it was the cause of death." This statement appears to have been carefully composed. Bransby Cooper seemed to be signalling that he was not completely in agreement with Guthrie. He was only agreeing on the nature of the wound and that the wound was the cause of death.
- The *Weekly Chronicle* of 29 January 1843, reported that: "It is stated that considerable difference of opinion as to the extent of the wound inflicted by the ball existed among the medical attendants. Mr Cooper took one view of the case, Dr Chambers, Mr Guthrie and Mr Jackson an opposite." This does not particularly come as surprise and it would have been helpful if the nature of their differences had been revealed.

The surgeons' team had issued regular bulletins on their patient from very shortly after the wounded Drummond was taken back to his house. There was no mention then, or subsequently while Drummond was alive, that, in the surgeons' opinion, this type of wound was invariably fatal. When the autopsy was carried out, it was then that the surgeons changed their opinion and expressed the views in the bullet points above. One would have expected the surgeons to have made it clear that they could only see the true extent of the injury during the autopsy – if that was indeed the case – but this did not happen.

Guthrie gave the view, on oath, that the wound to the diaphragm was "certainly a mortal wound". He then qualified this view by saying that the wound might not have been fatal if caused by "a lance, sword or spear." No details of why that should not be the case for a small pistol ball were given. Bransby Cooper also gave evidence that he "perfectly agreed" with Mr Guthrie regarding Drummond's wound. He made no comment on Guthrie's claim about wounding by other weapons.

Given the firm and clear evidence that Guthrie and Bransby Cooper gave – that this wound was not survivable – the optimism in the earlier medical bulletins is a nonsense. However, there was no examination of the two surgeons on this point by the coroner.

There was a letter to *The Times*[24] after the coroner's court received the evidence on Drummond's death. It raised the question as to why, of the six signatories to the post-mortem report, only the most junior signatory gave evidence. It continued,

> I think it was due to the friends of the unfortunate deceased, and also to the public, amongst whom this unfortunate case has excited so intense an interest, that medical evidence should have been given clearly and distinctly by one of the responsible agents instead of the (somewhat confused) particulars detailed by the gentleman whose duty wholly consisted of sitting up with Mr Drummond the two or three nights preceding his decease. That on the forthcoming trial the medical evidence will be given by Mr Guthrie, sen. and Mr B Cooper & co and not be wholly entrusted to Mr Guthrie's son….

While this plea made much sense, no one was to hear evidence from any one of the senior surgeons, as none of them were called to give evidence about the shooting or the treatment.

Cause of Death

Looking at the outcome of this shooting, it becomes much more likely that the cause of death would today be given that Drummond died from a loss of blood in his abdomen (and possibly chest cavity). In a modern analysis, it is likely that his death would be found to be due to hypovolemic shock. This is a condition caused by severe blood (or other fluid) loss that results in the heart being unable to pump enough blood to maintain adequate circulation. It would be fair to note that the amount of blood found in the chest cavity would not, by itself, be sufficient to cause death in the case of a reasonably fit man. However, when the amount of blood removed by the surgeons bleeding their patient is also taken into account, it shows a significant depletion of Drummond's blood supply, so much so as to endanger his life. Drummond's pulse remained between 108 and 112 BPM throughout the treatment and this strongly suggests that during his treatment he was short of circulating blood.

During the time that Drummond was being treated by his surgeons, it was noticed that he was having breathing difficulties and this would also point to hypovolemic shock. It can be caused by blood loss of one fifth of the normal amount of blood in circulation. When the body tries to respond to there being a lack of oxygenated blood it seeks to ensure that whatever blood has been retained is fully oxygenated. The conclusion that hypovolemic shock was originally caused by the pistol shot wound, exacerbated by copious bleeding, becomes quite compelling. It should be added that it is within the bounds of possibility that there could have been more damage to Mr Drummond's organs than was found by a nineteenth century post-mortem.

Hypovolemic shock is now widely considered to have been the cause of George Washington's death in December 1799. In his case, approximately 82 ounces of blood are thought to have been removed from him. If correct, this would be equivalent to 5 pints of blood. An earlier death, that of King Charles II in 1685, was also noted for copious bleeding. After suffering an incapacitating seizure, Charles was bled to the extent of at least 24 ounces of blood. In addition, there were many other "medicines" put into his system and this meant the exact cause of death cannot be determined – other than an overdose of treatment.

A Public Challenge to the Surgeons

Shortly after the trial of Drummond's assassin, the conduct of the medical team was directly challenged by Dr Samuel Dickson, writing under the pseudonym of 'An Old Army Surgeon'. His book was entitled *What killed Mr. Drummond, the Lead or the Lancet?*[25] Dickson started by explaining that Mr Guthrie and Dr Hume, at the time, were both inspectors of army hospitals and that Mr Bransby Cooper had also seen military service. He dismissed the other surgeons who signed the autopsy report as mere civilians who, in his view, would have known nothing of the practice of treating gunshot wounds. His challenge to the signatories of the post-mortem report was:

> In the course of their experience and reading, will any of these gentlemen say that they do not, or they have not, read of cases of gunshot wounds still more severe than this having perfectly recovered? – of the chest and lungs having been traversed from front to back – of the diaphragm having been perforated and the investing membrane of the heart even abraded, and yet the patient having survived the accident and been completely restored to HEALTH?

Dickson rose to greater heights of scorn when he came to the question of blood-letting – "few men even in the highest health could survive such repeated evacuations of their living blood." He further observed that:

> Every successive bleeding brought the unfortunate gentleman nearer the grave. The relief from each bleeding was said to be slight – the loss of blood admitted to be considerable; and still it was this practice madly persevered in by Army Surgeons and Civil Doctors acting under the influence of authority and custom.

This, again, is a core issue – was the blood-letting excessive and were the medical team aware of the point at which loss of blood would threaten life?

As commented earlier in this chapter, the loss of blood certainly seems to be a crucial factor in his death and we have a contemporary condemnation of the practice. *John Bull*[26] published some correspondence it had received on this subject:

> …of two persons wounded, each of them wounded by the pistol of an assassin, the ball taking in each a similar direction, the worst wounded sufferer of the two recovered and did well, while the other, who was subjected to frequent and severe bleeding, died at the end of a few days. It was open to this practitioner, whether surgical or medical, to show, if he was capable of doing so, by what this fatally opposite result was occasioned? As a champion of the system which his medical brethren adopted, it behoved him to demonstrate that where an individual has been so severely wounded by a pistol ball that the bodily functions are well-nigh unable to carry on the operations of life – that this fast wasting energy is to be repaired by copiously draining away the blood by which alone the action of the heart is maintained and which cannot be drawn of without the whole intestinal action being deranged…. The instances which testify against blood-letting are flagrant and deplorable … if momentary relief is given by the use of the lancet, does not the cause of the inflammation again return; and return, too, when the system, weakened by loss of blood, is less able than before to contend against it? Is not this debility of the vital power increased the oftener this diminution of the vital fluid is depleted?[27]

The writer of this denunciation, writing under the penname of "SYPHAX", concluded with a clear statement of his own preferences in the matter:

> I look upon the application of the lancet and leech as death-warnings, and I should never willingly trust my life to the point of one or the proboscis of the other.

There was another press attack on the use of bloodletting. This was in *The Times,*[28] in the form of a letter, but in fact, when read, it was clearly a commercial advertisement from two "hygeists" at the British College of Health. It contained criticism of the bloodletting ("bleeding under any circumstances whatever can never be attended with benefit"). While the "letter" made a valid point against bleeding as a cure, its force was undermined by the core belief of hygeists – that vegetable pills were a cure for all diseases.[29] The credibility of this cure by vegetable pills was already under attack well before the events of 1843.[30]

Gunshot Wounds

Much was made at the time of the expertise of Guthrie and Bransby Cooper when it came to dealing with pistol and musket ball wounds. Their experiences during the Napoleonic War were cited in support of this. But, in 1817, shortly after the end of hostilities, a report on wounds of soldiers and their treatment during the Waterloo campaign was prepared and published.[31] The section in this report on wounds to the diaphragm quite clearly states that wounds to the diaphragm were

> ...certainly not necessarily fatal, since, in several cases, seen in the Belgic Hospitals, the diaphragm must have been perforated once, if not twice, by musquet [sic] balls. In one case the ball entered the right Hypochondriac region, under the edge of the false ribs, and came out on the right side of the spine, on a level with the superior edge of the os ilium. This patient spat blood for some days, and voided it also by stool.

The *Lancet* was well aware of this report and, quite sarcastically, suggested that the surgeons who treated Drummond would be well advised to read it. But, there is an important point to be drawn from this. If the surgeons were unaware of this report, it strengthens the argument that they should not have been in sole charge of Drummond's treatment. But, if they were aware of the report and its contents then there is a *prima facie* case for concluding that:

- Those who signed the autopsy report perjured themselves in the evidence given to the coroner's court.
- Guthrie gave perjured evidence at M'Naghten's trial on a diaphragm wound by pistol ball being inevitably fatal.
- Bransby Cooper could have perjured himself by saying, on oath, at the same trial, that "I perfectly agree with Mr Guthrie on the nature of the wound".

The legal responsibility of medical professionals for negligent treatment is very much a twentieth century development. At the time of this trial there would have been little point in pursuing this idea. Even if the medical treatment did cause death, it would not have helped the accused assassin at trial, because of his initial action in firing his pistol. However, from our twenty-first century perspective, the optimism of the surgeons did not match their later evidence. Guthrie not giving evidence at the coroner's inquest does smack, more than a little, of an unwillingness to answer questions on his own work (although in the event it appears that no such questions were asked).

The Lancet Has Its Say

The issue of *The Lancet* on 18 March 1843 raised serious questions about Drummond's treatment and other actions taken (or not taken) by the surgeons. The leading article in this issue contained some very blunt criticism of the treatment that Drummond had received.

> We must observe then, at once, that the medical attendants of MR DRUMMOND, in their reports upon his case, did not do justice to the public or themselves. The uncircumstantial [sic] nature of those documents leaves us in complete darkness on certain points, the elucidation of which might have justified the proceedings of the surgeons, while their own statements apparently convict them of an omission which, by rendering the diagnosis obscure, in all probability misled them in their practice.
>
> The surgeons, when first called in might have been justified, by appearances, in thinking it possible the ball had coursed round

> the left side of the body, but we think all our readers who know anything of gunshot wounds will agree with us that, at the first blush of a case, on such a point can only be arrived at where the course of the ball can be distinctly traced under the integuments.
>
> We do not blame the surgeons for surmising that the ball had taken a circuitous course, but we say that they acted most imprudently in committing themselves by a positive opinion to that effect, while there were yet no sufficient data for forming one.

The Lancet drew attention to the surgeons (principally Guthrie and Bransby Cooper), making an assumption that the pistol ball had travelled round the left side of the body. Whilst the surgeon's assumption might well have been correct, they should, in the view of *The Lancet*, have only concluded this point with a proper examination of the ball's progress. Instead the surgeons proceeded solely on the basis of their original surmise. Why did the surgeons not try harder to verify the path of the ball, in particular examining more closely where the ball had come to rest, rather than merely extracting it?

On the question of Drummond's breathing difficulty, *The Lancet* was again critical – why was the chest not examined by auscultation? Auscultation was the use of an instrument, such as a stethoscope, to listen to the sounds produced by the internal organs of a patient, in order to form an opinion of their condition. As *The Lancet* damningly commented:

> ...we hear of no auscultation in this case. It seems to have been made an affair of pure surgery and the surgeons appear to have had no idea of what was really going on until a post-mortem examination enlightened them.

It is of course debateable that the post-mortem really did enlighten them, given that it did not establish the track of the bullet in Drummond's body.

Further condemnation came from the *Lancet* as to the suitability of surgeons alone undertaking the treatment of Drummond:

> We have again and again affirmed, and we now repeat, assuredly without fear of refutation from the case before us, that a "pure" surgeon, as such, is not fit to take charge of any case of injury or disease whatsoever – not even one which appears to be simply surgical.

This was not an anti-surgeon rant, but a sensible acknowledgement that a wound such as Drummond's required a wider range of skills and knowledge than those that the surgeons would have possessed.

In passing, it is worth considering what the bulletins actually revealed about what the surgeons did, of a surgical nature, when treating Drummond:

1. They probed the wound at the back and at the chest of Drummond, but neither yielded any information.
2. They bled the patient.
3. They listened to his chest.
4. They took his pulse and temperature.
5. They decided not to remove fragments of clothing taken into the body by the pistol ball.

That the above five actions/inactions were specifically mentioned, it seems to be a reasonable assumption that nothing else as major as these were undertaken. There is little in this list that actually qualifies as a surgical procedure. This does tend to reinforce the *Lancet*'s point about the need to involve physicians; something that would be alien to the surgeons of that time.

Why was auscultation not used to help identify where the inflammation might be? If the "purity of their surgical attainments [rendered] them ignorant of auscultation" why did they not obtain the service of one who could assist? More despairingly, *The Lancet* also asked:

> What, in the name of surgery, was Mr Guthrie dreaming of when he asserted that gun-shot wounds of the diaphragm were invariably fatal? It would be absurd to suppose a man of his experience as a military surgeon to be ignorant on such a point; his assertion, therefore, must have arisen from sheer carelessness.[32]

It should not be overlooked that the above observation by *The Lancet* states that his assertion must be the result of Guthrie's carelessness. A serious accusation which does not appear to have been answered by Guthrie.

The surgeons' bulletins on Drummond's health did not escape criticism. The anger of *The Lancet*'s view came through strongly in its condemnation of the bulletins. It does not make for comfortable reading.

> But carelessness and inaccuracy on the part of the medical attendants seem to be as predominant features in the reports on Mr Drummond's case as in its diagnosis. The bulletins issued in this case are absolute nonsense. The report of the post-mortem examination has been drawn up in a very clumsy manner, although it had reference to a case of extraordinary legal interest, and is the production of a teacher of military and forensic surgery, and a physician who examines surgeons for the East India Company service. We can make allowance for reserve and caution with which it may sometimes be wise to frame such documents; but it is not unreasonable to demand that, whatever meaning they have shall be distinctly stated, and that one bulletin shall not contradict or stultify another.[33]

Unfortunately, this direct criticism of the surgeons will not have been read by the wider public, unless they chanced to see a copy of the *Lancet.*

It should be noted that the treatment provided by Guthrie and Bransby Cooper would have been well understood by other surgeons in London. So, in some respects, the treatment of Drummond would have met with a level of approval, at least within a number of the surgeons of this country. Whether it would have met with that level of approval from other physicians is more questionable, particularly given the coruscating comments of the *Lancet*. There was also a change developing within the medical professions about the practice of bleeding patients. While there was no doubt that many clung to the long-standing practice of bleeding, there were other voices being raised against it on very clear grounds.

Mr Guthrie's Lecture

To try to throw some further light on Guthrie senior and his evidence, it is useful, but rather despairing, to read the text of the public talk that Guthrie gave at Westminster Hall, very soon after the end of the M'Naghten trial.[34] His lecture included his comments on Drummond's injury and death.

> It would, however be wrong in me, who knows better, and it would lead you into error, if I were to allow you to suppose that a penetrating wound of the chest and lungs could ordinarily be treated with success in so simple a manner. Mr Drummond was wounded in the back, near the spine, and the ball was found half an inch under the skin, nearly at an opposite point in front. From

> the absence of all those symptoms which usually indicate the lesion of a vital part, I was willing to hope the ball might not have penetrated the cavity of the chest, and as the opening made by the ball was too small to allow the finger to follow it, I did not choose to run the risk of examining it by a probe, which if the ball had run around, might have done much mischief.

The underlined passage above is difficult to understand. The ball had entered Drummond's back and halted just under the surface of the skin of Drummond's chest. No human finger could reach from the wound in the back to the bullet's resting place, even if it had followed a straight line, particularly as Mr Drummond was known to be a portly man.

> I could not however trace its passage in any direction, nor could I do it in a satisfactory way on examination after death.

While this may very well be correct, it is surprising that a surgeon with extensive experience of pistol and rifle ball injuries (in the Napoleonic Wars) could not establish more when observing the autopsy (or even doing it himself?).

1. Why was the autopsy left to his far less inexperienced son?
2. Guthrie, referring to the ball, said that he could not explain how it arrived at its final resting place.
3. Is not the purpose of the autopsy to discover how Mr Drummond was injured internally and how that caused his death?

Guthrie then proceeded with his talk and suggested, bizarrely, that if anyone wanted more information on explaining the path of a bullet through a body, they should apply to the then Lord Mayor of London. Guthrie suggested contacting the Lord Mayor as:

> His Lordship was able from hearing a statement of the case of Mrs Magnus, according to the report in the papers, to decide without knowing anything of the nature or treatment of Mr Drummond's wound, that these two cases were exactly alike in all respects. Now his Lordship could only have discovered this from that omniscience which naturally falls on a chief magistrate on his attaining office, and which, I trust he will exercise on this

> point also for your edification and mine, and that of all other ignorant people who are willing to rely upon his knowledge and discretion on so delicate a subject.

This paragraph was a very personal, offensive, sarcastic and unprofessional attack on an important London figure. To make the attack in a public lecture at Westminster Hall makes his comments even more reprehensible. Arrogance and abuse never did enhance the standing of a professional person.

Guthrie moved on to the treatment of Drummond:

> The ball was extracted at five o'clock on Friday evening, and I saw Mr Drummond again at eight and at twelve, as he was quite easy, I left him with the hope that our best wishes might be realised. At five in the morning of Saturday, I was sent for and I found him suffering from great uneasiness and difficulty in breathing accompanied by a particular catch or jerk, which, from my previous knowledge of the symptoms, made me aware that the ball had penetrated the cavity, and that the diaphragm was wounded. The chest sounded well to the ear in every part, and I had no doubt of the substance of the lung having escaped any serious mischief, although it might be injured by the ball passing between it and the diaphragm. I opened two veins in each arm, and obtained with great difficulty about twelve ounces of blood, the veins being small, and the arm very fat. It gave him some relief.
>
> At ten o'clock Mr Cooper and Mr Jackson decided as the difficulty of breathing had increased and his pulse was 112 (they [sic] only varied from 108 to 112 during the remainder of his life) he ought to be bled again. Mr Cooper tried and failed to draw blood from either arm, and I requested him to open the left temporal artery. This he did with his usual dexterity, but the artery would not bleed, nor another branch, which I opened myself, and only four or five ounces at most, could be obtained.
>
> He [Mr Drummond] had taken four grains of calomel overnight and was to have an aperient draught[35] every six hours: the nurse, however, who obeyed my direction to examine carefully all the excretion, informed me that he had passed a tea-spoonful or two of blood, and the aperients were immediately suspended. I had reason to believe that the ball had not only wounded but had

> penetrated the diaphragm, and probably opened an intestine, and that the cavities of the chest and abdomen had both been injured and must become inflamed.

Guthrie's comment was that he became aware "…that the ball had penetrated the cavity and that the diaphragm was wounded". This was odd as he had made no previous comment on damage to the diaphragm in the surgeons' briefings to the press about the wound. Was it a post-event embellishment to give the impression of inevitability for the death of a patient? Further, there was no mention of intestinal damage given at the inquest, nor was it mentioned in the bulletins while Drummond was alive. Notwithstanding this, Guthrie "had reason to believe" that not only had an intestine been opened, but also the cavities of the chest and abdomen had both "been injured". This more detailed view of Drummond's prognosis was apparently reached on the Saturday – the day after the shooting. This does not match the information released to the public after the shooting. It is unfortunate that Guthrie did not give any reason for his suspicion that an intestine was opened and the chest and abdomen had been injured.

What Was the Drummond Family Told?

> With a constitution apparently unequal to bear an inflammation of the most dangerous character which I knew must ensue or the remedies necessary to subdue it, the prospect was a melancholy one and I did not conceal it from his family. Three dozen leeches were applied to the side, but they drew very little blood, and the bites would not bleed afterwards.

If the above is correct, Guthrie told the family on the Saturday that either the wound was mortal or that the chances of survival were very slight. The problem with this claim is the number of persons closely interested in Drummond's condition:

- The Drummond family
- Sir Robert and Lady Peel
- Members of Peel's Cabinet
- Prince Albert and Queen Victoria

Colonel Drummond was a Groom in Waiting to Queen Victoria, and was, obviously, most concerned about the shooting of his brother. He could not have withheld the information on Drummond's condition from the wider Drummond family, which was numerous and of no little importance. Further, it is inconceivable that, if he was told of this gloomy prognosis, he could have withheld the facts from the queen or Prince Albert – as both were most anxious about Edward Drummond's survival. If Queen Victoria knew of this prognosis, it would have been recorded in her *Journal* – but she did not do so. Sir Robert Peel was greatly attached to Drummond and again it is inconceivable that information of this importance could have been withheld from the Prime Minister (and other senior Cabinet members), particularly if Guthrie was telling others. It seems more likely that Guthrie did not tell the family and the remarks in his lecture were intended to support his reputation.

> The symptoms of inflammation, which appeared on the Saturday morning, did not increase during the whole of Sunday, and, at the consultation at ten on Monday morning, we entertained some hope that they would remain within reasonable bounds. At twelve, Miss Drummond sent to tell me that he was much worse. I found him suffering great pain and uneasiness at and under each wound, with a greater jerk and oppression in breathing.

There were, of course, two apparent surface wounds, one on entry and a second where the pistol ball was extracted (by lancet and fingers). That there was inflammation at the site of the extraction of the ball indicated that either the inflammation from the original wound had spread quite rapidly through Drummond's system or that the extraction of the ball had introduced a further infection into Drummond's system where the ball was extracted.

> I determined to try again to bleed him, and the same vein, which would not bleed before, now yielded 12 ounces when the fat interfered and no more could be obtained. The blood, before it separated into its solid and fluid parts, was actually like size in colour (?) and its abstraction gave him relief. Calomel and opium were ordered every two hours.[36]
>
> At ten at night Dr Hume, Mr Cooper and Mr Jackson saw him again with me, and, as the oppression and painful uneasiness had returned with even greater severity, he was again bled to the amount of about 12 ounces, when the blood ceased to flow, though the pulse remained unaffected, apparently from the same cause –

> the fat intervening. This again greatly relieved him: but at five o'clock next morning (Tuesday) Mr Jackson and I were sent for in consequence of the return of all the symptoms, and particularly of the catch and the breathing, in a more aggravated state. He had dozed but little from the opium, and it was not to be doubted that he would soon die unless relief could be obtained; twelve ounces more blood were accordingly drawn from the other arm. This time he bled freely, and more might have been obtained, had it been prudent to let it flow. It was equally as yellow as cupped and as firm on division when coagulated, and the solid part was in as due proportion with the fluid as on the two previous occasions, and the relief obtained was equally satisfactory.
>
> I had seen Mr Drummond six times in each twenty-four hours, besides an hour or two spent with him during the night. I had ascertained by ear three times a day the state of his chest, and when we met on Tuesday, at the usual hour of ten, I knew that our patient could bear no further loss of blood with advantage – that fluid was collecting in his chest and that if he lived, it must soon be evacuated to prevent another evil more certainly fatal than even inflammation. [This reveals that a total of 36 ounces of blood were taken within 24 hours.]

It is unfortunate that the threat of "another evil" was mentioned, but was not identified, nor explained, by Guthrie.

> It was with very mournful feelings I said to Mr Cooper and Mr Jackson, for whose able and cordial co-operation I am grateful, "If I bleed our patient again, we shall lose him, and we shall lose him equally if we do anything else."
>
> "We met again at four o'clock at which time [Mr Drummond] had had some sleep… We thought him better and I expressed our hope to the family that when we met at 10 o'clock at night we should be able to give a more positive assurance or real amendment. At seven o'clock Miss Drummond sent to say some change had taken place, and that he was worse. I went to him directly, and found that he had no pulse at the wrist. At ten, when the [other surgeons] arrived, they were no less surprised than I had been at so sudden an alteration.

That it should now be a surprise, for the surgeons, that there was a sudden worsening in Drummond's condition is perplexing. Given the evidence delivered at the inquest on Drummond's death on 26 January that "We consider such a wound to be inevitably fatal" there should have been no surprise at his deterioration by this stage. In addition, this version is not compatible with Guthrie's claim that the surgeons were now "surprised" at Drummond's condition.

More Thoughts on Bloodletting

That blind faith in bloodletting continued well into the nineteenth century is quite astonishing. William Harvey, an English physician, who published his treatise on the circulation of the blood in 1628, doubted the value of bloodletting. Thereafter there was a small number of practitioners who would not use it. By the 1840s this number had grown, but the majority of the healing profession still stood by the old practice, despite the complete absence of any proof of benefit. By this stage in Drummond's treatment, he had reached the point where any further bloodletting would kill him.

In 1968 the *Bulletin of the History of Medicine* (Vol.42 No 1 (Jan-Feb 1968) pp.24-42) carried an article by Charles S. Bryant. He calculated that it was likely that a total of 56 fluid ounces of blood was taken from Drummond during his treatment. This would have represented at least 25 per cent of his total blood and the additional amount of blood within the body cavity probably made the bloodletting at least a significant contributory factor in his death.

Guthrie's Views on Wounds

> The treatment of a wound made by a knife or sword is diametrically opposite to that made by a musket-ball and the treatment of a wound made by a musket- ball is usually much more simple and requires much less aid from scientific surgery than that made by the small ball of a pocket or duelling pistol.

This was a highly contentious view from Guthrie and it was challenged quite quickly after he expressed it. Guthrie had admitted in the past to recommending that duelling pistols should be of bigger bore, with a greater powder-charge being used, so that a duelling shot would always go through a man rather than remain in the body. Guthrie's claim that a larger bore ball would always go through the body was not necessarily correct.

The duelling career of Andrew Jackson (later 7th president of the USA) is instructive in this area. He fought a duel with Charles Dickinson in May 1806. The two duellists used identical pistols which fired a 1-ounce ball. This was larger than the most commonly encountered ball size in duels which were around 0.49 ounces or 13.9 grams. Jackson's shot hit his opponent in the abdomen, causing a fatal injury to his intestines. Dickinson's shot severely damaged Jackson's chest wall and broke two ribs. The ball embedded itself deep in the left lung, probably carrying with it bone fragments and bits of cloth. It was not thought possible to extract the ball safely, and Jackson was left a semi-invalid for the rest of his life. Abscesses formed around the bullet, which contained the infection to a degree. In 1813, Jackson was shot in the back and shoulder from close range by Jesse Benton. Both balls remained in Jackson's body as his doctors feared for his life if they tried to remove the two pistol balls. Sometime later, when Jackson was president, he asked a visiting doctor to remove the ball from his shoulder. The doctor made the first incision and the ball dropped to the floor with no further assistance. President Jackson survived another assassination attempt when Richard Lawrence planned to shoot him and the attack failed. Both of Lawrence's pistols failed to fire. The two pistols were fully and correctly loaded. The following day the pistols were cleared and reloaded and they worked correctly. Guthrie's statement suggesting larger balls would have made a larger wound and passed through the body was not always correct.

That sword and knife wounds were less dangerous to the victim would be accepted and modern medicine would consider them less dangerous than bullet wounds. The cutting or thrusting of a sword or knife only injures along its path, whereas projectiles from muskets or pistols can injure more extensively. As well as inflicting injury along their path, the velocity of pistol or musket balls have a greater chance of causing cavitation injuries outside of the direct path of the ball. The re-examination by a modern surgeon of the injuries found in Lieutenant Seton after his duel with Lieutenant Hawkey brought forth the strong suggestion that the pistol ball, in passing close to the back wall of the bowel but not hitting it, produced blunt trauma by blast effect to the bowel wall.[37]

A further issue is that, although it was not included in the post-mortem report, the surgeons believed that the pistol ball had hit one of Mr Drummond's lower left-hand ribs and that this had changed its trajectory. Modern trauma knowledge would regard this as a complicating factor in treatment, as deflection can cause a projectile to yaw, or tumble, dissipating its energy into soft tissue causing greater injury.

Consensus of Treatment?

That the other surgeons concurred with Guthrie and Bransby Cooper in the treatment of Mr Drummond would seem to point to the treatment applied being as a result of a general consensus. However, it seems quite clear that Guthrie and Cooper both had national reputations for their treatment of Napoleonic War casualties, which would include a large number of gunshot wounds. Of the two, Guthrie's reputation was the greater. (See the endnote to this chapter.)

The manner of Guthrie's address at Westminster Hall is illuminating, not only for his sarcasm and his manifestly high opinion of himself, but also for his very superior attitude to other members of the medical fraternity. His forceful character probably dominated the choice of medical treatment for Drummond, and Bransby Cooper was unlikely to argue for any other treatment, given his less than forceful nature. That Guthrie was prepared to deride other practitioners in a well-publicised public address tends to show that he was not used to having his opinions challenged and was confident that his reputation would make him immune from any challenge. There is no doubt, whether deserved or not, that Guthrie had a high reputation, or at least a reputation in high places, but how well-deserved it was must be open to question.

Bransby Cooper v *The Lancet* (1828)

Prior to the assassination of Drummond, Bransby Cooper had already clashed with *The Lancet* over a question of his ability as a surgeon. Bransby Cooper was a nephew of the then famous surgeon Sir Astley Cooper. By 1827, Sir Astley was recognised as one of the most eminent surgeons in Britain. Bransby Cooper admired his uncle immensely and he tended to regard him as infallible. Unfortunately, Bransby Cooper lacked confidence in his own judgment and ability as a surgeon. As a lecturer, he was competent, but he lacked the ability to excite or captivate his audience. Despite this, he was a popular figure within Guy's Hospital – but mainly for his good nature and sporting prowess.

Sir Astley[38] was a greatly esteemed figure at Guy's and he did much to promote Bransby Cooper's progress as a surgeon. Bransby Cooper had served time with the British Army in the Peninsular War and therefore should have gained valuable experience in the treatment of gunshot wounds.

In 1817, Sir Astley had arranged for Bransby Cooper to be appointed as demonstrator of anatomy to the Borough Hospitals Medical School. This appointment was made without any consultation with the other hospitals involved with this medical school – therefore his high handedness had serious consequences. The relationship between Guy's and St. Thomas's was already strained, and Sir Astley's action increased the tension between these two hospitals. The outcome was that the treasurer of Guy's decided to sever the relationship between the two hospitals.[39] Bransby Cooper was then appointed, with Sir Astley's backing, to the new chair of anatomy at Guy's.

In 1825, Sir Astley was appointed consulting surgeon at Guy's, while Bransby Cooper was elected assistant surgeon on the same day. There were no other candidates for either post, unsurprisingly, as neither post had been advertised, which prevented anyone else from applying. Sir Astley's conduct reflected a long-held view by senior surgeons, that a person holding a chair at one of the main hospitals had the power to name his chosen successor to that chair. Sir Astley himself had benefited from this type of patronage being exercised in his favour by his uncle, William Cooper. When William Cooper resigned his surgeon's appointment at Guy's, he arranged for Astley to replace him. Appointments made in this way did not go down well with other members of the hospital staff. Despite this, Bransby Cooper kept his appointment as chair of anatomy – and in the same year, he was elected assistant surgeon and then full surgeon. He also obtained an appointment as consulting surgeon at the Western Infirmary.

Bransby Cooper's career in surgery was so far unspectacular, but he clearly had benefited from Sir Astley's patronage. In 1827, Sir Astley's wife died so he decided to retire abroad, leaving his highly lucrative private practice in Bransby Cooper's hands. Unfortunately for Bransby Cooper, Sir Astley regretted his decision within a year. He returned to England, remarried, and took back his private practice from his nephew.

The Lithotomy Debacle

In 1828, Bransby Cooper's reputation received a severe blow when he botched a lithotomy[40] before a large audience in the operating theatre at Guy's. The great majority of surgeons would have been able to perform this operation easily in 5 minutes. Indeed it would usually take a competent practitioner less time. Speed was important in this operation as patients then were neither sedated nor anesthetised.

On this occasion, Bransby Cooper took between 50 and 55 minutes to remove the not particularly big stone, with his patient screaming at him to stop; such was the patient's pain.[41] But Bransby Cooper continued until he was finally successful. The patient, a healthy man, apart from his fairly small stone, died the following day. *The Lancet* published an article on this operation and quite clearly suggested that as the operation progressed there were clear signs of panic in Bransby Cooper's comments and behaviour.

This whole fiasco in the operating theatre was recorded by one of the attendees who observed this surgery closely and took notes. The notes were handed, for a fee, to Thomas Wakley, editor and proprietor of *The Lancet*. An article was prepared on Bransby Cooper's debacle and it was then published in *The Lancet*. The article, it must be said, was sensational and, at times, in lurid language. The public accusation of Bransby Cooper's ineptness left him with no option but to instigate a libel action against Wakley to try to save his reputation. The damages claimed were for the then substantial sum of £2,000. Bransby Cooper had no alternative but to litigate, as it would have been very difficult, if not impossible, to continue his career if he did not, or if he failed to win the action.

There was another issue that would come out during the trial and that was the issue of nepotism. Although it was widely known within the medical profession, the general public would have had little knowledge of it. Wakley, being strongly in favour of ending the power of patronage within the medical profession, was happy to use this opportunity to expose how staff appointments and promotions could be managed. Wakley's conviction of the necessity of reform within the hospitals made much of Sir Astley's patronage and the fact that three of his nephews held four positions at Guy's between them through their uncle's influence.

Wakley represented himself in court, although he was aided outside of the court by two barristers. Significantly, one of these barristers was Henry Brougham,[42] who was then one of the most highly regarded barristers of his generation. At this time, Brougham was closely connected with the Whig party (Liberals) and was quite amenable to help to throw light on how hospital staff appointments were managed. The barrister Sir James Scarlett appeared for Bransby Cooper. Sir James had a reputation as a good barrister, but his performance during this trial went against his reputation, and much of his address in court was merely wind-bagging.[43] Wakley was a Whig and Bransby Cooper a Tory – a political alignment that reflected the politics of their counsel.

The jury found against Wakley but, more importantly, awarded a mere £100 pounds in damages to Bransby Cooper. This award of damages almost certainly saved Bransby Cooper's career, but the meagre sum of the damages (it was only 1/20th of the claim) meant that Wakley was very widely regarded as having been vindicated in publishing the article.

Another View of Bransby Cooper

A barrister, Sergeant Ballantyne, later wrote of Bransby Cooper having had "the misfortune to fail in an operation, which cost the patient his life" which was rather generous to Bransby Cooper and dismissive of the patient (or perhaps it merely reflected the spin put on the operation by Bransby Cooper's friends). Ballantyne also referred to Bransby Cooper as having ability, "but never having any hold on the public".

Ballantyne also recalled that, later in life, Bransby Cooper often complained about how a fishbone had lacerated his throat and left him with long term discomfort there. Bransby Cooper died suddenly at the Athenaeum Club in 1853. The cause of death was a major haemorrhage at the base of his tongue, which was found to have been caused by cancer of the throat.[44]

Why Were Guthrie and Cooper in Charge of Drummond's Care?

The assassination attempt was, obviously, a significant political incident, as Edward Drummond was an important person within the British political system. He was highly thought of by all of the prominent Tory politicians he had worked for. But at that time, the assassination of British politicians was sufficiently rare for there to be no standing procedures for their safety or for managing the treatment of wounded politicians or royalty.

The decision to take Drummond to his home appears to have been taken at Drummond's Bank, presumably by his brother. If the shooting had occurred today, there would have been no such choice and the victim would have been taken to the nearest hospital with a trauma centre. In 1843, there were no trauma centres, and the choice was simply between home and hospital. How this choice was actually made is unclear, and going home, as a matter of course, was quite possibly the natural assumption by those treating him. There might well have been little to choose between the two in terms of cleanliness and suitability for nursing. Either Jackson or the Drummond family probably made the choice. Political input into the choice would seem to have been nil.

The contemporary press reports give no clue as how the team of surgeons was put together. Jackson was the first involved, as he was the closest available surgeon to Drummond's Bank and it was an emergency. He gave the first assessment of Drummond's condition. Guthrie appears to have taken the lead around 5 pm and it may be that the other surgeons had been chosen by him, although some may have arrived before he did – but there is no proof of this. Indeed there is no information as to how anyone other than Jackson became a member of the team.

None of this provides a reason for selecting Bransby Cooper to join the team. Given his well-publicised error in 1828 with the botched lithotomy, he would not seem to have been a suitable candidate to join and help to supervise the treatment of such an important patient. As previously noted in this chapter, Sir Robert Peel told Queen Victoria of Guthrie's apparent skill in dealing with gunshot wounds, but there was no corresponding advice about Bransby Cooper's suitability other than that.

The press releases by the medical team appear to be almost exclusively about the actions of Guthrie and Bransby Cooper, which gives the impression, rightly or wrongly, that the other surgeons did not contribute very much. *The Lancet*'s criticism of the treatment of Drummond reinforces this impression of Guthrie and Bransby Cooper leading in directing Drummond's treatment.

It is difficult to believe that Guthrie and Bransby Cooper were the best qualified to manage the treatment of Drummond. It also seems that, instead of the posse of surgeons, the treatment should have been improved by the presence of at least one experienced doctor. However, there was probably too much rivalry between these professions for that to be feasible – very regrettably for Edward Drummond.

End Notes[45]

1. **George James Guthrie** (1785–1856) entered training as a surgeon's apprentice at 13 and made rapid progress with his learning. When 15, he passed his Royal College of Surgeons examination and was posted to the 29th Regiment of Foot and he later went to Nova Scotia with them. The army were impressed with his skills and he was promoted to full surgeon. He saw extensive action in the Peninsular War and in 1812 became deputy inspector of hospitals, although this was not confirmed until 1814. In 1815 he returned to the colours in Belgium, five days before Waterloo. After his return to England, he helped found the Westminster Hospital.

   The Royal Army Medical Corps continues the award of the Guthrie Medal for outstanding contributions made by consultants to the British Army.

2. **Bransby Blake Cooper** (1792–1853) went to sea as a midshipman in 1805, but soon decided this was not the right path. He returned to shore and after six years training, he joined the Ordnance Medical Department as a temporary assistant surgeon. He served with Wellington's Army in the major battles of the Peninsular War from Vittoria (1813) to the French surrender (April 1814). He then joined his uncle, Sir Astley Cooper, at Guy's Hospital as his assistant. On the separation of Guy's and St Thomas's Hospitals, Bransby Cooper was appointed to the chair of anatomy at Guy's. At the time of Drummond's shooting, Bransby Cooper was professor of human anatomy and surgery at the Royal College of Surgeons. He has been described as being "warm-hearted and jocular but with little confidence in himself".
3. **Samuel Dickson**, MD (1802–1869), author of the 'Chrono-thermal System of Medicine,' studied medicine at Edinburgh and at Paris, qualifying at the Edinburgh College of Surgeons in 1825. Having obtained a commission as assistant surgeon in the army, he went to India to join the 30th Regiment of Foot at Madras. During five years' service in India, he acquired a large amount of surgical experience (he speaks of performing forty operations for cataracts in one morning), became distrustful of the current rules and maxims of medical treatment, and speculated on the nature of cholera.

   On his return home he graduated MD at Glasgow in 1833, and began private practice, first at Cheltenham and afterwards in Mayfair, London. His first published work was *Hints on Cholera and its Treatment*, Madras, 1829, in which he traced the phenomena of the disease to influences acting on the nervous centres and the pneumogastric nerve. An English edition, with new matter, appeared under the title *The Epidemic Cholera and other prevalent Diseases of India*, London, 1832. When the next epidemic came, he returned to the subject in *Revelations on Cholera*, London 1848, and *The Cholera and how to cure it*, London 1849. Shortly after settling in London, where he had no connection with medical corporations, societies, hospitals, or schools of medicine, he began a series of clever polemical writings, in which he cast ridicule both on the intelligence and on the honesty of contemporary practice by way of recommending his original views. The following is a list of them:

   In 1850 he started a monthly journal, *The Chrono-thermalist, or People's Medical Inquirer*, which ran for twenty-two months, being entirely from his own pen, and, like all the rest of his writings, devoted to the dual purpose of advocating Dicksonian truth and exposing other people's errors. Several of his writings went through more than one edition, at home as well as in the United States; under their various titles they all cover much the same ground. The central idea of the chrono-thermal system is the periodicity and intermittency of all vital actions, ague being regarded as the type-disease. The system is, of course, very inadequate, both as an analysis and as a synthesis; but its author's writings are often instructive, both for theory and practice, here and there truly profound, and always lively and entertaining in style, some parts of his later polemic being in spirited rhymed couplets modelled on Pope.

He was early in the field against bloodletting, and even got credit for his originality and sagacity in that matter in an article in the *British and Foreign Medico-Chirurgical Review* (1860). He was ignored by most of the leaders of medicine, several of whom he circumstantially accused of plagiarising the ideas that he had long advocated on vital chronometry and other points. His tone towards the medicine of the schools was met by intolerance. According to his own statement, the leading medical journal refused even to insert the advertisement of his writings on the money being tendered; and it is certain that none of the English journals of the profession referred to his death, or gave any sketch of his career. Although he was not without supporters at home, his chief following was in the United States, where the Penn Medical College of Philadelphia was founded to teach his doctrines, the entire staff of ten professors subscribing a prospectus, or confession of faith, on behalf of 'the system for which we are indebted to that master mind, Samuel Dickson of London.'

He died at Bolton Street, Mayfair, on 12 October 1869.

From DNB 1885-1900

Chapter 10

THE REACTION

A significant and vocal section of opinion was outraged that M'Naghten should have been acquitted on the ground of insanity. In their anger at the court's verdict, many threw both rational thought and humanity out of the window. This can be explained by posing the question – did the majority of physicians at that time know much about mental illness? The answer is that they knew very little, and surgeons would have known much less. The knowledge of the average educated person would also have been insignificant, as was to be seen in some of views expressed about punishing a mentally ill person or his family, if the mentally ill person committed a criminal act. While this is to some extent understandable, it is difficult to accept, let alone explain, that human compassion for a person so afflicted could be abandoned in favour of advocating brutal treatment or execution.

1. Queen Victoria's Views

Someone who, understandably, was closely concerned with the outcome of M'Naghten's trial was Queen Victoria. Having survived four attempts on her life, it is not surprising that she held strong views on the subject. Regrettably, Queen Victoria recorded in her *Journal* an early view of M'Naghten's acquittal:

> …a letter relative to him, from a person in Glasgow, trying to show that [M'Naghten] was odd in the head, & by that means, mad – but this he is *not*. I wrote to Sir Robert Peel that no one's life would be safe, if people were continually being let off on the plea of insanity, & that I am anxiously hoping this will not be the case in this instance.[1]

Her emphatic statement that M'Naghten – a person she had never met and knew nothing about – was not mad reflects rather badly on her.

The queen returned to the subject in a later *Journal* entry, praising Sir James Mansfield's infamous charge to the jury in Bellingham's trial, adding:

> …had this been the line pursued in Oxford's case, I think, with certainty, the other attempts would not have taken place. It seems that Mac Naughthen still maintains that he shot Sir Robert Peel & showed but little feeling on hearing that his poor victim was dead.[2]

While, no doubt, many people would have agreed with the queen, it is unfortunate that she could not have more understanding of M'Naghten's plight and that she was not able to set an example by showing compassion for a mentally ill person.

A later entry in the queen's *Journal* contained condemnation of M'Naghten, but it is possible that the views expressed to the queen might have been tailored a little to match her views. The last point about the actions of the sheriff of Glasgow is hard to understand. Was Peel really advocating that evidence of insanity from Scotland should be suppressed?

> The wretch, Mac Naugthen, Sir Robert said, showed the greatest intelligence & was evidently not the least mad. That he owned at least £1,000, & that he was evidently a man of literary acquirements, which extracts from Voltaire &c, found in his lodging go to prove. Mr Allison, the author, & Sheriff for the County of Glasgow (really it must be sheer folly & madness) has, without being in the least acquainted with the wretched [sic], collected all the evidence, he can, in order to prove Mac Naughten's insanity, & sent it officially to the Sec^{y} of State. This, Sir Robert Peel says, is highly embarrassing to the Gov^{t}. How anyone can do such a thing, is quite inconceivable![3]

It is quite reprehensible that the queen should have been advocating the suppression of evidence of mental illness, presumably in order to allow M'Naghten to be hanged. This puts her in a thoroughly bad light.

Sir Robert Peel wrote to the queen with the news of M'Naghten's acquittal:

> Sir Robert Peel presents his humble duty to your Majesty, and begs leave to acquaint your Majesty that the prisoner MacNaghten

> was acquitted last night, after a trial which lasted two days, upon the ground of insanity.
>
> The fuller account of the evidence which Sir Robert Peel has seen is on the accompanying newspaper.
>
> The only other information which has reached Sir Robert Peel is contained in a note (enclosed) from Mr Maule, the solicitor to the Treasury, who conducted the prosecution. The three Judges appear to have concurred in opinion, that the evidence of insanity was so strong as to require a verdict of acquittal – and the Chief Justice advised the Jury to find that verdict without summing up the evidence or delivering any detailed charge upon the facts of the case and the law bearing upon them.
>
> It is a lamentable reflection that a man may be at the same time so insane as to be reckless of his own life and the lives of others, and to be pronounced free from moral responsibility, and yet capable of preparing for the commission of murder with the utmost caution and deliberation, and of taking every step which shall enable him to commit it with certainty.[4]

Later, the queen replied:

> The law may be perfect, but how is it that whenever a case for its application arises, it proves to be of no avail? We have seen the trials of Oxford and MacNaghten conducted by the ablest lawyers of the day – Lord Denman, Chief Justice Tindal, and Sir Wm. Follett – and they allow and advise the Jury to pronounce the verdict of Not Guilty on account of Insanity, – whilst everybody is morally convinced that both malefactors were perfectly conscious and aware of what they did! It appears from this, that the force of the law is entirely put into the Judge's hands, and that it depends merely upon his charge whether the law is to be applied or not. Could not the Legislature lay down that rule which the Lord Chancellor does in his paper, and which Chief Justice Mansfield did in the case of Bellingham; and why could not the Judges be bound to interpret the law in this and no other sense in their charges to the Juries?[5]

Despite the queen's previous personal experience of assassination attempts, the thought that she was advocating that the law should be changed so that in future a man who was insane could be executed is really unacceptable. As is the idea that none of those around her were prepared to explain that Mansfield's conduct in Bellingham's trial was equally unacceptable.

> Mac Naughten is acquitted, on the ground of insanity! How dreadful, & how unexpected! *What* security is there left now! Something ought to be done to alter the law, which is indeed very defective.[6]

A meeting with Peel no doubt mollified the queen, but, as she would later find, the judges and Parliament did not follow the course the queen hoped for.

> I heard from Sir Robert Peel, in answer to my strong expressions of disapproval, regarding Mac Naughten's acquittal, Sir Robert says, besides other things, that "he will communicate with the Law Officers & others qualified to form a sound opinion on the important subject of the additional precautions by legislation, against the violence of persons labouring under insanity, & will not fail to report to Y^r^ Majesty."[7]

The queen commented further in her *Journal*:

> Albert gave a long audience to Sir Robert Peel upon many topics. He told him, that he was displeased with the way in which Mac Naghten's trial had been conducted, also that Dillan had been seized, as well as one or two other suspicious people. Great vigilance was being now observed.[8]

The queen aired her views further when she observed later in her *Journal*, after a dinner at Buckingham Palace:

> I heard from Sir Robert Peel besides other things that "a Debate took place in the H^{se} of L^{ds} on the subject of Mac Naghten's trial & acquittal. Regret was justly expressed at the sudden termination of that trial without a speech in reply from the Solicitor Gen: & a Charge from the Judge. The proposed Conference may lead to something or to some uniformity of Proceeding. Sir Robert Peel fears that considering the circumstances of each case vary,

> it would be very difficult to prescribe by law any general rule for the guidance of the Judges before whom the trials of Criminal Lunatics may take place."[9]
>
> He sent me on the 11th, what we think a most unsatisfactory paper, from the Ld Chancellor, inasmuch as it only said the Law was perfect, & citing Ld Mansfield's, & the opinions of others, which however never are followed. I wrote strongly to Sir Robert Peel on the matter, saying that the Judges ought to be bound to interpret the Law in this way & no other. Every Party is crying out for improvement, – yet each criminal escapes, from the folly & fear of changing our "perfect Laws", & I fear more victims will be sacrificed, ere people do something for the improvement of the Laws.[10]

In a dinner at Windsor on 16 March 1843, Peel and other notables dined with the queen. In a short journal entry she recorded that Peel "...told me how ill Mac Naughthen's trial had been conducted, but that it had the effect of making people very vigilant". Lord Clarendon also made it clear that he shared the feelings of the queen and Prince Albert as to the acquittal.[11]

2. Dr J.G. Davey, medical officer at Hanwell Asylum and later a superintendent at Colney Hatch Asylum

After the trial, Davey wrote a pamphlet entitled *Medico-Legal Reflections on the Trial of Daniel McNaughten*, which provided an antidote to some of the crasser publicly expressed views.

> It would be a perfect waste of time to enter into the various and contradictory statements, made both by physicians and lawyers, relative to the real nature of insanity; its characters and criteria; suffice it to say, and we do without the slightest fear of a rationale contradiction, that the general ignorance of the structure and uses of the brain, in a state of health, necessarily prevented all parties, whether medical or not, from making anything more than a very slight approach to the elucidation of those several phenomena which constitute disease.
>
> ...no insane person has every mental faculty diseased. I believe there is not one within the walls of Hanwell, even including the idiotic and fatuous, who does not retain some few powers of the mind...every case of insanity, is more or less partial.

This was a well-deserved bucket of cold water poured over the more extreme opinions that were expressed by those with no real knowledge of insanity.

3. *The Times*

> **6 March 1843** *(extract from a letter to the editor)*
> Sir, If the result of M'Naghten's trial satisfies the end of justice, by proving the moral irresponsibility of the murderer, it undoubtedly leaves the security of Her Majesty's subjects from similar murderous attacks in a very unsatisfactory state ... Is there no responsibility on the part of the relatives in leaving such dangerous lunatics at large?
>
> [Extract from an editorial]
>
> ...in a spirit of humble and honest earnestness...ask those gentlemen to define, for the edification of common-place people like ourselves, where sanity ends and madness begins....
>
> Mr Cockburn laid it down that a man might be mad on one point and sane on all others....
>
> We only want to know for the benefit of simple folks, what in future is to be considered sanity?

Doubtless this question posed in the paper was honestly and openly put, but it was also quite naïve. One thing that the trial had made abundantly clear was that now a new field of human science was opening up and that it concerned a subject that was beyond those who were not educated in this field. Thus the paper's plea for something that "simple folks" would understand was not possible. Science, in all its diverse areas, was then starting on a course away from something "simple folks" could understand.

> **7 March 1843**
> Sir,
> I have in contemplation the accomplishment of a certain pet project, which unfortunately involves some degree of violence in its attainment; I mean, however, to retain beforehand some of the most eminent medical men of the day as witnesses in proof of my monomaniacal possession, and in the meantime I hope, through the assistance of your journal, to ascertain when the public (who I understand considers itself rather outraged

by the acquittal of my friend Mr M'Naghten) are sufficiently tranquillized to render it safe and expedient for a British court of justice and a British jury to reward my perseverance with a comfortable and permanent abode in Bethlem Hospital at the expense of the nation. I confess this latter consideration has much weight with me, as I am at present out of work and have the much more disagreeable alternative of a union workhouse staring me in the face.

I have the honour to remain
Your very insane servant
KILLING IS NO MURDER

No doubt this was intended to be humorous, but was it really worth publishing?

4. *The Morning Post*

8 March 1843

It appeared, by the evidence of Dr. Munro that M'Naughten said, that when Sheriff Bell, of Glasgow, did not relieve him from his persecutors, he would have shot Sheriff Bell as he sat in his Court, if he had had a pistol. Therefore (supposing this to be true), the morbid delusion leading to homicide had nearly reached its climax before Mr. Drummond became M'Naughten's victim. But they who are disappointed at the result of M'Naughten's trial should consider whether, if he were condemned to be hanged for shooting Mr. Drummond, he could now perceive the connection between the punishment and the offence. Would any one wish that a man should be hanged as a dog is hanged, merely to get rid of him, and without grounding the punishment upon the supposition that the culprit is conscious that it comes upon him as a consequence of his crime? If M'Naughten were hanged, would he not, his mind being disordered as it is, contemplate the hanging as the crowning act of his persecutors, just as Dr. Monro said the homicide was the crowning point of his morbid delusion? It is not intended to assert positively that the inability of the man distinctly to connect punishment with his homicidal act should exonerate him from all punishment, but it may be thrown out as a reason why the public should not be disappointed at the acquittal which has taken place. (Extract)

5. An Early (Intolerant) Reaction

The *Morning Post* of 23 January published a letter from "Life for a LIFE".

> The feeling against taking away the life of a fellow creature is so prevalent, that not one person in a hundred will believe that the wretch who attempted, in the high street and in broad daylight, to assassinate Mr. Edward Drummond, will meet with the fate he deserves, if ever murderer deserved execution yet. In one journal, on Saturday, it was stated, "no symptoms of insanity had appeared yet." And the defence offered by the criminal himself already is, that he is mad – conclusive evidence to every man of common sense, that he is, unfortunately too sane.
>
> Sir, I maintain that no individual is safe, if the laws are to be evaded, as in the like cases they have been. Because the man who fired at, or who was supposed to have fired at her Majesty escaped his just and legal due, pray do not let the public continue to imagine that such a dangerous precedent is to nullify the law of the land we live in. That the man fired at Mr. Drummond with intent to kill is as clear a fact as evidence made clear, in the face of which the magistrate remands him a fortnight for further examination! Is the man to have time to perfect his insanity, for really the first attempt has been a terrible failure?

This, no doubt, reflected a widely held view of how the insane should be treated – but it is based on near absolute ignorance of madness.

6. The *State Trials* Essay

The introductory essay to the *State Trials* report of *R v M'Naghten*, contains a sharp dig at a Tory MP for advocating the abolition of a plea of insanity in murder cases. Fortunately, his proposal for reform was ignored by the entire House of Commons:

> With the impulsive energy of his nation, Sir Valentine Blake[12] moved for leave to bring in a bill to abolish the plea of insanity in cases of murder, except where it could be proved that the person accused was publically known and reputed to be a maniac, and not afflicted by partial insanity only, and to ask the House to suspend the standing orders to accelerate the progress of the bill.

> The eagerness of the worthy baronet that not a day's delay might interpose between the danger and the remedy, was baffled by the sad accident of the motion not finding a seconder!

The same essay also condemned the infamous haste with which Bellingham's trial had been organised and the extent to which the judge, Sir James Mansfield, ignored his duty to be impartial in Bellingham's trial.

7. Not the Poet Laureate

M'Naghten's acquittal inspired a piece of doggerel which was widely printed in newspapers, and no doubt widely read, despite its vicious sentiments. That the mainstream newspapers would publish this verse is probably an indication of how widely the sentiments expressed therein might be held – or perhaps how little the public, in 1843, ever considered the plight of those afflicted by mental illness.

> CONGRATULATION ON A LATE ACQUITTAL.
> BY T. CAMPBELL.
> Ye people of England! exult and be glad
> For ye're now at the will of the merciless mad.
> Why, say ye but three authorities reign –
> Crown, Commons, and Lords – You omit the insane!
> They're a privileg'd class, whom no statute controls,
> And their murderous charter exists in their souls.
> Do they wish to spill blood – they have only to play
> A few pranks – get asylum'd a month and a day –
> Then heigh! to escape from the mad-doctor's keys,
> And to pistol and stab whomsoever they please.
> Now the dog has a human-like wit – in creation
> He resembles most nearly our own generation:
> Then if madmen for murder escape with impunity,
> Why deny a poor dog the same noble immunity?
> So, if dog or man bite you, beware being nettled,
> For crime is no crime – when the mind is unsettled.

8. *Punch*[13]

Punch's humour was much admired in the nineteenth century, but in early editions it tended to be rather leaden. However, *Monomaniac Academy* can still raise a smile even today. Making humour out of monomania will no doubt have offended many when these two parodies were produced.

MONOMANIACS

An unfortunate creature was brought up charged with having a mania for splitting open policemen's skulls, without any cause whatsoever. This unhappy individual, for whom every one present felt the deepest commiseration, had broken the heads of two policemen, and threatened to do the same thing for the whole division to which they belonged. The policemen whom the poor fellow had attacked, came into court to give their evidence, and the state of their heads made everyone feel sincerely for the unhappy man, whose state of monomania must be pitiable indeed, to have hurried him into infliction of such extensive injuries as the policemen's heads presented.

The following examination of the prisoner, whose unfortunate condition was the object of general commiseration, was then gone into.

Magistrate – *What induced you to perpetrate this unaccountable piece of violence?*

The prisoner returned no answer

Magistrate – *What books do you read?*

Prisoner (sullenly) – *Boxiana*[14]

Magistrate (shaking his head) – *Poor creature! What an awful condition of monomania he seems reduced to.*

A medical witness was then called

Magistrate – *Be good enough to state to me the result of a professional examination of the unfortunate person at the bar,*

Medical witness – *When I examined him at the station house, I found his eyes fixed but his head rolling about, and, pathologically speaking, I think the action of the cerebellum was increased to a high state of irritation.*

Magistrate (somewhat wonder-struck) – *Go on sir, if you please.*

Medical witness – *The perceptive organs were no doubt a good deal obscured; and this, acting on the moral propensities, added a degree of excitement which was probably local – considering that he came from a public-house – would in my opinion account for what has happened.*

Counsel for the Prisoner – *May not a coagulation of moral agencies existing coequally with a highly inflammatory condition of the muscular fibres, produce such a result as that which is now the subject of inquiry?*

Medical witness (after a few minutes' consideration during which the whole court was in a state of breathless suspense) – *I think it may!*

Magistrate – *Then there is an end to the case. The unhappy man at the bar is a subject of pity, not of punishment.* (To the prisoner) *You will be taken where every comfort will be provided for you. Have you any objection to go!*

The victim of monomania answered mechanically that he had not, and has since been placed in the infirmary, where every indulgence will be granted him, until he is in a fit state to be restored to liberty.

The decision seemed to give perfect satisfaction to everyone, except to the two policemen; but as they are since dead, their dissent can be of little consequence.

The friends of the monomaniac have applied to have him restored to them; and if they give proper assurance that they will take care of him, their request will of course be readily acceded to.

Monomaniac Academy
Bethlem Hospital

Messrs Oxford and Macnaughten beg to announce that they have opened an Academy for the instruction of youth in the art of insanity. This very desirable and necessary acquirement will enable persons who have committed any crime or offended against the laws of their country, to escape punishment. Messrs O. and M'N. beg particularly to address persons who expect to receive legacies or reversions on the death of rich relations; as such parties will be enabled, after receiving a few lessons, to remove all impediments to their fortune. Young gentlemen who are studying the art of picking pockets will also find this a desirable addition to their education; as should they be detected,

> and tried at the Old Bailey, two or three lessons will teach them how to become monomaniacs pro tempore. Terms – One Guinea per lesson.

9. A Dandy's View

Thomas Raikes, dandy, man about town and diarist, was acquainted with most of the men who mattered in London society in 1843. After his death, his diaries were published and widely read. It is a reasonable assumption that his views were not wholly out of tune with his social circle. However important his friends might have been, he showed little understanding of the issues involved with insanity when he wrote about M'Naghten in his journal: "It is feared he will get off on the plea of madness; in which case no man's life will be safe."[15]

Raikes returned to this issue a little later, but regrettably he had understood nothing pertaining to M'Naghten's defence.

> Macnaghten has been acquitted on the plea of insanity. It is a trait of the canting philosophy of the times. The man might have been under the delusion that he was persecuted; but he had sense somehow to waylay his imaginary persecutor, to provide himself with pistols and slay him. Ergo, he shot wilfully and deserved to be hanged. [16]

10. An Unusual Christian View of Punishment

The clergy were not immune from abandoning Christian principles, as shown when the *Times* of 11 March 1843 published an extract from Archbishop Whately's[17] thoughts:

> In fact, although no one considers the brute animals as moral agents, everyone is well aware that it is possible to operate on them through fear of punishment. It is not reckoned an useless cruelty or an absurdity to teach a dog by beating it to abstain from worrying sheep. Anyone therefore who well knowing that irrational animals may be trained by fear of punishment to check their impulses, yet would proclaim impunity to any man who may be partially or wholly reduced to the state of an irrational animal, such as one plainly shows that he is allowing his views to be influenced by irrelevant consideration.
>
> *Archbishop Whately's Thoughts on Secondary Punishments* page 29.

11. A Sane and Unprejudiced Listener

On the same day that Whately's view was published, a much more thoughtful piece appeared in a letter to the *Morning Post* which confirmed that there were voices of reason:

> The sentiments which are going the rounds of the newspapers marking M'Naughten's acquittal to be a dangerous precedent, appear to me to be fraught with much more peril than the acquittal itself! Sir, none can grieve more deeply than I do for the calamity which the public deplore; but it must be far more satisfactory that Mr. Drummond's friends should know that their irreparable loss was not brought about by the determined atrocity of an assassin, but was the result of a delusion under which the mind of the man whose hand struck the blow, had laboured for two years, and which same delusion was the occasion of the most racking torture to the unhappy being himself. Sir, I went to M'Naughten's trial with the conviction that he must and ought to suffer! I listened to every detail of the evidence on both sides, and I narrowly watched the prisoner during the eighteen hours which his trial lasted. (Of him I shall merely say that I never saw absence of mental capacity more strongly marked in any human countenance. He appeared perfectly unaware, even of his acquittal.) I went, certainly believing he deserved hanging and I came away thankful that the dread crime had not been committed by a responsible being, and proud of the fearless and impartial justice which mark the proceedings of a British Court of Law, and which is unequalled in any other country of the world. I saw every vestige of political feeling cast aside, and yet who can say that such feeling did not exist? Aye, and struggled hard in the breasts of many concerned. I saw the horror of the act, the acuteness of private feeling, which reigned paramount in the hearts of the able and learned men, who proved their anxiety to investigate and pursue, to the utmost, every fact which could, by possibility, serve to render the culprit amenable to the law. I even heard it said around me, "the Crown is pushing this prosecution too far." I saw all the natural horror and bias of mind against him who did the deed overmastered by conviction in the minds of administrators of justice, and heard that infallible lawyer, our Solicitor-General, declare that he could

> not ask "the gentlemen of the Jury to find the prisoner guilty, after such incontrovertible evidence had been adduced of his insanity".
>
> *A Sane and Unprejudiced Listener*

12. A Barrister Who Had Faith in the Public

A barrister of Lincoln's Inn, who signed himself simply CM, wrote on 11 March 1843 in the *Morning Post* to suggest a quite reasonable approach to the problem. He was quite clear in his belief that the public would not accept the execution of the insane or partially insane.

> While, however, I admit that monomaniacs are sensible of the salutary effects of example, I do not believe that the public feeling in this country would ever tolerate the execution of an insane or monomaniac criminal; but there is a still higher consideration, and a more anxious feeling in the public mind, and that is, security for the valuable life of the innocent and the sane. There should be, as I began by stating, a serious responsibility attached to the parents or guardians of the unhappy persons labouring under this awful visitation. There should be an authority vested in some competent hands for taking the steps necessary to guard against mischief.[18]

Also on 11 March the *Oxford Journal* added some words of wisdom now the trial was finished:

> Amid the regret we feel for the loss of such a valuable life which has been sacrificed, and the affliction we are under to find an intellect shattered, we yet rejoice that Mr Drummond's life was not taken by a cold-blooded murderer, but has been taken by one who, deprived of reason at the time of his committing the deadly act, cannot be supposed to have been cognizant of the awful act he was at that instance committing. With these few observations we dismiss this melancholy subject from our further consideration.

13. The Columnist

The *Morning Post* of 17 March 1843 in its *Table Talk* column went with a very different view of the public mood towards execution.

The M'Naughten madness affair is one of great painfulness and perplexity. Most people, and sensible people too, think that M'Naughten ought to be most indubitably and effectually hanged; that the doctors whose evidence led to his acquittal ought to be privately whipped; and that the Judge and Jury who tried the accused ought to be reprimanded, and cautioned to be less favourable to the plea of insanity for the future.

This seems to me to be rather too strong a feeling upon the matter. It seems incredible that the fellow could have been acting insanity, though Mr. Guthrie[19] seems to hint a suspicion to that effect. All this, however, is but conjecture. That which is certain in the affair is, that the doctors deposed with astonishing confidence to the state of the man's mind, and to his being beyond the power of moral control. The Jury were sworn to decide according to the evidence; and the Judge (whose sagacity is unquestionable) was satisfied that the insanity to which the doctors deposed was that kind of insanity which, in the contemplation of law, renders a man incapable of legal crime, by which I mean crime according to the legal definition.

Nothing, however, seems to have occurred which should reasonably reconcile the public to such a death-dealing maniac being treated as a person who had done no harm. The very language of the law, which declares such a man as M'Naughten not guilty on the ground of insanity, seems an offence to common sense.

He should be convicted of the fact at all events, and let a conviction of insanity be recorded at the same time, if that fact has been proved. And such a double conviction as this being obtained, it seems but reasonable that the convict should then be sent to some criminal prison, there to be dealt with, as the Judge might direct, according to the circumstances which appeared at the trial. Even madmen, who perpetrate atrocities, should be treated with much more severity than mad men who have been harmless. It would be wrong to hang M'Naughten if there be a serious doubt whether he is capable of understanding the connection between such punishment and the homicide which he committed; but close confinement, with hard work, and a bread and water diet, and no permission to strangers to visit him, might very safely and reasonably be his potion.

It is a mercy that more of his class do not grow as mad and mischievous as he. The lower orders in Scotland are, by the habits of the nation, indulged and encouraged in such an uncontrolled licentious exercise of the reasoning faculty, with, for the most part, so narrow a range of sound knowledge and experience to work upon, that the wonder is that more of them do not strain their minds into madness. To suspect their own judgment is a piece of philosophy which is never taught them. The time was when they had reverence for the Bible, but now they have little reverence for anything divine or human, save their own powers of judging and deciding. I remember in the days when the Rev Edward Irving was remarkable, hearing him pour forth an eloquent lamentation upon the progress of overweening self-confidence among his countrymen. He described with wonderful force their smatterings of science, their magazine literature, and the conceited habit of rash judgment thereby engendered. "This," he said, or rather cried with a loud voice, while he towered in the pulpit, and reared his lone arm into the air above his head," This is what, in the affairs of civil society, is called liberality, and in religion judging for myself. The lower orders of the west of Scotland are always judging for themselves – always disputing – always criticizing – always indulging in the most licentious bitterness of reproach whatever their crude judgments do not approve. If they go to church it is to criticise the prayers and to sit in judgment upon the preaching. Possibly this may sharpen their minds and give them a habit of thinking, which when properly used, is a useful habit; but used with unbridled licentiousness, it an odious habit, which breed ill-humour, strife and much unhappiness. Presbyterianism and absolute independence of judgment, may appear to practical advantage in a rude and thinly people country, where frequent encounters with the awfulness force a sense of reverence upon the mind. But when people congregate in great masses and get the conveniences of mechanical civilization about them, and become separated from the wild simplicity and occasional awfulness of nature, then the bare system of Presbyterianism, and the training to judgment, is found in practice to work ill. If the people have

> prosperity they become stiff-necked and preposterous – their tongue walketh through the earth. If they are touched by adversity, they become sullen, moody, fierce and miserable. If they light upon bad books, they are apt to become infidels, and to go mad and do mischief.

So much bile in one column!

14. Antidotes to Table Talk
The Weekly Chronicle, 11 March 1843

> The plea of insanity was completely made out, as Sir Robert Peel must have known it would be, at the very time he founded on M'Naughten's act a diabolical insinuation against Mr Cobden. Indeed, but for the form, M'Naughten need not have been put on trial, so well assured were all parties in the secret of his insanity.

This was more perceptive than much of the views expressed on M'Naughten.

15. More Balanced Approaches
Oxford Journal, 11 March 1843

> We have carefully looked over the body of evidence adduced to establish [insanity] and perfectly agreeing with the Learned Judge, who thought it proper to stop the case, such was the plea made out, we are glad the original time fixed upon for the trial of the prisoner was departed from, as we feel convinced had not such a departure taken place a conviction for murder would have been the result and the unhappy wretch would have forfeited his life upon the scaffold for the commission of an act the guiltiness of which he was not conscious of, owing to the monomania under which he laboured in respect of certain matters....
>
> Amid the regret we feel for the loss of such a valuable life which has been sacrificed, and the affliction we are under to find an intellect shattered, we yet rejoice that Mr Drummond's life was not taken by a cold-blooded murderer, but has been taken by one who, deprived of reason at the time of his committing the deadly act, cannot be supposed to have been cognizant of

> the awful act he was at that instance committing. With these few observations we dismiss this melancholy subject from our further consideration.

The Scotsman also took a much more balanced approach to the trial and its outcome:

> THE acquittal of M'Naughten has created a great sensation throughout the country; a verdict of guilty of murder was all but universally expected, nay, we may say desired; and the non-gratification of this wish has led to the abuse of the medical witnesses by the press in no very measured terms. This strong condemnation of the "mad doctors" as they are contemptuously styled, implies either that they must be culpably ignorant of the condition of the insane mind – greatly more ignorant of it than those who so unceremoniously denounce them – or that they have been guilty of flagrant perjury….
>
> With every respect for the intelligence of the public, we are constrained to express our conviction, that on the subject of insanity they are still less enlightened than the "mad doctors." As we approve of the verdict, we shall endeavour to express as briefly as possible the grounds of our opinion in its favour. All respectable medical authorities are agreed that insanity is a disease, not of the immaterial soul, but of the brain.[20]
>
> In M'Naughten's case, however, the evidence demonstrated that diseased impressions existed in his mind. These are styled delusions in the evidence; but they indicate diseased feelings. There were suspicions of conspiracies against him, and a fear of enemies. Suspicion and fear are not intellectual but emotional states of the mind. The intellect seems to have been so far enfeebled that it became incapable of detecting their insane character; for M'Naughten, under the belief that the dangers were real, applied to influential persons for protection against them. At the same time, his intellect retained so much of the character of sanity that it dictated to him a course of action which was quite rational, on the assumption that the danger did, as he believed, actually exist. His claims for protection were unheeded. The morbid state of the feelings increased, the destructive propensity

> also seems to have become involved in disease, and the result was the catastrophe for which he was tried. In our opinion, the act of shooting Mr Drummond proved that the feelings had at last completely overpowered the intellectual faculties. There was no rational bond of connection between the impressions and the act which he committed. The act itself is explicable only on the hypothesis of disease. It has been said that "the acquittal of M'Naughten, on the ground of the medical evidence that lie was incapable of self-control, was, in effect, a verdict that he could not help murdering Mr Drummond, and that this is a doctrine of most dangerous example."

16. Everything is Right, Yet Something is Wrong

However, the *Morning Post*[21] returned to the fray with an opinion piece from a medical doctor. He did rather cheapen the debate when he suggested that irresistible impulses accounted for 90 per cent of female shoplifting. While this medical doctor joined others in lamenting that the law did not ensure punishment for the partial insane, he did alight upon one particular valid issue – what is the way forward?

> Learned doctors have come to be so liberal in their interpretations of the mental impulses of criminals that it is almost likely to be much harder, one of these days, to say who is not insane than to say who is. Men of law and men of physic unite in declaring that a "deluded" man must be a demented one, and that the most atrocious of outrages, if perpetrated under the influence of undefined monster, called "morbid delusion," may not subject the perpetrator to the slightest responsibility for purpose either of punishment or of example.
>
> Cases of recent occurrence – more especially the question raised by the slaughter of Mr. Drummond – have turned people's thoughts not a little to the state of law, or, rather to the tendency of the professional theories that govern the decision of juries in criminal lunacy cases. There is one very general feeling – a feeling of discontent and insecurity. Lawyers and "mad doctors," with faces the most profoundly grave, may expatiate on the wisdom of the doctrines that make criminal investigations the mere cat's paw puppets of technical abstractions; they may do

this but men are not the more pleased. It does seem a prima facie case of fraud and absurdity that any individual susceptible of the sensation of fear – that any one capable of understanding the difference between ease [sic] and punishment, be; no matter how devoid of sound moral discrimination and control – should be given to understand (and persons in this situation are often found to understand most thoroughly the fact, and the extent of their immunity), that, commit what deadly crime he may, he is responsible to no authority, and subject to no chastisement. . . .

Noble Legislators, learned in the law, see plainly that in the present system of dealing with the "partially insane" – with the "morbidly deluded" – there is, somewhere or other a glaring violation of good sense. The Lord Chancellor of England says that something must be done – he has a Bill to bring before Parliament. We read the Learned Chancellor's speech – we gather from it that his something is likely to be nothing. The law, he says, is right; the practice of the law is right; and so is its interpretation by the Judges. The mystifying, confounding, labyrinthal "explanations" of the mad doctors – their extraordinary claims of exemptions for varying degrees of eccentricity – all these, says the Chancellor, are quite right; but something is wrong. We shall be glad to know, when Lord Lyndhurst's proposition is before us, where he takes the wrong lie. All that he has yet said leaves our queries as to his meaning in most admired disorder. We are only told that he thinks everything is right, but that something is wrong. Time does wonders, and may, peradventure, elucidate this riddle.

Chapter 11

THE ASYLUMS AND M'NAGHTEN'S DEATH

This chapter was written with an invaluable contribution from Robin Jacoby, Professor Emeritus of Old Age Psychology, Oxford University, on issues of schizophrenia. He has, throughout the work on this chapter, freely given his advice and his participation – for which I have been most grateful.

After his trial ended, M'Naghten, having been found not guilty by reason of insanity, was removed from Newgate Prison by Mr Cope, the governor. Given the determination of the court as to his insanity, M'Naghten could now be transferred to Bethlem Hospital, in St George's Fields.[1] This transfer was made under an order signed by Home Secretary Sir James Graham, pursuant to his powers under the Criminal Lunatics Act 1800. M'Naghten was to remain in Bethlem until 1864.

Bethlem

There was, understandably for the time, considerable criticism of M'Naghten's acquittal. Much of the criticism was against the supposed comfort M'Naghten would receive there at the state's expense. However, the *Times*[2] reported a rather different story:

> He was constantly watched by two turnkeys who were relieved every 12 hours and with these individuals the wretched man at all times entered into conversation with considerable alacrity. He frequently made inquiries as to the political movements which were going on, and manifested great anxiety when in the performance of their duty the officers attempted to evade answering his questions. His excitement when conversing on this subject appears to have impressed all those who were

> brought into contact with him, with a belief that his mind was effected.
>
> His conversation is generally stated to have been extremely interesting, frequently turning on mechanical subjects; but it is a curious circumstance that on only one occasion did he allude to the fearful crime committed by himself, and then only in the most unconcerned manner. He appeared to have no anxiety as to his defence, and saw his solicitor only two or three times.
>
> He was impatient of confinement and would sometimes pace his cell backwards and forwards for half an hour at a time. He slept remarkably well, generally retiring about 10 o'clock and seldom waking during the night. Since his acquittal, he has been visited by his father twice, but no other relative has seen him.

A week after this comment in *The Times*, the *Spectator*[3] also carried an article attempting to bring further balance into the reporting of M'Naghten's situation. The *Spectator* started by quoting Lord Brougham's view that M'Naghten's confinement would be:

> …the next thing to capital punishment…. Many depraved creatures may know little of madhouses beyond what is contained in such paragraphs as the Press issues; and upon their authors, in case it should by their falsehood tempt some destitute wretch to crime, must rest an unenviable accountability. Since the law is not altered – since insanity is still regarded as a pitiable disease to be treated by restraint rather than killing – and since the power of deciding upon its existence is still left to a jury, it should be at the present moment the object of all who sincerely deplore M'Naghten's deed, to paint as vividly as possible all the terrors to which, under the merciful sentence he is doomed.

On M'Naghten's admission to Bethlem, the following information was noted in his record:

> Name .... *Daniel McNaughton*
> Age .... *29 on admission*
> Admission .... *March 13th 1843*
> From whence brought .... *Newgate*

Married, single or widowed	*Single*
How many children	
Age of Youngest	
Whether first attack	
When previous attacks occurred	
Duration of existing attack	
State of bodily health	*Moderate*
Whether suicidal or dangerous to others	*No and No*
Supposed cause	
Chief delusions or indications of insanity	*Imagines the Tories are his enemies: shy and retiring in his manner*
Whether subject to epilepsy	*No*
Whether of temperate habits	*Yes*
Degree of education	*Fair*
Religious persuasion	*Episcopalian*
Crime	*Murder*[A]
When and where tried	*Central Criminal Court* 1843
Verdict of jury	*Found insane*
Sentence	*Her Majesty's Pleasure*

On 18 March, a few days after M'Naghten's admission to Bethlem, he was joined there by James Stevenson, a fellow Scot. M'Naghten made no attempt to talk with Stevenson or, for that matter, any other inmates, preferring instead to talk with the staff. Stevenson, a native of Beltrees, was a religious maniac who sought the removal of Queen Victoria from the throne. This was on the basis that the Scriptures did not support the right of any woman to rule over the country. He was, like other new inmates, held in a cell on the ground floor, like M'Naghten.

> It is not generally known, perhaps, that those committed as criminal lunatics are, on their first admission, confined on the ground floor; and are continued there until a careful observation of their habits and conduct – such as their cleanliness and harmlessness – shall satisfy authorities that it is safe to remove them to the apartments on the first floor, and that if they continue to gain further in the

> confidence of the authorities they are removed to the second floor. Oxford has already attained this envied eminence, and we think we may say, without fear of contradiction, that there is not a man in or about the prison capable of judging, who does not regard him as perfectly sound in his mind on every subject. The same impression prevails as to M'Naughten, though not with the same certainty, as the means of observation have not been of the same duration.[5]

At the same time a Scotsman by the name of M'Coleman was committed to an asylum in Lanarkshire. He claimed that he was M'Naghten's father, which he certainly was not. He threatened, if his wishes were not complied with, to "make skeletons" of all and sundry. M'Coleman was in fact an ex-soldier who had suffered a serious head wound while in the army and the press reported that "since then has never rightly been settled." M'Coleman was another who sought the assassination of Sir Robert Peel. The number of would-be assassins caused the *Glasgow Chronicle* to observe that it was at the time, "somewhat remarkable that so many madmen should at the same time concentrate their notions on one individual and he the Prime Minister of England".

There is one contemporary newspaper description of M'Naghten, on 25 March 1843, very soon after he had arrived in Bethlem:

> We accompanied a party on Tuesday last, and passed through the criminals' exercising ground as the patients entered. Oxford[6] was busily engaged, with three others, in playing fives: and as the recent regulation of the Governors of the hospital precludes the keepers from pointing out any individual among the criminals, he was observed only by those who had previous knowledge of his person. McNaughton was also in the yard but, probably from the novelty of his situation, he appeared ill at ease, and was seated alone, under a covered shed in the centre. As our party entered, he purposely averted his face, seeming anxious to avoid observation, and, fortunately, none were curious enough to intrude upon him further.[7]

On 28 March 1843 the *Morning Post* carried a report about the workings of Bethlem:

> We hear that M'Naghten keeps up no intercourse with his fellow prisoners, but evinces a disposition to get into conversation

> with his keepers. It is not generally known, perhaps, that those committed as criminal lunatics are, on their first admission, confined on the ground floor; and are continued there until a careful observation of their habits and conduct – such as their cleanliness and harmlessness – shall satisfy authorities that it is safe to remove them to the apartments on the first floor, and that if they continue to gain further in the confidence of the authorities they are re-moved to the second floor. Oxford has already attained this envied eminence, and we think we may say, without fear of contradiction, that there is not a man in or about the prison capable of judging, who does not regard him as perfectly sound in his mind on every subject. The same impression prevails as to M'Naghten, though not with the same certainty as the means of observation have not been of the same duration….

There is very little more within the Bethlem records that would help to show the state of M'Naghten's mental health while he was there, but one illuminating description has survived:

> He is a man of so retiring a disposition and so averse to conversation or notice of any kind that it is very difficult even for his attendant to glean from him any information as to his state of mind or the character of his delusions, but one point has been made out that he imagines he is the subject of annoyance from some real or fanciful being or beings; but more than this is not known, for he studiously avoids entering into the subject with any one. If a stranger walks through the Gallery he at once hides in the water closet or in a bedroom and at other times he chooses some darkish corner where he reads or knits. . .[he] imagined that the Tories were his enemies and annoyed him. He has refused food and had been fed with the stomach pump.[8]

It is unfortunate that there are not more such observations recorded later in his time in Bethlem. The above entry, limited though it might be, is helpful in that M'Naghten's behaviour apparently remained very much as it was before his arrest and during his trial. For those who thought that M'Naghten had faked his insanity, this entry suggests quite the opposite. The entry was made eleven years after the trial and his behaviour was consistent with that recorded when he first arrived. In fact, if anything, it shows some further deterioration which would be consistent with the progress of his illness. Henry R. Rollin[9] considered that these observations of M'Naghten led him to conclude:

- M'Naghten still showed evidence of his paranoid delusions;
- He appeared to be emotionally "flat", as the emotional concomitants that were previously associated with his delusions had gone;
- He chose to hide away from human contact (as far as he could within an asylum) and,
- His refusal of food indicated a degree of negativism or stupor.

Rollin concluded his diagnosis:

> The whole clinical picture is therefore consonant with that of severe, chronic schizophrenic illness now affecting every department of the mind. The picture finally gives the lie to the diagnosis of Monomania; there is nothing at all "partial" about his mental disintegration.

A Conversation with M'Naghten

In 1852, there had been another journal article on M'Naghten's psychiatric state:[10]

> M'Naghten was standing in the courtyard, dressed in the costume of the place (a pepper-and-salt jacket and corduroy trousers) with his hat on, knitting. He looks about forty years old, and in perfect health. His features are regular, and their expression is mild and prepossessing. His manner is tranquil. Usually he wears his hat somewhat slouched over his eyes, and sidles slowly away from any one approaching him, as if anxious to escape observation; but on this occasion he at once entered into conversation with our companion, calmly and cheerfully, and afforded us a full opportunity of watching him. Had we seen him casually elsewhere, and as a stranger, we should have thought his countenance indicative of a certain sort of cheerful quiet humour, especially while he was speaking; but to us it seemed to exhibit a feeble intellect, shown chiefly by a faint flickering smile, even when he was speaking on

the gravest subjects. When asked what had brought him where he was, he replied "Fate". "And what is fate?" "The will of God, or perhaps" he added quickly "of the devil – or it may be of both?" and he half closed his eyes and smiled. When told that Sir Robert Peel was dead, he betrayed no emotion, nor exhibited the slightest interest. "One should have thought that, considering what has happened, you would have felt some interest in that gentleman." He looked rather quickly at the speaker, and said, calmly with a faint smile, "It is useless to speak to me on that subject; you know quite well I have long and long ago made up my mind never to say one word about it. I never have and I never will; and so it would be quite childish to put any questions."

"How are you, M'Naghten?" He slightly sighed and said "I am very uncomfortable, I am very ill used here; there is somebody or something always using me ill here. It really is too bad! I have spoken about it many, many times; but it is quite useless. I wish I could get away from this place! If I could just get out of this place and go back to Glasgow, my native place, it is all I would ask for: I should be quite well there! I shall never be well and happy here, for there is always someone ill-using me here." "Well, but what do they do to you?" "Oh" shaking his head and smiling "they are always doing it; really it is too bad". "Who are they?" "Oh, I am always being ill-used here! My only wish now is to get away from this place! If I could only once get to Glasgow, my native place!" This is the continual burthen of his song. It is needless to say that his complaints are altogether unfounded; he is treated with the utmost kindness consistent with his situation; and, as he has never exhibited violence nor ill-behaviour, it has never been necessary to resort to personal coercion, with one exception. Two or three years ago, he took it into his head that, as he could not get away, he would starve himself; and he persevered for such a length of time in refusing all kind of food that he began to lose flesh fast. At length he was told by the physician that, since he would not eat voluntarily, he must be made to eat; and it was actually necessary to feed him for a considerable time mechanically, by means of the stomach-pump. Under this treatment he presently regained his flesh, in spite – as it were – of himself; and at length suffered himself to be laughed out of his obstinacy, and has ever since taken his food voluntarily. He seemed himself to be tickled by

> a sense of the absurdity of which he was guilty. Not a doubt of his complete insanity was entertained by my acute companion, who has devoted much observation to this case. Shortly after we had quitted him, and were out of sight, he put away his knitting, placed his hands in his jacket pockets and walked very rapidly to and fro, his face bent on the ground; and he was somewhat excited. Whatever may have been the state of M'Naghten at the time to which our inquiries have been directed in this article, we entertain little, if any, doubt, that he is now in an imbecile condition.

This article chimes with the 1854 note in the Bethlem records as to M'Naghten's mental decline. It is unfortunate that there is so little further relevant information in M'Naghten's case notes at Bethlem. After the 1854 entry, there are seventy-four entries in the case notes, all of which simply say "No change". It is impossible to accept that these entries were an accurate reflection of M'Naghten's state of health, but probably no one cared much by now. There was a note on his physical condition in January 1863, which recorded ominously "He complains very much of palpitation of the heart and at present is keeping to his bed. Appetite is not good."

Broadmoor Hospital and Death

Broadmoor was a new criminal lunatic asylum that was completed in 1863. Transfers of Bethlem patients to the new establishment started in May 1863. M'Naghten was transferred to Broadmoor on 26 March 1864 and recorded as patient No. 75. He was then aged 50 and in very poor health, quite likely near to death. On 28 March, the only entry in Broadmoor records which touches on his mental health was recorded:

> A native of Glasgow, an intelligent man, states he must have done something very bad or they would not have sent him to Bethlem, gives distinctly the sentence of the Chief Justice – "Acquitted on the ground of insanity, to be confined during Her Majesty's pleasure". When asked whether he now thinks he must have been out of his mind – he replies "Such was the verdict – the opinion of the jury after hearing the evidence." Has been suffering from rheumatism lately. Has an anaemic appearance, ancles [sic] swell a little. Appetite tolerably good, pulse 84, regular.

The following entries in his records were solely concerned with his declining physical health. The final entry in his case sheet is for 3 May 1865: "Gradually sank and died at 1.10 am". M'Naghten was 52 years old.

From *The Times*, 6 May 1865

> The Assassin of Mr Edward Drummond
> On Wednesday (3rd May) an inquiry took place before Mr. Rupert Clarke, coroner for Berks, at the Criminal Lunatic Asylum, Broadmoor, respecting the death of Daniel M'Naughten, who died at that establishment on the same morning. The deceased, by trade a turner, formerly lived in Glasgow, and afterwards proceeded to London, and while there he appears to have been affected in his intellect. On Friday, the 20th of January 1843, he fired twice at Mr. Edward Drummond, private secretary to Sir Robert Peel, who was walking in the street, and who had been pointed out to him as Sir Robert Peel. The wound was fatal, inflicted by the pistol ball which produced fatal results. M'Naughten took his trial at the Central Criminal in the following March, when he was acquitted on the ground of insanity, but the Lord Chief Justice ordered him to be detained during her Majesty's pleasure. He was removed to Bedlam, and subsequently confined in the Criminal Lunatic Asylum at Broadmoor, where his health latterly failed, and it was proved that he died from natural causes. A verdict in accordance with the medical testimony was returned.
>
> (Reprinted from the *Globe*)

The post-mortem information recorded for M'Naghten:

1. He was aged 52;
2. He suffered from chronic mania and dementia;
3. He was in feeble health;
4. The causes of death were reported as: "anaemia, brain disease and gradual failure of the heart's action";
5. His heart was enlarged and all chambers were "filled with colourless gelatinous clots" which were also found in the pulmonary vessels;
6. Gall bladder was extended with gall stones.

There was no reference in this report concerning the diabetes that M'Naghten suffered from and which was noted during his time in Bethlem, although this would have been sure to have helped to weaken his general health. His insanity was described as "chronic mania and dementia", which, applying today's knowledge, would not be correct. The correct diagnosis would today be considered to be schizophrenia.[11]

Schizophrenia

From what mental disorder did Daniel M'Naghten suffer? The classification of mental disorders at the time of Drummond's assassination was somewhat rudimentary and bore little relationship to what we would recognise today. The phenomenology, i.e. the clinical manifestations of the illness as a whole, had been well described, but the understanding of specific mental disorders was less advanced. Thus, phenomena such as delusions, hallucinations and disturbances of mood were well recognised, but the categories into which constellations of symptoms could be fitted were not.

Specific treatment for mental disorders was effectively non-existent, and management consisted of physical control of disturbed behaviour – straight-jackets and other forms of physical restraint, even with chains. In some more enlightened institutions, patients were restrained as little as possible and given things to do, by way of a precursor to modern occupational therapy.

In current terminology, as set out in Henry R. Rollin's chapter in *Daniel McNaughton: His Trial and the Aftermath* (see Bibliography), M'Naghten's disorder was clearly a schizophrenic illness that would today be classified in the International Classification of Diseases 11th Revision (ICD-11) as 6A20 Schizophrenia.[12] In its description of this illness, ICD-11 states:

> Schizophrenia and other primary psychotic disorders are characterised by significant impairments in reality testing and alterations in behaviour manifest in positive symptoms such as persistent delusions, persistent hallucinations, disorganised thinking (typically manifest as disorganised speech), grossly disorganised behaviour, and experiences of passivity and control, negative symptoms such as blunted or flat affect and avolition, and psychomotor disturbances. The symptoms occur with sufficient frequency and intensity to deviate from expected cultural or subcultural norms.

Rollin considered that Alexander Cockburn, M'Naghten's defence counsel, described features of a schizoid personality in his client before his removal to Bethlem. In court, Cockburn spoke of:

> ...gloomy, reserved and unsocial habits...a man of singularly sensitive mind – one who spent his days in incessant labour and toil, and at night gave himself up to the study of difficult and abstruse matters; but whose mind notwithstanding, was tinctured with refinement.

Such traits in adolescence and early adulthood often precede the appearance of florid schizophrenia. Nowadays a schizoid personality would be classified in ICD-11 as 6A22 Schizotypal Disorder. The description from ICD includes:

> Schizotypal disorder is characterised by an enduring pattern (i.e. characteristic of the person's functioning over a period of at least several years) of eccentricities in behaviour, appearance and speech, accompanied by cognitive and perceptual distortions, unusual beliefs, and discomfort with – and often reduced capacity for – interpersonal relationships. Symptoms may include constricted or inappropriate affect and anhedonia.[13] Paranoid ideas, ideas of reference, or other psychotic symptoms, including hallucinations in any modality, may occur, but are not of sufficient intensity or duration to meet the diagnostic requirements of schizophrenia, schizoaffective disorder, or delusional disorder. The symptoms cause distress or impairment in personal, family, social, educational, occupational or other important areas of functioning.

What Positive Features of Schizophrenia Did M'Naghten Show?

Clearly, the homicide of Drummond was primarily motivated by one or more delusions. A delusion is defined as a fixed, false belief of morbid origin that is inconsistent with the believer's cultural or religious background. 'Of morbid origin' in this context means arising from a known or presumed mental disorder. M'Naghten believed he was persecuted by several individuals and organisations who had followed and harassed him everywhere, even when he went abroad, probably in an attempt to escape them. He almost certainly experienced auditory hallucinations and passivity phenomena: the experience of mental and physical integrity being interfered with by external forces. M'Naghten was described by one witness at the trial as getting up at night "uttering incoherent sentences" and "his conversation was not so connected as formerly". This is consistent with 'formal thought disorder', which refers to a disorder in the logical *form* of thinking (as opposed to a disorder in the *content* of thought, as occurs in delusions). A patient with formal thought disorder may initially show a loosening of logical associations that may progress to logical connections at one remove – so-called 'Knight's move' thinking. Eventually, speech or writing may be wholly incomprehensible.

In 1843, the Term Schizophrenia Had Not Yet Been Coined

The diagnosis at M'Naghten's trial given by Dr Thomas Monro, a physician from the Bethlem Royal Hospital, was that of Monomania, a term introduced by the French psychiatrist Esquirol.[14] It seems likely, however, that the particular label was not of interest to the court; and the defence was simply at pains to establish "insanity".

The modern history of schizophrenia dates back to Emil Kraepelin, professor of psychiatry in Munich who, in the last decade of the nineteenth century, in a series of revisions of his textbook *Allgemeine Psychiatrie*, described various types of what he called dementia praecox (precocious dementia) – hebephrenic, catatonic and paranoid. Before describing the Kraepelinian sub-types of schizophrenia, it is important to emphasise that in modern times psychiatrists tend not to use them as set in stone, but consider the clinical manifestations of the patient's illness as a whole. Thus, ICD-11 does not adhere to Kraepelin's classification. The description of the sub-types below uses the present tense to avoid the false implication that such clinical manifestations are no longer encountered. They are indeed, but simply not firmly partitioned from each other.

Hebephrenic schizophrenia, derived from the ancient Greek words for *youth* and *mind* is characterised by formal thought disorder as described above, delusions and hallucinations, usually auditory. Patients often showing inappropriate emotional expression. For example, a young man laughing when told of the death of his mother. In severe cases there is prominent personality deterioration, such that patients are unable to care for their most basic needs. The peak age of onset is about 20 in males and 25 in females.

Catatonic schizophrenia was much more common at the time Kraepelin described dementia praecox than today, when it is uncommon. The condition is characterised by motor manifestations, such as excitement or stupor often with an abnormal posture. Stupor is a technical term meaning a state of inaccessibility without loss of consciousness. A catatonic patient might stand on one leg for hours at a time and not respond to speech or any other interaction.

Paranoid schizophrenia is characterised by prominent delusional beliefs, usually of persecution. The age of onset tends to be later than with hebephrenic schizophrenia, and may be marked with so-called *primary delusions* that emerge from nowhere without any apparent reason, and from which a subsequent complex delusional system may be derived. For example, a patient experienced a primary delusional perception whereby she saw a man wearing a red pullover and became convinced it meant that Soviet spies were out to persecute her. From this she concluded that everything that subsequently happened to her in life was connected to persecution from Russia.

Whilst Kraepelin's clinical descriptions still form a basis for our modern understanding of the disease, schizophrenia is neither dementia, in the modern meaning of the word, nor precocious, in the sense that it comes on only at a young age.

Eugen Bleuler in Zurich was the psychiatrist who introduced the term schizophrenia in 1908. The literal meaning of the term, derived from ancient Greek, means splitting of the mind. However, this has given rise to the entirely erroneous understanding, held by much of today's general public, that patients have a "split personality" as exemplified by Dr Jekyll and Mr Hyde. Schizophrenia should be correctly understood as a disintegration of mental function.

As already mentioned, there was no specific treatment for schizophrenia in M'Naghten's lifetime. His medical records after his acquittal are extremely scant, and we do not know whether he was subjected to any of the interventions, such as bleeding, which the surgeons used when treating poor Mr Drummond. However, there is no evidence, with one exception, from the medical records that he exhibited disturbed behaviour requiring physical restraint.

One account from an article on M'Naghten's behaviour appeared in *Blackwood's Magazine* in 1851 stated: "as he has never exhibited violence nor ill-behaviour, it has never been necessary to resort to personal coercion, with one exception…" This occurred when M'Naghten began to refuse food. He began to lose weight and the hospital responded by force-feeding him via a tube into his stomach. It is not known when this started or for how long it lasted, but there is a reference to it in a Bethlem Hospital note of 21 March 1854. The article in *Blackwood's Magazine* records: "it was actually necessary to feed him for a considerable time mechanically, by means of the stomach pump." It seems that M'Naghten spontaneously resumed eating normally. So, by and large, he was probably left for much of the time to his own devices, but also given things to do as a form of occupational therapy. For example, we know from the *Blackwood's* article that he did spend some of his time knitting.

Modern Treatment

It was not until the 1950s that specific pharmacological treatment for schizophrenia emerged with the arrival of Chlorpromazine. This drug was synthesised first by the French drug company Rhône-Poulenc and was not specifically intended as a treatment of mental disorders, but as an antihistamine for allergies, among other things. It was noted to have sedating effects, and Delay and Deniker at the St Anne psychiatric hospital in Paris were the pioneers who first used it for the treatment of major mental illness, including schizophrenia. Since that time many other drugs with similar neuropharmacological actions have been developed and used to treat schizophrenia. They all act by antagonising the neurotransmitter, Dopamine, in the brain. These drugs have been variously labelled "major tranquillisers, neuroleptics and anti-psychotics", the latter tending to be the term mostly used currently. They are all liable to cause serious unwanted side-effects, but there can be little doubt that they have revolutionised the treatment of schizophrenia. For example, without them, it would not have been feasible to close the large mental hospitals, as happened between the 1970s and the 1990s. Again, without antipsychotics, far fewer sufferers would have been able to return home and lead much more normal lives.

What Would Happen to Daniel M'Naghten Today?

Perhaps psychiatrists would declare him mentally unfit to stand trial, or he would have pleaded guilty to manslaughter on the grounds of diminished responsibility under Section 2 of the Homicide Act 1957. If he were found to have acted with diminished responsibility, the disposal by the court would be the same as if he had been found mentally unfit to stand trial. He would be sent to a secure hospital, such as Broadmoor, or possibly to a medium secure unit, such as exists today at the Bethlem Royal Hospital.[15] The big difference between now and then is that he would have received antipsychotic medication either by agreeing to take it, or by compulsory treatment under the Mental Health Act 2007.

Would He Recover Completely?

Probably not, but his mental state would most likely improve such that auditory hallucinations would remit and formal thought disorder would also either disappear or be less prominent. As to his delusions, they might well undergo what psychiatrists term “encapsulation”. That is to say that they might not disappear altogether, but they would no longer be prominent in his thinking, or lead him to act on them as he did towards Edward Drummond. Encapsulated delusions can sometimes be elicited only with careful mental state examination by a psychiatrist.

Today, Would He Be Confined For the Rest of His Natural Life?

The problem here is the political dimension. Would the government risk the opprobrium of the press and mass media were he released? This is not a question that can be answered. It can, however, be said that, in an ideal world, he would be treated and carefully moved into progressively less secure settings. Then he might be able to apply for release, and his case be reviewed by a tribunal. If that tribunal were to consider him no longer a risk to the public, release under supervision could theoretically happen.

Appendix A

THE HOUSE OF LORDS AND LAW REFORM

Parliamentary Concern

The acquittal of M'Naghten necessarily gave rise to a discussion as to where the law then stood.[1] This took place in the House of Lords on 6 March 1843 and the opening comments were from Lord Brougham. He felt it necessary to see if the Lord Chancellor (Lord Lyndhurst) or the Lord Chief Justice of Queen's Bench (Lord Denman) thought it unnecessary to call for a debate on the state of the law regarding partial insanity. It was unnecessary for him to have raised this point, as it was clear that the state of the law after M'Naghten's acquittal must be addressed by the legislature. Lyndhurst replied that he had already turned his mind to finding out if "anything could be done to remedy this evil." He planned to consult with those who were most likely "to afford correct information upon the subject." This did seem to be a less than enthusiastic response, but Brougham was by now a person that many politicians and lawyers were not enthusiastic about.

Brougham acknowledged Lyndhurst's answer and suggested that Lord Chief Justice Denman would be the person best qualified to undertake this review. Lyndhurst replied that if he had been aware of Brougham's intentions he would have spoken to him earlier. At this point, Lord Denman spoke to explain that he had not yet given any thought to the subject, although he was aware that it would require careful consideration. The distinct lack of enthusiasm on the part of their Lordships seems to indicate a reluctance on their part to face the intricacies of what many regarded, wrongly, as an arcane area of the law,

On 13 March, the House of Lords[2] returned to the issue when Lord Lyndhurst made a long statement about his consultations. The first important point was that as partial insanity took so many forms, any attempt to define partial insanity:

> ...would be altogether futile and that the only course we can pursue is to lay down some general and comprehensive rule, and to leave to those who administer the laws of the country to apply that rule to the different cases as they may arise.

This appears, at first reading, to indicate that the House of Lords intended to pass the buck, to avoid tackling this difficult subject – and there must have been an element of this involved. But, in fairness to their Lordships, it is doubtful that they had sufficient knowledge or experience of partial insanity to produce much that could be useful and practical. The wider medical profession would be in the same position, but really should have been involved (particularly given how important their evidence in M'Naghten's trial was).

What is important to note is that the approach of the House of Lords was intended to be exclusively based on law. Little notice was taken of the overwhelming importance of the medical evidence in the outcome of M'Naghten's trial. It should have been obvious to them that medical evidence was now of paramount importance, and any reform of the judicial process should include this.

The 5 Questions from the Lords

The House resolved[3] that the judges would be asked to consider, collectively, five questions. On 19 June 1843, the judges attended on the Lords and the following questions were put to them:

1. What is the law respecting alleged crimes committed by persons afflicted with insane delusion in respect of one or more particular subjects or persons; as, for instance, where at the time of commission of the alleged crime, the accused knew he was acting contrary to law, but did the act complained of with a view, under the influence of insane delusion, of redressing or revenging some supposed grievance, or injury, or of producing some supposed public benefit?
2. What are the proper questions to be submitted to the jury when a person, alleged to be afflicted with insane delusion respecting one or more particular subjects or persons, is charged with the commission of a crime (murder, for example) and insanity is set up as a defence?

3. In what terms ought the question to be left to the jury as to the prisoner's state of mind when the act was committed?
4. If a person under an insane delusion as to existing facts commits an offence in consequence thereof, is he thereby excused?
5. Can a medical man, conversant with the disease of insanity, who never saw the prisoner previously to the trial, but who was present during the whole trial, and the examination of all the witnesses, be asked his opinion as to the state of the prisoner's mind at the time of the alleged crime, or his opinion whether the prisoner was conscious at the time of doing the act that he was acting contrary to law, or whether he was labouring under any and what delusion at the time?

The First Answer from a Reluctant Mr Justice Maule

One of the judges, Maule J., then gave details of why he felt unable to join with his brother judges in answering the five questions.

- There was no matrix of fact and events on which to consider a point of law.
- As a judge, he would expect to base his opinion on specific circumstances and events.
- Answering points of law, without having specific facts, carried the risk of causing future embarrassment to a court when a future specific case arose in a criminal trial.
- In matters of insanity or partial insanity, Maule J. correctly drew their Lordships' attention to the fact that these were more a question of physiology [sic] rather than law.

Maule J. was showing welcome independence in refusing to follow a course that he thought was both unwise and impractical.

The Findings of the Other 11 Judges

The other judges came up with five answers:

1. *Criminal responsibility of persons labouring under partial delusions*: A person labouring under partial delusions only, and not otherwise insane, who did the act charged with a view, under the influence of insane delusion, of redressing or revenge some supposed grievance or wrong,

or of producing some public benefit, is punishable, if he knew at the time that he was acting contrary to the law of the land. If a party labouring under an insane delusion as to existing facts, and not otherwise insane, commits an offence, he must be considered in the same situation as if the facts in respect to which the delusion exists were real.

2. *Direction to the jury in such cases*: To establish a defence on the ground of insanity it must be clearly proved that, at the time of committing the act, the party accused was labouring under such a defect of reason from disease of the mind as not to know the nature and quality of the act he was doing, or if he did know it, that he did not know that what he was doing was wrong. If the accused was conscious that the act was one which he ought not to do, and if that act was at the same contrary to the law of the land, he is punishable.
3. *Evidence*: *Medical witnesses present at the trial*: Where the defence of insanity is set up, a medical witness who never saw the prisoner before, but was present during the whole of the trial, cannot, in strictness, be asked his opinion of the state of the prisoner's mind at the time of the alleged crime; or whether the prisoner was conscious at the time of doing the act that he acting contrary to law; or whether he was labouring under any and what delusion at the time. Such questions involve the determination of the truth of the facts deposed to, which it is for the jury to decide. But where the facts are admitted or not disputed, and the question becomes one of science only, such questions may be allowed to be put in that general form, though this cannot be insisted on as a matter of right.
4. *Right of the House of Lords to consult the judges*: The judges cannot be required by the House of Lords to give their opinion upon a bill not yet passed into law, but may be called on to assist the House by giving their opinions on abstract questions of existing law.[4]

Chief Justice Tindal then presented an agreed statement of the other eleven judges:

> …her Majesty's judges…have forborne entering into any particular discussion upon these questions, from the extreme and almost insuperable difficulty of applying those answers to cases in which the facts are not brought judicially before them. The facts of each particular case must of necessity present themselves with endless variety, and with every shade of difference in each case; and it is their duty to declare the law upon each particular case, on

> facts proved before them, and after hearing argument of counsel thereon, they deem it at once impractical, and at the same time dangerous to the administration of justice, if it were practicable, to attempt to make minute applications of the principles involved in the answers given by them to your Lordships' questions.

The Views of the Eleven Judges

The answer to the 1st question:

> …we are of opinion that, notwithstanding the party accused did the act complained of with a view, under the influence of insane delusion, of redressing or revenging some supposed grievance or injury, or of producing some public benefit, he is nevertheless punishable according to the nature of the crime committed, if he knew at the time of committing such crime that he was acting contrary to law; by which expression we understand your Lordships to mean the law of the land.

The answer to the 2nd and 3rd questions:

> ….jurors ought to be told in all cases that every man is to be presumed to be sane, and to possess a sufficient degree of reason to be responsible for his crimes, until the contrary be proved to their satisfaction; and that to establish a defence on the ground of insanity, it must be clearly proved that, at the time of the committing of the act, the party accused was labouring under such a defect of reason, from disease of the mind, as not to know the nature and quality of the act he was doing; or, if he did know it, that he did not know that what he was doing what was wrong.*
>
> The mode of putting the latter part of the question to the jury on these occasions has generally been, whether the accused at the time of doing the act knew the difference between right and wrong:

* The underlined passages above are those that became generally applied and are regarded as the core of the test. However, as formulated in this rather unconventional way, it took time to settle on this expression of the test.

> which mode, though rarely if ever, leading to any mistake with the jury, is not, as we conceive, so accurate when put generally and in the abstract, as when put with reference to the party's knowledge of right and wrong in respect to the very act with which he is charged. If the question were to be put as to the knowledge of the accused solely and exclusively with reference to the law of the land, it might tend to confound the jury, by inducing them to believe that an actual knowledge of the law of the land was essential in order to lead to a conviction; whereas the law is administered upon the principle that every one must be taken conclusively to know it, without proof that he does know it. If the accused was conscious that the act was one which he ought not to do, and if that act was at the same time contrary to the law of the land, he is punishable; and the usual course therefore has been to leave the question to the jury, whether the party accused had a sufficient degree of reason to know that he was doing an act that was wrong: and this course we think is correct, accompanied with such observations and explanations as the circumstances of each particular case may require.

The answer to the 4th question:

> …we think he must be considered in the same situation as to responsibility as if the facts with respect to which the delusion exists were real. For example, if under the influence of his delusion he supposes another man to be in the act of attempting to take away his life, and he kills that man, as he supposes, in self-defence, he would be exempt from punishment. If his delusion was that the deceased had inflicted a serious injury to his character and fortune, and he killed him in revenge for such supposed injury, he would be liable to punishment.

The answer to the 5th question:

> …we think the medical man, under the circumstances supposed, cannot in strictness be asked his opinion in the terms above stated, because each of those questions involves the determination of the truth of the facts deposed to, which it is for the jury to decide, and the questions are not mere questions upon a matter of science, in

> which case such evidence is admissible. But where the facts are admitted or not disputed, and the question becomes substantially one of science only, it may be convenient to allow the question to be put in that general form, though the same cannot be insisted on as a matter of right.

The Reaction of the Lords

Lord Brougham thought that the answers from the eleven judges were presented in a "very able" manner. He also seemed anxious to ensure that it was understood that there was a precedent for asking judges to answer questions without argument by counsel. Lords Campbell, Cottenham, Wynford and Lyndhurst all agreed with the ability of the House of Lords to call on the judges for opinions in abstract on a point of law, but this right did not extend to asking for views on proposed legislation.

The Legal Position Created by the Advice of the Judges

From two passages in the answers to question 2 and 3, the so called M'Naghten Rules came to be expressed as:

> Every man is to be presumed to be sane, and to possess a sufficient degree of reason to be responsible for his crimes, until the contrary be proved to their satisfaction; and that to establish a defence on the ground of insanity, it must be clearly proved that, at the time of the committing of the act, the party accused was labouring under such a defect of reason, from disease of the mind, as not to know the nature and quality of the act he was doing; or, if he did know it, that he did not know he was doing what was wrong.
>
> If the accused was conscious that the act was one which he ought not to do, and if that act was at the same time contrary to the law of the land, he is punishable; and the usual course therefore has been to leave the question to the jury, whether the party accused had a sufficient degree of reason to know that he was doing an act that was wrong.

Appendix B

ASSASSINATION

Assassination is generally thought of, within Britain, as being a very un-British crime. As has already been mentioned in the main text, the urge to assassinate was more frequent in the nineteenth century than is often supposed. With British influence extending widely across the then known world, there were many British officials who were seen as targets for those who sought to challenge British power or dominion. There were also those within Britain who resorted to assassination, often against the monarchy.

The names set out below give an indication of some of the more important assassinations and attempted assassinations connected with Britain in the nineteenth century.

The names in **bold** denote deaths.

Year	Target/Where	Assassin	Punishment
1800	George III (London)	Sergeant Hadfield	Insane
1801	**Pemulwuy, aboriginal leader** (New South Wales)	Henry Hacking, following NSW Governor's orders, for Pemulwuy to be taken dead or alive (i.e. without trial)	none
1802	King George III (London)	The Despard Conspirators	**7 executed**
1810	Ernest, Duke of Cumberland (St James's, London)	John Sellis	Committed suicide
1812	**Spencer Perceval MP Prime Minister** (Lobby of House of Commons)	**John Bellingham**	**Executed**, but most likely insane

Year	Target/Where	Assassin	Punishment
1812	**Emmanuel de Launay, Comte d'Antraigues and his wife** (Barnes)	**Lorenzo, a servant**	Committed suicide
1817	George, the Prince Regent (the Mall near Carlton House). In January, the Prince Regent attended the Houses of Parliament for the formal opening of the new session of Parliament.	Not identified	None
1818	Duke of Wellington (Paris)	Cantillon, a French soldier	No action taken
1818	Lord Palmerston (London)	Lieutenant Davies	Insane
1820	The entire government Cabinet (London)	The Cato Street Conspiracy	**5 sentenced to hanging and beheading** and 3 transported for life
1831	**Thomas Ashton** Mill owner's son	**Mosely brothers**	**Executed**
1832	King William IV (Ascot)	Dennis Collins	Execution commuted to transportation for life
1833	**Nathaniel Sneyd,** Irish politician (Dublin)	John Mason	Insane
1833	**Lieutenant Colonel J.M. Coombs** (Palaveram now part of Chennai, India)	**Sergeant Emam Ally**	**Executed**
1835	**William Fraser Commissioner, Delhi territory**	**Kureem Khan & Frozepur Jhirka**	**Both hanged**
1839	**Hector Graham-Toler, 2nd Earl of Norbury** (Durrow, Ireland)	Unknown	None
1840	Queen Victoria (Hyde Park)	Edward Oxford	Insane

Year	Target/Where	Assassin	Punishment
1840	**Lord William Russell** (Norfolk St (now Dunraven St), London)	**Francois Benjamin Courvoisier** (Swiss valet)	**Executed** (before a 40,000 crowd)
1841	Henry Grey, Viscount Howick MP (later 2nd Earl Grey)	Unknown	None
1841	**Sir Alexander Burnes, Resident Political Officer (Kabul)** and **Sir William MacNaghten, Political Agent (Kabul)** (also killed were **women, children** and **servants of Burnes** and **MacNaghten)**	Afghan mob	None
1842	Queen Victoria (The Mall and Constitution Hill)	John Francis (two attempts)	Transportation for life
1842	Queen Victoria (The Mall)	John William Bean	18 months hard labour
1843	**Edward Drummond** (Charing Cross)	Daniel M'Naghten	Insane
1849	Queen Victoria (Constitution Hill))	William Hamilton	7 years transportation
1850	Queen Victoria (Piccadilly)	Robert Pate	7 years transportation
1851	**Captain James Milne, Bombay Army, Deputy Commissary-General**	**Name unknown**	**Killed**
1852	Sir Robert Peel, 3rd Baronet MP (Tamworth)	Election mob of Whig supporters	None arrested
1853	**Lieutenant Colonel Mackeson, Deputy Commissioner, Peshawar**	**Local petitioner**	**Executed**
1857	Rt. Hon. Robert Lowe (Kidderminster)	Rioters	none
1858	**Mr Page, Acting British Vice Consul** (Jeddah) (also killed were **his wife** and **children** and **the French Consul** with **his wife and children)**	**Religious riot**	none

Year	Target/Where	Assassin	Punishment
1858	Mr Fonblanque, British Consul-General (Belgrade)	Turkish soldier	None known
1860	**Walter Plowden, British Consul, Massawa (**Gondor, Ethiopia)	**Stabbed by Ethiopian rebels**	None known
1861	Rutherford Alcock KCB, British Consul-General (Japan)	**Japanese ronin**	**At least four attackers killed** and seven wounded
1864	**Major G.W. Baldwin** and **Lieutenant R.N. Bird 20th Reg. of Foot**	**Unknown**	None known
1865	**G.W. Gordon, magistrate and politician** and **Paul Bogle, deacon and civil rights activist**	**Both unlawfully executed by British authorities in Jamaica**	none
1868	Prince Alfred, Duke of Edinburgh (Clontart, Sydney)	**Henry O'Farrell**	**Executed**
1868	Sir Harry Parkes, Envoy Extraordinary, Minister Plenipotentiary and Consul General, (Japan)	**3 Japanese Swordsmen**	**Killed**
1870	**Edward Herbert, Secretary, British Legation** (Athens)	Greek brigands	Unknown
1870	**G.J.W. Hayward, explorer**	**Unknown**	Unknown
1871	**John Norman, Acting Chief Justice,** (Calcutta High Court)	**Shot by Indian patriot**	**Executed**
1871	**John Coleridge Pattison, Bishop of Melanisia** (Soloman Is.)	**Nukapo Islanders**	Not known
1872	**Richard Bourke, 6th Earl of Mayo and Viceroy of India** (Port Blair, Andaman Is.)	**Stabbed by Sher Ali Afridi**	**Executed**

Year	Target/Where	Assassin	Punishment
1872	Queen Victoria (Outside Buckingham Palace)	Arthur O'Connor	Whipping and 1 year in jail.
1874	Colonel Robert Phayre, British Resident Baroda	Maharajah of Baroda (arsenic)	Deposed and exiled
1875	**Commodore James Goodenough RN**	**Poisoned arrow, Santa Cruz Islands**	None
1875	**Augustus Margary, British Diplomat** (Bhamo, China)	**Unknown**	None
1876	**Sir Henry Abbott, German Consul,** (Thessaloniki)[1]	**Killed in religious riot**	None
1878	**William Clements, 3rd Earl of Leitrim** (Cratlagh, Donegal)	**Unknown**	None
1878	**Charles Ogle, *Times* reporter** (Mount Pelion)	**Orders of Amouss Aga commander of Turkish army**	None
1879	**Major Sir Pierre Louis Napoleon Cavagnari, British representative** (Kabul)	**Members of Afghan Army**	None
1879	Robert Bulwer-Lytton, Earl of Lytton, Viceroy and Governor-General of India	Buss	Insane
1880	**William de Montmorency, 5th Viscount Montmorres** (Galway)	**Unknown**	None
1882	Queen Victoria (Windsor Station)	Roderick MacLean	Insane
1882	**Lord Frederick Cavendish, Chief Secretary for Ireland** and **Thomas Burke, Permanent Under-Secretary, Irish Office** (Phoenix Park, Dublin)	**Tim Kelly and others**	**Executed**
1882	Mr Cookson, British Consul, (Alexandria)	Riot	None

Year	Target/Where	Assassin	Punishment
1885	**Major-General Charles Gordon CB** (Khartoum)	**Sudanese rebels**	None
1885	**John Hannington, Bishop of Eastern Equatorial Africa**	**On orders of Mwanga II**	None
1897	**Walter Charles Rand, Plague Commissioner Pune** and **Lieutenant Charles Ayerst**	**Damodar Hari Chapekar, Balkrishna Hari Chapekar, Vasudeo Hari Chapekar, Mahadev Vinayak Ranade** and **Sathe**	**None**
1900	Edward, Prince of Wales (Brussels-North Railway Station))	Jean Baptiste Spirido	Too young under Belgian law to stand trial

This list represents only some of the British figures assassinated during the nineteenth century. There were many more, often holding lesser positions, who were assassinated, particularly within the Empire's territories and in Ireland. However, this list is sufficient to support my point that assassination of British figures was more common in the nineteenth century, than is often supposed.

Blue Plaques?

London has well-developed systems for identifying and celebrating places where notable residents of London have lived. It seems to me to be odd, and a bit disrespectful, that London is not prepared to acknowledge those in political offices who were assassinated in London. Spencer Perceval, the only British prime minister to have been assassinated, has a plaque in the lobby of the House of Commons,[2] but there is no plaque for Drummond in Whitehall, nor where he lived in Lower Grosvenor Street. When considering this issue further it is worth noting that those listed below were politicians who were assassinated and had connections with London.

1. **Sir Richard Lyons** PC MP London merchant, financier, monopolist who was beheaded at ***Cheapside*** on **14 June 1381** during the Peasants' Revolt.

2. **Sir Robert Hales,** Lord High Treasurer, was beheaded on **14 June 1381** on ***Tower Hill*** during the Peasants' Revolt.
3. **Simon of Sudbury,** Archbishop of Canterbury and Lord Chancellor of England, was beheaded on ***Tower Hill*** during the Peasants' Revolt on **14 June 1381.**
4. **Sir John Cavendish,** Chief Justice of the King's Bench was beheaded at ***Bury St Edmunds*** on **15 June 1381** during the Peasants' Revolt.
5. **Sir John Ipstones** MP, a quarrelsome Staffordshire MP, was murdered by Roger Swynnerton near ***Charing Cross*** in **February 1394**.
6. **James Fiennes,** 1st Baron Saye and Sele and his son-in-law **William Cromer**, deputy-sheriff of Kent were handed over to rebels during Jack Cade's rebellion. Fiennes was beheaded by a mob in ***Cheapside*** **4 July 1450** and **Cromer** was executed the same day outside the ***City walls***. Their heads were then paraded through the street of London.
7. **Thomas Thorpe,** Speaker of the House of Commons, escaped from imprisonment in the Tower of London, but he was beheaded by a London mob at ***Harringay*** on **17 February 1461**.
8. **William Catesby,** Speaker of the House of Commons, was summarily executed after capture at ***Bosworth Field*** on **25 August 1485**.
9. **Robert Pakington** MP, was shot outside the Mercers' chapel in ***Cheapside*** on **13 November 1536.** The assassin was never identified. This is thought to have been the first murder in London by a firearm.
10. **Fulke Greville**, 1st Baron Brooke MP was murdered by a servant in his house in ***Holborn*** on **30 September 1628**.
11. **Thomas Thynne** MP murdered in ***Pall Mall*** by Charles George Borosky, **12 February 1681**.
12. **Spencer Perceval** KC MP for Northampton and Prime Minister, assassinated in the ***House of Commons*** Lobby by John Bellingham, **11 May 1812**. There is a memorial plaque in the Lobby.
13. **Edward Drummond.**
14. **Lord Frederick Cavendish** MP, Chief Secretary for Ireland, murdered in ***Phoenix Park, Dublin***, **6 May 1882**.
15. **Field Marshal Henry Wilson**, former CIGS assassinated by the IRA outside his house in ***Eaton Square*** on **22 June 1922**.
16. **Sir Michael O'Dwyer** was shot in ***Caxton Hall, Westminster*** on **13 March 1940**. He was shot by Udham Singh, an Indian freedom fighter, because of his role in the Amritsar Massacre, 1919.

17. **Ross McWhirter,** right-wing political activist (and co-author of the *Guinness Book of Records*) was assassinated in ***Bush Hill Park***, Enfield, North London on **27 November 1975**, by two IRA members of the Balcombe Street Gang.
18. **Airey Neave** DSO MC TD MP, murdered at the ***House of Commons*** by an IRA bomb placed in his car on **30 March 1979**.
19. **Robert Bradford** MP died on **14 November 1981** at a constituency meeting in a community centre, when he was shot by an IRA gunman (who also shot the caretaker of the centre).
20. **Sir Anthony Berry** MP Conservative Deputy Chief Whip died on **12 October 1984** at the bombing of the ***Grand Hotel Brighton*** (MP for Enfield South).
21. **Donald Kaberry, Baron Kaberry of Adel,** a former Conservative MP who retired in 1983. He was seriously injured in the IRA bombing of the ***Carlton Club*** in 1990 and **died on 13 March the following year**.
22. **Jo Cox**, MP for Batley and Spen, was assassinated on **16 June 2016** outside the library in ***Birstall*** shortly before her constituency surgery. She was killed by a constituent who held extreme right-wing views.
23. **David Amess,** MP for Southend West, stabbed on **15 October 2021 outsid**e Belfairs Methodist Church Hall ***Leigh on Sea.*** The assassin was Ali Harbi Ali.

All the above are connected with London in that they were killed in London, were London MPs (with the exception of Catesby), or had strong, usually political connections with London. Please note that this list is representative, rather than exhaustive, and additional names could be added with further research.

Appendix C

DANIEL M'NAGHTEN'S DISCHARGE PAPERS FROM BETHLEM HOSPITAL

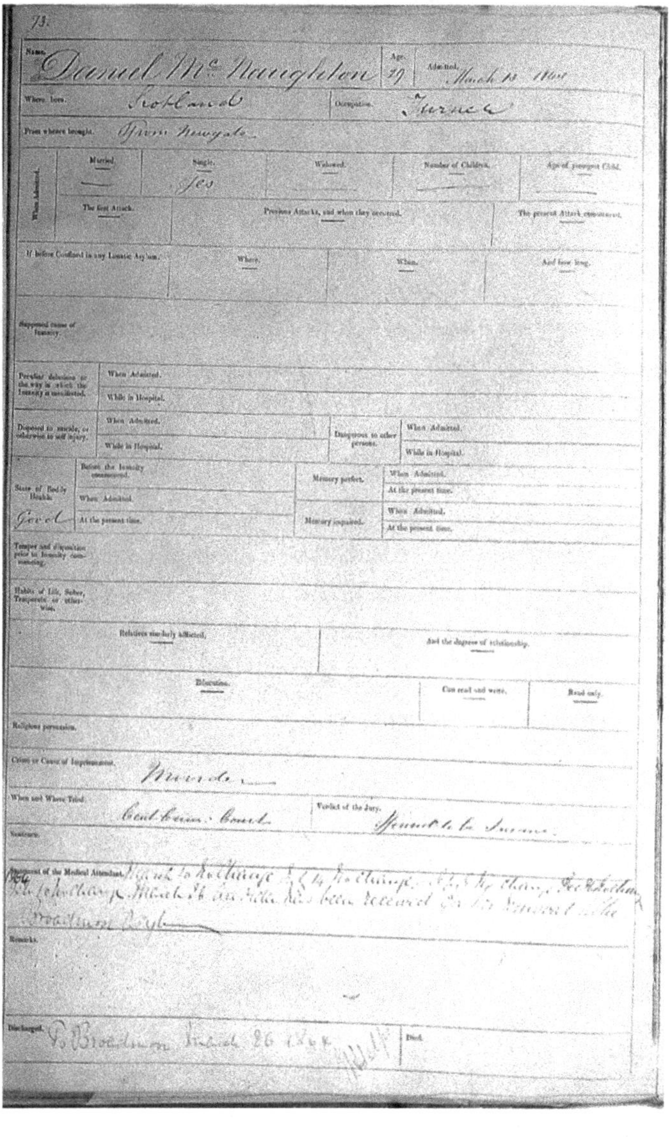

73.

Name. Daniel Mc Naughton — Age. 29 — Admitted. March 13 1843

Where born. Scotland — Occupation. Turner

From whence brought. From Newgate

When Admitted. Married. — Single. Yes — Widowed. — Number of Children. — Age of youngest Child.

The first Attack. — Previous Attacks, and when they occurred. — The present Attack commenced.

If before Confined in any Lunatic Asylum. — Where. — When. — And how long.

Supposed cause of Insanity.

Peculiar delusions or the way in which the Insanity is manifested. — When Admitted. — While in Hospital.

Disposed to suicide, or otherwise to self injury. — When Admitted. — While in Hospital. — Dangerous to other persons. — When Admitted. — While in Hospital.

State of Bodily Health. Good — Before the Insanity commenced. — When Admitted. — At the present time. — Memory perfect. When Admitted. At the present time. — Memory impaired. When Admitted. At the present time.

Temper and disposition prior to Insanity commencing.

Habits of Life, Sober, Temperate or otherwise.

Relatives similarly afflicted. — And the degree of relationship.

Education. — Can read and write. — Read only.

Religious persuasion.

Crime or Cause of Imprisonment. Murder

When and Where Tried. Cent Crim. Court — Verdict of the Jury. Found to be Insane.

Sentence.

Statement of the Medical Attendant. 1864 [illegible] has been [illegible] Broadmoor [illegible]

Remarks.

Discharged. To Broadmoor March 26 1864 — Died.

March 21st 1854. He is a man of so retiring a disposition and so averse to conversation or notice of any kind that it is very difficult even for his Attendant to glean from him any information as to his state of mind or the character of his delusions, but one point has been made out that he imagines he is the subject of annoyance from some real or fanciful being or beings; but more than this is not known for he studiously avoids entering into the subject with any one. If a stranger walks through the gallery he at once hides in the water closet or in a bedroom and at other times he chooses some darkish corner where he reads or knits. His crime created great commotion at the time. In mistake for the late Sir Robert Peel he shot Mr Drummond as he was going into the Treasury or some Government Office and at that time imagined that the Tories were his enemies and annoyed him. He has refused food and been fed with the stomach pump.

July 26th No change
Sept 30th No change
Dec 2nd No change
1855 Jany 24th No change March 2 No change
May 17 No change June 27 No change
Augt 9 No change. Sept 15 No change
Oct 31 No change. Dec 12 No change
1856 Jan 23 No change. March 17 No change
April 28 No change June 12 No change
Augt 4 No change. Sept 16 No change
Nov 3 No change Dec 16 No change
1857 Jany 22 No change. March 9 No change
April 20 No change June 9 No change
July 11 No change Augt 24 No change
Sept 23 No change. Oct 27 No change
Nov 23 No change Dec 22 No change
1858 Jany 29 No change Feb 27 No change
March 29 No change May 3 No change
June 2 No change July 8 No change
Augt 2 No change Sept 7 No change
Oct 4 No change Nov 8 No change
Dec 21 No change.
1859 Jany 31 No change. March 3 No change
April 13 No change. May 26 No change
July 12 No change. Augt 7 No change
Sept 27 No change. Oct 17 No change
Nov 15 No change. Dec 20 No change
1860 Jany 30 No change. March 14 No change
April 17 No change. May 22 No change
July 9 No change. Augt 13 No change
Sept 10 No change. Oct 14 No change
Nov 5 No change Dec 20 No change
1861 Jany 28 No change March 6 No change
April 15 No change. May 21 No change
July 10 No change. Augt 29 No change
Oct 8 No change. Nov 9. No change.
Dec 11 No change.
1862 Jany 27 No change. March 26 No change
May 6 No change. June 10 No change.
July 21 No change. Sept 9 No change.
Oct 12 No change.
1863 Jany 31 He complains very much of palpitation of the heart and at present is keeping his bed. Appetite is not good.
Feb 24 In much the same state.

ENDNOTES

Author's Preface

1. *The Plea of Insanity in Criminal Cases*, Boston Med. Surg. 1843: 29:14-18 ("...*excited more attention than any other of modern times*...").
2. Compiled during the third to sixth centuries. The quotation is from the *Babylonian Talmud: Tractate Baba Kamma* Folio 87a.

Chapter 1: A Dinner at Windsor Castle

1. Her Coronation was one year later.
2. *Letters of Queen Victoria Vol 1* (1837–1843), 20 January 1843.
3. At this stage nothing had been established as to the path the bullet took through Drummond's body
4. Edward Oxford (1840), John William Bean (1842) and John Francis (1842), who made two attempts. There would be eight unsuccessful assassination attempts during her reign, by seven different assassins.
5. He was a colonel in the Scots Fusilier Guards (previously the 3rd Foot Guards).
6. The contemporary style for this and many other streets was Lower Grosvenor Street.
7. *Queen Victoria's Journals*, 20 January 1843.
8. This news, important as it was, could not travel rapidly any distance, as there was not, as yet, a readily available national telegraph service.
9. This was long before a British prime minister would have been accompanied by bodyguards as a matter of course.
10. Launched on 1 January 1785 as *The Daily Universal Register* the title was changed on 1 January 1788 to *The Times.*
11. The youngest son of Francis, Duke of Saxe-Coburg-Saalfeld. He married Princess Charlotte of Wales, and took British citizenship in 1816. Charlotte died after 18 months of marriage. He was offered the throne of newly

independent Belgium and accepted in July 1831. Queen Victoria was his niece and remained close to him.

12. Letter of 10 February 1843 to Queen Victoria.
13. There were five sons born to Peel and his wife, Lady Julia. Four of them had distinguished careers:
    Sir Robert Peel 3rd Baronet GCB PC MP was chief secretary for Ireland (1861–1865). Sir Frederick Peel KCMG PC MP was a Liberal politician and railway commissioner. Captain Sir William Peel VC KCB distinguished himself in the Crimean War and the Indian Mutiny. He died of smallpox aged 33. Arthur Peel PC 1st Viscount Peel MP was a Liberal politician and Speaker of the House of Commons.
14. *The Times*, 23 January 1843

Chapter 2: The State of Britain in 1843

1. *Liberty Equality Fraternity*. The start of the French revolution is usually reckoned to have been 5 May 1789 and its end to have been 9 November 1799 (The Coup of Brumaire).
2. Henry Thomas Cockburn of Bonaly (1779–1854), lawyer, judge, solicitor general for Scotland (1830–1834) and author.
3. (1729–1797), economist, philosopher and initially a Whig. Later in life his opposition to the French Revolution led him to develop more conservative views.
4. Paine fled to France to avoid arrest in England on a charge of seditious libel. He was tried and convicted *in absentia*. He never returned to Britain.
5. On the island of Sumbawa, part of present-day Indonesia.
6. The Tambora eruption had between 4 and 10 times more energy than the more well-known eruption of Krakatoa in 1883 in the same region.
7. On the island Luzon in the Philippines.
8. The figures usually given for civilian causalities are 18 dead and estimates of the wounded range from 400 to 700. It is not known how many died later from their wounds.
9. (1795–1881) Scottish philosopher, historian and man of letters.
10. Properly, the Representation of the People Act 1832.
11. This replaced the Poor Law 1601.
12. And Charles Dickens (see *Oliver Twist*, 1838).
13. Enfranchisement of women on equal terms with men was realised in Britain in 1928.

14. In 1841 the Manchester and Leeds Railway crossed the Pennines, the Great Western Railway completed its line from London to Bristol, the London and Brighton Railway opened throughout its route and Thomas Cook ran his first excursion (Leicester to Loughborough) for a Temperance rally.
15. As illustrated by the Welsh pioneer Pryce Pryce-Jones and the development of his business into the first mail-order company.
16. It also provided much work for the Bar as each new railway proposal required Parliamentary approval and the merits and demerits of each proposed line were argued before Parliamentary committees by a select group of members of the Bar.
17. This word derived from the workmen who built the eighteenth century canal network. An alternative name for canal was a navigation. Navvy describing a workman working on the navigations and, later on, railways, was a contraction of navigation.
18. 1839 *Nemesis*, a British ocean-going iron warship was launched at Birkenhead for the East India Company. HMS *Tartarus* was launched in 1834, the first Royal Navy warship powered by steam.
19. Within Christian Millennialism, there was a belief that the Kingdom of God on earth was close at hand. Most of the belief was derived from the Book of Revelations, in particular Revelation 20.
20. The court was unable to commit Hadfield to confinement, as the law then contained no provision for an acquitted lunatic to be confined. Hadfield was held, without authority, pending the passing of the Criminal Lunatics Act 1800. Hadfield was then confined in Bethlem until his death in 1841. He had escaped in 1802, but was caught and sentenced to 14 years in gaol. While in Bethlem, Hadfield killed Benjamin Swain, by punching him – this was held to be an accident. A better side of his nature was to be found in his care for pets. He also wrote and sold illustrated poems.
21. Character evidence was given on Despard's behalf by Horatio Nelson who had become acquainted with Despard when they were both serving in the Caribbean.
22. Henry John Temple, 3rd Viscount Palmerston (1784–1865) who was twice prime minister and three times foreign secretary.
23. Some reports said "backside".
24. Then Robert Jenkinson, later 2nd Earl Liverpool (1770–1828).
25. One of the members of this government was the Duke of Wellington (Master-General of the Ordnance).

26. One of those executed was William Davidson. He was the illegitimate son of Robert Sewell, the attorney general of Jamaica and a black woman. After a chequered career, he became involved in this conspiracy. When the police captured the conspirators Davidson was armed with a blunderbuss. As he had been armed during the fight with the police, Davidson was executed.
27. Introduced by William Pitt the Younger in his December 1798 Budget to raise £10m, but in its first year produced only around £6m. The rates were 2d in the £ on incomes over £60p.a. rising to 2/- in the £ on incomes over £200p.a.
28. (1757-1844) later 1st Viscount Sidmouth. His low standing as a prime minister was reflected in the then current rhyme – "Pitt is to Addington as London is to Paddington" – which was attributed to George Canning (1770–1827). Addington left office after 119 days (which was the shortest tenure of any prime minister until the administration of Liz Truss, which lasted 45 days in 2022).
29. This led to the return of Pitt as prime minister and Addington being sent to the House of Lords.
30. The tax was at a rate of 7d in the £ on incomes over £150 pa. Income tax has remained a permanent feature of British taxation ever since.
31. An estimated 1,600 slave ships were seized in this way, resulting in preventing some 150,000 Africans being taken for slavery.
32. (1762–1812) He is the only British prime minister to have been assassinated.
33. 29 January 1843 p.3.
34. 4 February 1843 p.2.

Chapter 3: The Victim

1. The link between goldsmiths and bankers was not uncommon in the early 1700s. Those who held gold for their businesses, required a higher degree of security than most other businesses could afford. Therefore, bankers often sought, for a payment to the goldsmith, to use the greater security available from a goldsmith's premises. However, as the banks grew and needed to hold larger sums for their clients, it became much more convenient for the banks to provide security to their customers, as well as holding their own assets in their own, increasingly secure, safes and strong-rooms.
2. *Morning Post*, 31 January 1843 (reprinted from the *Oxford Herald*).
3. Frederick John Robinson, the Viscount Goderich, later 1st Earl of Ripon, was prime minister for five months ending January 1828. In 1815, his

support for the Corn Laws had caused a mob to loot his house. He was also Chancellor of the Exchequer Jan 1823 – April 1827.

4. Canning (1827), Goderich (1827–1828) and Wellington (1828–1830, and 1834).
5. Drummond's successor as chief private secretary was a Mr William Stephenson, then the junior private secretary.
6. *Morning Post*, 26 January 1843.
7. *Letters of Queen Victoria* Vol. 1 p460. Melbourne (1779–1848) was a former Whig Prime Minister (1834 and 1835–1841)
8. 21 January 1843
9. Raikes was a diarist, dandy and man about town (1777–1848). He was a near neighbour of Drummond in Lower Grosvenor Street. This street, now Grosvenor Street, runs from the south-east corner of Grosvenor Square to Bond Street. When Drummond leased a house there it was regarded as a more superior neighbourhood, favoured by the gentry and politicians.
10. *The Spectator*, 28 January 1843.
11. Letter to Sir Robert Peel on 30 January 1843.
12. In late April 1843, Peel wrote a touching note to his wife regarding her road to recovery.
    "My own dearest love,
    You must not be dispirited by occasional checks to your immediate and complete recovery. Depend upon it, all will go well. Your constitution is an excellent one. I wish I could have said this to you, instead of writing it."
    Julia Peel did recover by the end of the summer and was well enough to cope with the strain of a visit by Victoria and Albert. Julia Peel suffered a much worse blow when, seven years later, Sir Robert died as a consequence of a riding accident on Constitution Hill.
13. Mr Guthrie the surgeon, in his evidence at M'Naghten's trial, referred to Drummond as being "very fat".
14. *Queen Victoria's Journal*, 28 January 1843.
15. Saturday, 25 January 1843.
16. *Queen Victoria's Journal*, 26 January 1843.
17. *Letters of Queen Victoria* Vol 1 (1837–1843), 25 January 1843. The use of upper floors for grace and favour apartments had started in the 1760s and the last person to be granted such an apartment was admitted in the 1980s.

Chapter 4: The Shooting

1. Letter to Lord Ashley, 31 January 1843.
2. There was no Charing Cross station yet, it was opened in 1864.
3. Thomas Hamilton KT PC FRSE (1780–1858) First Lord of the Admiralty (1841–1846) Lord Lieutenant of Ireland (1835) Lord Privy Seal (1846); 6th Earl of Haddington (17 March 1828).
   Despite having held these offices, Haddington was not a man of any remarkable ability. Charles Greville, after recording in his diary that the Governor-General-ship of India had been offered to Haddington, but which was refused by him, remarked in 1841:
   "It is a curious circumstance that a man so unimportant, so destitute not only of shining, but plausible, qualities, without interest or influence, should by a mere combination of accidental circumstances have had at his disposal three of the greatest and most important offices under the crown, having actually occupied two of them and rejected the greatest and most brilliant of all" – *Dictionary of National Biography* (1904).
4. *Queen Victoria's Journal* for Friday 20th gave the time of the shooting as 3.15 pm, but this is clearly too early.
5. Metropolitan Police Divisions A to F were created in 1829 with further divisions added in 1830. Scotland Yard was then at 4 Whitehall Place.
6. Early reports were that the second shot hit Drummond in the left thigh. This was incorrect. The *Mornington Post*, 21 January 1843 also reported incorrectly that M'Naghten fired two shots which both hit Drummond in the back.
7. At preliminary hearing at Bow Street court. *The Times*, 23 January 1843.
8. 21 January 1843.
9. Curiously, and erroneously, the *John Bull*, 4 March 1843 reported that two men were wounded in the shooting and that one had recovered after treatment.
10. Evidence given by Hodge before Bow Street Magistrates, Bow Street: *The Spectator*, 21 January 1843.
11. Evidence given by Weston before Bow Street Magistrates: *The Spectator*, 21 January 1843.
12. A Queen Eleanor cross erected in the 1290s and destroyed in 1647, but a bronze equestrian statue of Charles I was placed there in 1675.
13. *Morning Post*, Saturday, 21 January 1843.
14. 21 January 1843.
15. Reported in the *Morning Post*, 27 January 1843.

16. The *Annual Register* for 1843 (21 January) also puts the shooting being "close by the Salopian Coffee House".
17. He had been reappointed as commander-in-chief of the Army in 1842.
18. The *Times*, 25 January 1843.
19. *Queen Victoria's Journals*, 21 January 1843.
20. *History of the Peace: Being A History of England from 1816 to 1854.* Vol II by Harriet Martineau.

Chapter 5: Drummond's Funeral

1. Letter from Peel to Queen Victoria, 23 January 1843.
2. Mutes were paid mourners who kept vigil outside the house and then led the funeral procession. They would be dressed in black with a black top-hat, black sash and a black crepe-covered staff.
3. This church has a rare privilege of being allowed to fly the White Ensign that was in use by the Navy until the Act of Union 1800. This White Ensign can be flown on St Luke's Day and St George's Day at the church. This privilege was in recognition of its role as a navigation mark for ships on the River Thames.
4. A distant relative of the Drummond family.
5. It is more than a little baffling that the family did not want politicians to attend, despite so many being colleagues of Drummond, while inviting local people from Charlton-near-Woolwich.
6. Although this report was taken from *The Times*, its original source was the *Observer*.
7. The First Lord of the Treasury is the head of the Lords Commissioners of the Treasury and he exercises the ancient office of The Lord High Treasurer of the United Kingdom. The office of the First Lord is always held by the current prime minister of the United Kingdom. The Chancellor of the Exchequer is always The Second Lord of the Treasury.

Chapter 6: The Culpability of the Police and Civil Service

1. Later Sir Richard Mayne KCB, barrister: he had a long career and was largely responsible for creating the Metropolitan Police. During his time in charge of the Met the force grew from 1,000 to 8,000 men and its operational area grew to ten times its original size. Other counties and cities followed the examples that he introduced.
2. *Morning Post*, 21 January 1843.

3. 28 January 1843.
4. Evidence given to Bow Street Magistrates (*The Times*, 23 January 1843).
5. Walter Montagu Douglas Scott, 5th Duke of Buccleuch (1806–1884), Lord Keeper of the Privy Seal (1842–1846). Played twice for the MCC in 1841, and resided at Montague House, Whitehall. His residence was close by Sir Robert Peel's.
6. Now Dover House, 70 Whitehall. Lady Dover was formerly Georgiana Agar-Ellis (nee Howard) before her marriage to George Agar-Ellis 1st Baron Dover PC.
7. Author's added emphasis.
8. Evidence given by Drake at M'Naghten's trial.
9. Monday, 23 January 1843.
10. Established by Act of Parliament, June 1829, the first patrols were on duty on 29 September 1829, and PC Joseph Grantham was the first policeman killed in the line of duty when he was beaten to death when trying to stop two drunks from fighting (28 June 1830). The inquest jury found it was "justifiable homicide." Grantham was said to have caused his own death through "over exertion in the discharge of his duty".
11. Hence the first nickname of the new policemen – "Peelers"
12. There is some uncertainty as to Beale's cavalry unit. The press variously reported this as the 2nd Dragoon Guards (Queen's Bays) or the 6th (Inniskilling) Dragoons.
13. Query: was this officer James Partridge of A division, who gave evidence against M'Naghten and who regularly patrolled this area?
14. *Morning Post*, 30 January 1843.
15. The Queen's abbreviation for the 10th Hussars.
16. *Queen Victoria's Journal*, 1 February 1843.
17. If the sentence of being hanged, drawn and quartered had been carried out he would have been the last person executed in Britain by this barbaric method.

    Two days after the commutation of this sentence, John Bean tried to shoot the queen. He failed as his pistol was only loaded with paper, tobacco and very little powder. He was sentenced to eighteen months hard labour.
18. There was another warning in the wounding of Viscount Palmerston, Secretary at War. He was shot by Lieutenant David Davies, a mentally deranged naval officer on half pay. Palmerston was only slightly wounded and he paid the legal costs of Lt Davies's trial.

Chapter 7: The Assassin

1. 23 January 1843.
2. Alexander Cockburn, who defended M'Naghten at his trial, would later successfully defend two Royal Marine officers Lt. Hawkey and Lt Pym in 1846. Hawkey was charged with the murder of an ex-Army officer called Seton in a duel, while Pym, Hawkey's second, was charged as an accessory. Cockburn then used similar words to denigrate "foreign" assassins, while referring to the "manly" approach of the English duel.
3. Jingoism was a later invention to describe brash patriotism and aggressive views against the foreign policies of others. The word comes from a popular music-hall song's chorus of the 1870s, written by G.W. Hunt and made famous by the singer G.H. MacDermott:
   We don't want to fight but by Jingo if we do
   We've got the ships, we've got the men, we've got the money too
   We've fought the Bear before and while we're Britons true
   The Russians shall not have Constantinople.
   (Known as *By Jingo* or *Macdermott's War Song*)
4. This police station in Westminster was replaced by a new station in King Street (A Division) in 1847. It was a sign of the times that an assassin was taken down by one officer who then walked him along Whitehall, apparently unaccompanied, to the police station. We must assume that he had at least been handcuffed.
5. *The Spectator*, Saturday, 21 January 1843.
6. *The Times*, Saturday, 21 January 1843.
7. At this time, no licence was required to purchase a pistol, nor was there any suitability assessment of anyone seeking to acquire a pistol.
8. *The Times*, 23 January 1843, reprinting material from *The Observer*.
9. Lady Mary Anne Chantrey, widow of renowned sculptor Sir Francis Chantrey (died 1841).
10. *Queen Victoria's Journals*, 4 February 1843.
11. *Queen Victoria's Journals*, 13 September 1842.
12. *The Spectator*, 4 February 1843.
13. *The Times*, 21 January 1843.
14. "drab" then referred to a thick grey cloth.
15. *The Spectator*, 21 January 1843.
16. *The Times*, 21 January 1843.
17. *The Times*, 21 January 1843.

18. *Morning Post*, 21 January 1843.
19. Article republished in *The Times*, 28 January 1843.
20. *Morning Post*, Saturday, 21 January 1843.
21. (1792–1861) Conservative politician, Home Secretary (1841–1846).
22. *Queen Victoria's Journals*, 21 January 1843.
23. Newspapers would have had stock portraits of members of the royal family members, famous soldiers etc.
24. *The Times*, 21 January 1843.
25. 23 January 1843.
26. 24 January 1843.
27. Woodturner – one who "turns" or shapes wood and supplies the finished product to furniture makers. Turned wood would be typically chair legs, spindles, tool handles, balusters, newels etc.
28. By this time, Alexander Cockburn, who would remain a bachelor all his life, had one, possibly two, illegitimate children. During his life he had eight children, possibly nine, that can now be identified. He appears to have looked after all these illegitimate children well.
29. *Reformer's Gazette,* 11 March 1843 "*Sketch of M'Naughten: By one who knew him.*"
30. 30 January 1843.
31. *The Glasgow Courier*, 28 January 1843.
32. *Morning Post*, 28 January 1843, quoting the *Glasgow Courier*.
33. 30 January 1843.
34. In Scotland the procurator fiscal is a public prosecutor.
35. The lord provost is known as Glasgow's first citizen. He is the principal civic representative rather like a lord mayor. In carrying out his civic duties, he is supported by a *Depute Lord Provost* and *18 bailies*. He is also the *Lord Lieutenant of Glasgow* and as such is the Sovereign's official representative in Glasgow.
36. *Glasgow Constitutional*, 28 January 1843.
37. *Glasgow Courier*, 28 January 1843. The letter was dated 5 May 1842.
38. Some press reports said 1839, but it is unlikely to have been this early.
39. *Daniel McNaughton His Trial and the Aftermath* ed. by West and Walk: Gaskell Books (1977) p91.
40. *The Times*, 1 February 1843 (from an original report in the *Glasgow Herald*).
41. It was soon noticed that M'Naghten had not told Mr Martin that he was acquainted with Mr Martin Jnr. M'Naghten had done business with him before.

42. A "mechanic" in 1843 would have meant an artisan of whatever trade. The change of use to apply to one who works with machinery was a later development of the word.
43. 23 January 1843.
44. The new building cost £186,000.
45. Which number included Charles Dickens and his fellow novelist William Makepeace Thackeray.
46. Now Dunraven Street.
47. Later 1st Earl Russell. He was one of the main architects of the Reform Act of 1832.
48. His throat was cut by Courvoisier.
49. Doctor William Palmer (1824–1856). In this trial, Sir Alexander Cockburn, then Attorney-General led successfully for the prosecution.
50. 24 January 1843.
51. 24 January 1843.
52. 28 January 1843.
53. Information taken from the *Morning Post*, 23 and 24 January 1843.
54. *Morning Post*, 24 January 1843.
55. *The Times*, 24 January 1843.

Chapter 8: The Trial

1. Sir Nicholas Conyngham Tindal PC (1776–1846).
2. Sir John Taylor Coleridge PC (1790–1876).
3. Sir Edward Vaughan Williams PC (1797–1875) – Ralph Vaughan Williams (1872–1958) composer, was a grandson of Sir Edward.
4. Daniel Good was hanged for murder 1842. His ability to evade capture for as long as he did provided some of the impetus for the creation of a detective force within the Metropolitan Police.
5. *The Times,* 4 March 1843 – the Court Circular announced that Prince Albert was shooting with Sir Edward Bowater, before lunch, on the 3rd.
6. *St James's Chronicle*, 4 March 1843.
7. *Canterbury Journal*, 4 March 1843.
8. *The Times*, 4 March 1843.
9. *Morning Post*, 4 March 1843.
10. The prosecution failed with the majority being acquitted and those found guilty of minor charges were not sentenced.

11. Charles Russell, Baron Russell of Killowen (1832–1900) Lord Chief Justice 1894–1900).
12. *North American Law Review*, 1894.
13. *A History of Our Own Times* Justin McCarthy (1903 edition) p.331.
14. From his essay *"The McNaughton Case and its Predecessors' in Daniel McNaughton: his Trial and the Aftermath.* (see bibliography).
15. *R v Ferrers* (1760) 19 State Trials 1281 –.
16. It has been claimed that he was hanged with a silken rope, the prerogative of a noble, but this is uncertain.
17. (1800) 237 *State Trials* (new series) 1281: see Chapter 2 for brief details of Hadfield.
18. Later 1st Baron Erskine, and Lord Chancellor (1806–1807). He was one of the great advocates of his generation and, with liberal views, he was not afraid of defending radical causes.
19. From *The Proceedings of the Old Bailey* reference no 18120513-5.
20. 2 February 1843 (*Queen Victoria's Letters* vol. I p.460).
21. Foss's *Dictionary of Judges of England* refers to his unpopularity and that the Sergeants in court took advantage "...towards the end of his career they worried to such a degree that he could not always refrain from venting in audible curses against his tormentors. So great was the annoyance that he resigned his post in Hilary vacation 1814."
22. Mansfield: (1734–1821) MP for Cambridge University (1779–1784) Solicitor-General (1780–1782 and 1783) Chief Justice of Common Pleas (1804–1814) offered but refused Lord Chancellorship (1806). He died in 1821.
    Spencer Perceval: Prime Minister (1809–1812) MP for Northampton (1796–1812) Solicitor-General (1801–1802), Attorney-General (1802–1806) Chancellor of Duchy of Lancaster (1807–1812) Leader of House of Commons (1807–1812) Chancellor of the Exchequer (1807–1812) Prime Minister (1809–1812).
23. *The Proceedings of The Old Bailey* On Line reference t18120513-5. Author's added emphasis.
24. *The Proceedings of The Old Bailey* On Line reference t18120513-5. Author's added emphasis.
25. *A Historical View of the M'Naghten Trial*: Jaques M. Quen.
26. Author's added emphasis.
27. 5 Car 7 168 (1831).
28. Lord Lyndhurst later expressed his complete agreement with Mansfield's summing up in *Bellingham.*

29. What is the definition of "the laws of God and nature"?
30. *Fraser's Magazine for Town and Country* vol. 22 p446.
31. *The Glasgow Chronicle* citing *The Times*, 28 January 1843, and also the evidence given at trial by William Gilchrist.
32. *A Treatise on the Medical Jurisprudence of Insanity* Dr Ray MD Boston 1838
33. Author's added emphasis.
34. *Morning Post*, 23 January 1843.
35. Dr Edward Thomas Monro was a member of the family Monro of Fyrish. The family had become distinguished through their skill as physicians. The first member of the family to practice in the area of insanity was Dr James Monro (8th of Fyrish). He was followed by Dr John Monro (9th of Fyrish) who, like his father, worked at Bethlem Hospital. Dr Thomas Monro also followed the family vocation and was involved in treating King George III in his final illness.
    Dr Edward Thomas Monro (1817–1856) followed his father in being appointed principal physician of Bethlem Hospital. During his career he is said to have given evidence in approximately 400 cases of insanity. Of these cases, only twice was his evidence not followed, although both of these decisions were later set aside. His evidence was noted for being both clear and forceful which may well explain why he was so often instructed to give evidence. Unfortunately he also followed some of his father's treatments of the insane and was dismissed after another inspection of Bethlem. He was later admitted as a patient to Brooke House (an asylum run by the Monro family) and he died there in 1856. His son Dr Henry Monro followed the same profession as his father.
36. In 1843, the East Coast Main Line had not been completed, it would be completed between Edinburgh and Berwick-on-Tweed 1846. The through route for the West Coast Main first ran a through route London to Glasgow in 1846.
37. Sir A. Morrison and Mr Forbes Winslow.
38. The phrase "two of the medical gentlemen sent by the Government" implies that the government had, before the trial, sent more than two doctors. That these other doctors were not called also implies that they must have agreed with the other two.
39. 21 June 1843.
40. Follett's cross-examination of Dr Monro.
41. Unfortunately the chamber's ledger recording the fees charged by Cockburn for this trial has not survived.

42. M'Naghten's father, William Gilchrist, John Hughes, William Carlo, Jane Patterson, Henry Bell (sheriff depute), Alexander Johnston MP, Sir James Campbell (Glasgow Lord Provost), Hugh Wilson (commissioner of Glasgow Police).
43. *Daniel McNaughton, His Trial and the Aftermath*, edited by Donald J. West and Alexander Walk (see Bibliography).
44. *Knowing Right From Wrong* Richard Moran (see Bibliography).

Chapter 9: The Surgeons and Drummond's Treatment

1. Lindsey Fitzharris: *The Butchering Art*, Allen Lane 2017.
2. The pioneering work in the use of sterilisation was undertaken by Ignaz Semmelweis (in Vienna) and by Oliver Wendell Holmes (in Boston). The lives of both these pioneers are worth reading.
3. Mr Freeman, a surgeon, was the usual medical adviser to the Drummond family, but he was away from home when sent for.
4. Guthrie had been consulted in 1812 on the fatal chest wound sustained by Major General Robert Crauford, the renowned commander of Wellington's elite Light Division, in the storming of Ciudad Rodrigo.
5. This includes the time that Jackson will have spent examining Drummond. Jackson's evidence at the trial was that the ball was removed within an hour of the shooting, but that is unlikely.
6. It is a curious coincidence that later, in 1850, when Peel was fatally injured by a fall from his horse on Constitution Hill, he too suffered a wound surrounding his left shoulder blade.
7. 23 January 1843.
8. Author's added emphasis.
   The Royal Navy, in the film *Master and Commander* (20th Century Fox, 2003), was portrayed as knowing all about this risk and how to remove it, 40 years before Drummond was shot!
9. In the absence of twenty-first-century cleaning methods for outer clothes in 1843, they would be far less clean than today and would provide another potential source of infection during treatment.
10. *The Times*, 21 January 1843.
11. 21 January 1843.
12. 22 January 1843.
13. 28 January 1843.
14. 21 January 1843.

15. The process whereby dead or damaged body tissue produces pus.
16. *Queen Victoria's Journal*, 23 January 1843.
17. The Wikipedia entry for '*bloodletting*' quite simply refers to it as being a pseudoscience – "statements, beliefs, or practices that claim to be both scientific and factual but are incompatible with the scientific method."
18. The surgical opening of a vein (phlebotomy).
19. *The Times* of 23 January 1843.
20. *Queen Victoria's Journal*, 24 January 1843.
21. *Queen Victoria's Journal*, 25 January 1843.
22. 25 January 1843.
23. The son of Mr Guthrie senior.
24. 28 January 1843.
25. (1843) Simpkin and Marshal (London) Octavo 5s. An advertisement for this book appeared in the *Morning Post* on 3 February 1843. The book contained the text of a lecture on inflammation and bloodletting by T.D. Hume published as Lecture IV in *Fallacies Of The Faculty* compiled by Samuel Dickson and published in 1841.
26. At this time *John Bull* was a Conservative supporting Sunday newspaper.
27. *John Bull*, Saturday, 4 March 1843, page 10.
28. Saturday, 28 January 1843.
29. Hygeism was the creation of James Morrison (1770–1840). He claimed to have found relief from years of pain by taking vegetable pills of his own invention. He then manufactured them and sold them as a universal cure on the basis that "bad blood" was the cause of all disease and that purgation by his vegetable pills was the only safe remedy!
30. In April 1836 an apothecary, Robert Salmon, was charged with the manslaughter of John M'Kenzie through the administration of excessive amounts of Morrison's pills. He was found guilty and fined £200 (*British Satire 1785-1840 vol. 1*, J. Strachan and S. Jones (pub. 2003 Taylor & Francis); also *The Times*, 19 February 1843 p.7.
31. *Report of Observations made in British Hospitals in Belgium* – The author was John Thomson MD.
32. *The Lancet* suggested Guthrie should refresh his memory by reading Dr John Thomson's "*Report of the Observations made in the British Military Hospitals in Belgium after the Battle of Waterloo*" pp93-4.
33. Author's added emphasis.

34. 11 March 1843.
35. An aperient is a mild laxative.
36. Calomel was a popular treatment in the nineteenth century. It was a mercury chloride mineral that was used to treat a wide range of ailments. The use of calomel began to decline in the early twentieth century when the real dangers of mercury became better understood.
37. *A Matter of Honour* by Martyn Beardsley, Bookline & Sinker (2010). The duel between Seton and Hawkey was the last fatal duel between Englishmen (1845) in England. Hawkey was acquitted of murder due mainly to the forceful defence by Alexander Cockburn QC.
38. Appointed surgeon to King George IV in 1828.
39. They shared administration and teaching functions.
40. The removal of a stone from the bladder.
41. John Bell (1763–1820) a notable Scottish surgeon, in his work *Principles of Surgery*, wrote of "long and murderous operations, where the surgeon labours for an hour in extracting the stone, to the inevitable destruction of the patient."
42. Brougham was a Scot, but he moved to England and was admitted to the English bar. He was a success as a barrister and in 1823 became a KC. He was later appointed Lord Chancellor and created Baron Brougham and Vaux.
43. Scarlett was later appointed Lord Chief Baron of the Court of Exchequer and was raised to the peerage in 1835 as 1st Baron Abinger. He was not a success as a judge. He had a reputation for unfairness and also for his domineering attitude towards juries.
44. *Serjeant Ballantine's Experiences* p.80.
45. Royal College of Surgeons online *Plarr's Lives of the Fellows*. https://lives online.rceng.ac.uk

Chapter 10: The Reaction

1. *Queen Victoria's Journal*, 24 January 1843.
2. *Queen Victoria's Journal*, 26 January 1843.
3. *Queen Victoria's Journal*, 28 January 1843.
4. *The Letters of Queen Victoria* Vol 1 1837-1843, 4 March 1843.
5. *The Letters of Queen Victoria* Vol 1 1837-1843, 12 March 1843.
6. *Queen Victoria's Journal*, 5 March 1843.
7. *Queen Victoria's Journal*, 6 March 1843.

8. *Queen Victoria's Journal*, 10 March 1843.
9. Peel was displaying better judgment than Victoria by pointing out the difficulty of proscribing punishment in a developing area of the law.
10. *Queen Victoria's Journal*, 14 March 1843.
11. *Queen Victoria's Journal*, 16 March 1843.
12. (1780–1847) 12 Baronet and Tory MP for Galway.
13. *Punch*, (1843) Volume 4 – *Monomaniacs* p121; *Monomaniac Academy* p132.
14. *Boxiana* – a series of volumes from the pen of Pierce Egan, reporting bare-knuckle prize fighting.
15. *Raikes Journal* Vol 4, 28 February 1843.
16. *Raikes Journal* Vol 4, 8 March 1843.
17. (1787–1863) Archbishop of Dublin, Bishop of Glendalough and Primate of Ireland.
18. *Morning Post*, 11 March 1843.
19. Guthrie was the surgeon who had the main role in treating Mr Drummond and it is very doubtful that he was capable, or even inclined, to distinguish between sanity and insanity. See Chapter 10 for more detail of his involvement.
20. *The Scotsman*, 22 March 1843.
21. *Morning Post*, 23 March 1843: page 6 – *On the Different Forms of Insanity in Relation to Jurisprudence* by J.C. Pritchard MD.

Chapter 11: The Asylums and M'Naghten's Death

1. In 1936, the site of the Bethlem Hospital was acquired by the Imperial War Museum as a new site for its main collection in London.
2. 14 March 1843.
3. 21 March 1843.
4. This entry is of course incorrect. M'Naghten had been found to be "not guilty by reason of insanity".
5. *Morning Post*, Tuesday, 28 March 1843.
6. See Chapter 1, endnote 3.
7. *London Illustrated News*, 25 March 1843. It was not accurate to refer to M'Naghten as a criminal as he had not been convicted of any criminal offence.
8. Bethlem case notes, entry for 21 March 1854.
9. Consultant Psychiatrist, Horton Hospital, Epsom, Surrey in *McNaughton's Madness*, his chapter included in *Daniel McNaughton his Trial and the Aftermath* – see Bibliography.

10. The article was first published in *Blackwood's Magazine* in 1851 and then reprinted in the *Journal of Psychological Medicine* in 1852. The writer is thought to have been Mr Samuel Warren, of a legal profession.
11. The term "schizophrenia" did not come into use until 1908. The word translates as "splitting of the mind". It is estimated to reduce life expectancy by 20–28 years.
12. International Classification of Diseases 11th Revision (ICD-11).
13. Anhedonia is a diverse array of hedonic function, including reduced motivation or ability to experience pleasure. Today it will also cover reduction in motivation, anticipatory pleasure, and consumatory pleasure.
14. Jean-Etienne Dominique Esquirol (1772–1840) was a French psychiatrist, reformer and architect of the French national law of 1838 relating to asylums.
15. In 1930 the hospital was moved to Croydon.

Appendix A: The House of Lords and Law Reform

1. House of Lords debate 6 March 1843, volume 67 cc288-90288.
2. House of Lords debate 13 March 1843 volume 67 cc714-44714.
3. House of Lords debate on 6 and 13 March 1843, Hansard, vol 67 pp. 288, 714.
4. The *Westminster Bank case* 2 Cl.& F.191.

Appendix B: Assassination

1. Despite his position, Abbott was a British citizen and merchant who had chosen to accept this appointment.
2. Also one in the Church of St Luke, Charlton, where he is buried.

SOURCES

Published Books and Papers

Appignanesi, Lisa, *Trials of Passion (Crimes committed in The Name of Love and Madness)*. Pegasus Books LLC, New York (2014)

Arnold, Catherine, *Bedlam*. Simon & Schuster (2008)

Ayton, Mel, *Plotting to Kill the President*. Potomac Books, University of Nebraska Press (2017)

Ayton, Mel, *Hunting the President*. Regnery History Washington D.C. (2014)

Ballantine, William, *Some Experiences of a Barrister's Life*. Richard Bentley & Son, London (1883)

Ballantine, William, *The Old World and the New: Being a Continuation of his experiences*. Leopold Classic Library

Bates, Stephen, *1815*. Head of Zeus, London (2015)

Beardsley, Martyn, *A Matter of Honour*. Bookline & Thinker Ltd (2010)

Bewley, Thomas, *Madness to Mental Illness: A History of the Royal College of Psychiatrists*. Online Archive 17 (James Hadfield)

Bolitho, Hector and Peel, Derek, *The Drummonds of Charing Cross*. George Allen and Unwin, London (1985)

Bousefield, R M. and Merrett, R., *Report of the Trial of Daniel M'Naughten*. Henry Henshaw, London (1843) (MOML edition)

Brown, Michael, *Rats, Bats and Barristers: The Lancet, libel and the radical stylistics of early nineteenth century English Medicine*. Social History,39.2, 182-209, DOI: 10.1080/03071022.2014.905277

Browne, Douglas C., *The Rise of Scotland Yard*. George G. Harrap & Co Ltd London (1956)

Cameron, H.C., *Mr Guy's Hospital 1726-1948*. Longman Green & Co, London (1954)

Carlyle, Thomas, *Letters 1826-1836*. Macmillan, London (1888)

Diamond, Bernard L. MD, 'Isaac Ray and the Trial of Daniel M'Naghten'. *The American Journal Of Psychiatry*: Vol 112 p.651

Dickson, Samuel, *What Killed Mr Drummond, the Lead or the Lancet?* Simpkin and Marshall, London (1843)

Fitzharris, Lindsey, *The Butchering Art*, Allen Lane (2017)

Foss, Edward, *A Biographical Dictionary of the Judges of England (1066-1870)*. Reprint by The Lawbook Exchange Ltd , Clark, New Jersey

Foss, Edward, *The Judges of England.* John Murray, London (1864)

Greenstone, Gerry, MD, 'The History of Bloodletting'. *British Columbia Medical Journal*, vol.52, issue 1

Hurd, Douglas, *Robert Peel.* Weidenfeld & Nicholson, London (2007)

Jones, Roger, 'Thomas Wakley, plagiarism, libel, and the founding of The Lancet'. *Journal of Royal Society of Medicine* (2009)

Kingston, Charles, *Famous Judges and Famous Trials*, Stanley Paul & Co, London (1923). (MOML edition)

Manson, Edward, *Builders of Our Law (2nd ed.)*. Horace Cox, London

Martineau, Harriet, *History of the Peace: Being A History of England from 1816 to 1854*. Vol 11. Scholarly Publishing Office, University of Michigan 2006

McDougall, Ian (editor), *Cases that Changed Our Lives*. LexisNexis (2010)

Moran, Richard, *Knowing Right from Wrong.* The Free Press New York (1981)

Morgan, Kate, *Murder The Biography*. Mudlark Publishing, London

Murphy, Paul Thomas, *Shooting Victoria: Madness, Mayhem and the Modernisation of the Monarchy*. Pegasus Books (2012)

Murphy, Paul Thomas, *Plarr's Lives of the Fellows.* https://livesonline.rceng.ac.uk

Porter, Roy, *Madness: A Brief History*. Oxford University Press (2002)

Queen Victoria, *Queen Victoria's Journals*. https://www.queenvictoriasjournals.org/home.do

Queen Victoria, *The Letters of Queen Victoria Vol 1* (1837-1843). https://www.gutenberg.org/files/20023/20023-h/20023-h.htm

Quen, Jacques, MD, *James Hadfield and Medical Jurisprudence of Insanity.* New York State Journal of Medicine Vol.69/Pt 1

Quen, Jacques, MD, 'An Historical View of the M'Naghten Trial'. *Bulletin of the History of Medicine*, 1 January 1968

Raikes, Thomas, *A Portion of the Journal Kept by Thomas Raikes Esq – from 1831 to 1847 Vol. 4*. Longman, Brown, Green, Longman's & Roberts, London (1857)

Rutherford Sarah, *The Victorian Asylum*. Shire Library (2008)

Schneider, Richard D. *The Lunatic and the Lords*. Irwin Law Inc. Toronto (2009)

Shenton, Caroline, *The Day Parliament Burned Down*. Oxford University Press (2012)

Thursfield, J.R., *Peel*. Macmillan & Co London (1891)

Wakley, Thomas, *A Report of the Trial of Cooper v Wakley*. The *Lancet,* London (1829)

Wallenborn, White McKenzie, MD, *George Washington's Terminal Illness: A Modern Medical Analysis of the Last Illness and Death of George Washington*. https://washingtonpapers.org/resources/articles/illness/

West, Donald J. and Walk, Alexander, *Daniel McNaughton: His Trial and the Aftermath.* Gaskell Books (1977)

Winslow, Benignus Winslow, *The Plea of Insanity in Criminal Cases*. Boston: C.C. Little and J. Brown (1843)

Wise, Sarah, *Inconvenient People: Lunacy, Liberty and the Mad-Doctors in Victorian England.* Vintage Books (2013)

Newspapers and Periodicals

The British Newspaper Archive

The Dictionary of National Biography (various editions)

Fraser's Magazine for Town and Country

The Illustrated London News Archive

The Lancet Archive

The Spectator Archive

The Times Archive

Other sources

House of Lords Debates:

6 March 1843, volume 67 cc288-90288

13 March 1843 volume 67 cc714-44714

Old Bailey transcript of M'Naghten's trial reference t18430227-874

INDEX